Practicing Baptism

Practicing Baptism

Christian Practices and the Presence of Christ

BÅRD EIRIK HALLESBY NORHEIM

☙PICKWICK *Publications* · Eugene, Oregon

PRACTICING BAPTISM
Christian Practices and the Presence of Christ

Copyright © 2014 Bård Eirik Hallesby Norheim. All rights reserved. Except for brief quotations in critical publications or reviews, no part of this book may be reproduced in any manner without prior written permission from the publisher. Write: Permissions, Wipf and Stock Publishers, 199 W. 8th Ave., Suite 3, Eugene, OR 97401.

Pickwick Publications
An Imprint of Wipf and Stock Publishers
199 W. 8th Ave., Suite 3
Eugene, OR 97401

www.wipfandstock.com

ISBN 13: 978-1-62564-175-5

Cataloguing-in-Publication data:

Norheim, Bård Eirik Hallesby.

    Practicing baptism : Christian practices and the presence of Christ / Bård Eirik Hallesby Norheim.

    xiv + 224 pp. ; 23 cm. Includes bibliographical references and index.

    ISBN 13: 978-1-62564-175-5

    1. Christian life. 2. Baptism. 3. Jesus Christ—Presence. 4. Theology, Practical. I. Title.

BV3 N75 2014

Manufactured in the U.S.A.

Contents

Preface | vii

Acknowledgments | xi

Abbreviations | xiii

1 Christian Practices in a Post-Christendom Era | 1
2 The Engagement in Christian Practices | 16
3 Christian Practices in the Light of Lutheran Theology | 54
4 Practicing Baptism | 153
5 The Diaconal Telos of Christian Practices | 203

Bibliography | 213

Index | 221

Preface

MY FIRST FULL-TIME INVOLVEMENT in ministry took place in Tallinn, Estonia, in the school year 1992–1993. Together with two other Norwegians I worked as a volunteer youth worker in the Estonian YWCA-YMCA—starting up a Christian creative arts group, called *ten sing*. Most of the young people we met had no relationship to church—or Christianity for that matter. Years of atheistic Soviet rule had estranged many from faith. But in the turmoil of a whole system breaking down, many of them became curious about faith and showed an interest in investigating further what Christianity was really about. They were asking fundamental questions like: Who was Jesus really? What does it mean to believe? And finally: What do Christians do?[1] Quite a few of these young people took on a journey of faith, which led them to being baptized and becoming members in a church—often the Estonian Evangelical-Lutheran Church (EELC).

My experiences that year in Estonia somewhat unwillingly convinced me to study theology, and finally to become an ordained priest in the Church of Norway. For four years I worked as a children and youth pastor in a suburban Oslo congregation. In 2003 my wife and I were sent for three years as missionaries to Estonia, working with youth ministry in the EELC. Obviously, much had changed since 1993, but for those young people still coming to church the same curiosity was evident: What does it mean to be a Christian? What do Christians really do? The young people we met wanted to experience this first hand—by testing out praying, the Lord's Supper, Bible reading, helping the needy, being and eating together. Youth ministry in Estonia also taught us to value practical ecumenical youth ministry, as we worked together with young

---

1. One of my friends from that time asked me seventeen years later: "The thing I really wanted to know all those years, was how do I actually pray?"

people from a large range of different congregations—Roman Catholics, Orthodox Christians, Methodists, Baptists, Pentecostals, and different free churches.

My experiences in ministry over all these years led me to study in more detail those engaging so-called *Christian practices* as a new curriculum for ministry. Several theologians both in US and in Europe argued for a renewed focus on so-called "Christian practices," as they claim that the traditional churches had largely neglected the challenges of the rapidly changing context, where fewer and fewer people have knowledge of the Bible and the Christian tradition. The engagement in Christian practices has emerged out of a critical and constructive reading of Alisdair Macintyre's appeal to Neo-Aristotelian virtue ethics. It focuses the Christian everyday life as a communtarian life shaped by Christian practices such as prayer, hospitality, forgiveness and caring for the sick and the poor. The idea behind this new paradigm was that in a context where fewer and fewer have any knowledge about Christianity, people have to learn about Christianity by participating in the practices that the Christian church has been practicing since the very beginning, the practices that made them recognizable publicly as Christians in the first place.

But as I studied this, two questions struck me: What makes a practice *Christian* after all? And: What is the role of baptism in a life where Christian practices is the curriculum? This reflection corresponded with what Miroslav Volf pointed to in *Practicing Theology* (2002), that not much attention has been given to some of the more crucial dogmatic questions involved, such as discussing what makes a practice Christian in the first place. This book takes as its point of departure the need to trace and discuss the theological limitations within the conversation on Christian practices. The engagement in Christian practices is fundamentally an attempt to answer the question of how to construct the life of a Christian in an era of secularization. This book analyses how this question have been answered within the practices conversation. Further, the book traces the question in order to develop answers to the more *normative* problems that arise from this conversation, focusing particularly on the anthropological, soteriological, and ecclesiological implications. The particular contribution of this book is how it engages Lutheran Incarnation theology and baptismal theology in a way, which both promotes and provokes theological reflection and seeks to be relevant to practical ministry. This leads to the developing of the concept *practicing baptism* as a formative concept for a communitarian theology of Christian practices.

When we worked as missionaries in Estonia, we experienced that the rite of confirmation often seemed to replace baptism as the *rite of passage*. This was true both for young and old, previously unfamiliar with the Christian faith, choosing to become members of the church. Baptism often then becomes more of a private ritual, celebrated on a Saturday evening among a small circle of friends, whereas confirmation was celebrated as the highlight of the Sunday Mass. For those choosing to become Christians and members of the church the importance of baptism seemed harder to get at then the rite of confirmation, which seemed to communicate in a more comprehensive and attractive way the subjective element of coming to faith, highlighting the choice made. Even in a post-Soviet context this seems like a version of what is referred to as "the subjective turn in culture."[2]

When we returned to Norway in 2006, I started working on my dissertation. During this time I was fortunate to spend time with young people in the area just outside Oslo, where my wife served as a pastor. These kids were in many ways similar to the youngsters we had been working with in Estonia. Most of them had no relationship to church or any faith community before being engaged in youth ministry, most often through confirmation training. So for most young people the practices of the Christian community were something exotic, but therefore also fascinating: Confirmands were using their cell phones to record or take photos of the evening worship at confirmation camp and posting it on Facebook to share with their friends.

This book tries to reformulate the importance of baptismal theology in an era of heightened personal autonomy. It starts and ends in practical ministry, but it is also an attempt to further the theological discussion on Christian practices by offering clarity and new insight to the question of how the Christian self is constructed. At the same time, the book is an invitation to a process of discerning and discussing the importance of this in the context of actual ministry. The chief conclusion in the book is that Christian practices are ways to *practice baptism*. The argument and ideas of this book is based on my dissertation, which I defended publicly in March 2012 at MF Norwegian School of Theology in Oslo, Norway. The full title of the dissertation is "Practicing Baptism: A Theological Investigation of The Presence of Christ in Christian Practices in the Context

---

2. Taylor, *The Ethics of Authenticity*.

of Youth Ministry." This book is an attempt to develop and sharpen this argument and make it accessible for a larger audience.

My experience in ministry, and in youth ministry in particular, have shaped my own motivation to discuss how baptism and baptismal theology relate to the shape of everyday Christian life in a changing context. Numerous books have been written over the last two decades discussing Christian practices, and what all of them have in common is their interest in how faith should shape a Christian way of life. This study investigates how the faith given in baptism should inform and shape the Christian way of life. More precisely, it investigates the shape of the Christian life, given in baptism, in the light of a Lutheran theology of the presence of Christ.

Bård Eirik Hallesby Norheim
Bergen, Norway, Jan 9, 2014

Acknowledgments

THERE IS A WHOLE bunch of people who deserve thanks as the work with this book comes to an end. First of all I would like to thank Pickwick Publications of Wipf and Stock Publishers for offering me the opportunity to publish the book. It has been a pleasure working with you. I would also like to thank the members of my doctoral committee, Christian Batalden Scharen, Pete Ward, and Svein Olaf Thorbjørnsen for all their effort. A special thanks to Chris Scharen for making the connection with Wipf and Stock. I am very thankful to MF Norwegian School of Theology, Oslo, Norway, where I was given the opportunity to work with the dissertation upon which the argument of this book is based. During the course of this study, I was blessed with two brilliant supervisors, Leif Gunnar Engedal (main supervisor) and Torleiv Austad (co-supervisor). In addition to this, a lot of people, at different stages of the work, offered valuable feed-back on the idea and argument of the study, and on the actual text: Oswald Bayer, Maria Bjørdal, Kirsten Busch-Nielsen, Kenda Creasy Dean, Tron Fagermoen, Kristin Graff-Kallevåg, Peder Gravem, Espen Andreas Hasle, Harald Hegstad, Jan-Olav Henriksen, Morten Holmqvist, Oddvar Johan Jensen, Tone Stangeland Kaufman, Roland Martinson, Sverre Dag Mogstad, Steven Paulson, Risto Saarinen, Kjell Olav Sannes, Astrid Sandsmark, Christian Batalden Scharen, Ola Sigurdson, Atle Søvik, Marius Timmann-Mjaaland, Knut Tveitereid, Pete Ward, and Fredrik Wenell.

An important conversation partner over the last few years has been Andrew Root. I met Andy through IASYM (the International Association for the Study of Youth Ministry). Special thanks also goes to my colleague at NLA University College, Bergen, Norway, Joar Haga, who long ago, mildly, but convincingly, pointed me in the direction of the theme of this study, with his appeal to investigate further theologically the presence of Christ.

Finally, I would like to thank my family, first of all my grandfather Helge, who was the first to encourage and discipline me in the art of theology, by teaching me Greek. My mother and father, Mia and Eirik, have never encouraged me to write a book—or to study theology, for that matter—but rather always performed the careful and balanced art of offering just enough freedom and encouragement along the way. My deepest gratitude goes to my wife Kjersti and our kids Hanna, Eirik, Selma, and Lina for being a chaotically beautiful practicing community in the midst of life as it is. You have been offering just enough freedom, just enough crazy questions, and just enough impatience and action in order for me to enjoy doing the same thing for such a long time. To acknowledge the importance of my wife, Kjersti, is as easy as making sure there are no typing errors in the footnotes. Here I restrict myself to simply thanking you for being the most inspiring discussion partner, a true pastoral colleague, an excellent proof reader, and the master of allowing crazy ideas to have their needed space and time to come to life. Last, but most importantly, I would like to thank all the people that I have met in youth ministry in Norway and in Estonia. You are a constant reminder of where this study starts and ends. I therefore dedicate this work to you.

Abbreviations

BC *The Book of Concord: The Confessions of the Evangelical Lutheran Church.* Ed. Robert Kolb and Timothy J. Wengert. Minneapolis: Fortress, 2000.

BELK *Die Bekenntnisschriften der evangelisch-lutherischen Kirche.* 11th ed. Göttingen: Vandenhoeck & Ruprecht, 1992.

CA Confessio Augustana, in BELK and BC.

LW *Luther's Works American Edition*

StA Luther, Martin. *Studienausgabe*: Ed. Hans-Ulrich Delius. Berlin: Evangelische Verlagsanstalt, 1979–1992.

WA *D. Martin Luthers Werke.* 70 vols. Kritische Gesamtausgabe. Weimar: Böhlau, 1883–.

1

Christian Practices in a Post-Christendom Era

WHY CHRISTIAN PRACTICES?

Christian Practices in a Time of Theological Anxiety

THERE IS A CERTAIN anxiety within Western theology on how to understand the construction of the (Christian) self in an era of heightened personal autonomy and secularization. The appeal to focus on Christian practices in ministry and theological education is an attempt to respond to that anxiety. The common ground for all those engaging theology with practice(s) is a mix of this ambition to rethink faith formation and a radical contextual impetus. The context of the Western church has been fundamentally altered over the last few decades. The church can no longer lean on a Christendom approach to theological education and Christian formation.[1] Church and theology have to rediscover the shape and nature of the Christian life in a radically and rapidly changing context.

---

1. The term post-Christendom is used to emphasize that the Western world, due to the emerging biblical illiteracy and vanishing knowledge of Christianity, and also due to the growing presence of other world views and religions (i.e., plural societies), is no longer to be understood simply as a Christian culture, a *Corpus Christianum*, in the strict meaning of the word, where Christianity as religion is hegemonic in both culture and government.

During the late 1980s and the 1990s various theologians, particularly in the US, started to discuss the role of so-called "Christian practices" in theological education and ministry.[2] This engagement grew out of a self-critical evaluation of the theological education and ministry offered by the traditional churches in the US, the so-called Mainline Protestant Churches.[3] The problem, according to many, was that the traditional churches had largely neglected the challenges of the rapidly changing context, where fewer and fewer people have knowledge of the Bible and the Christian tradition. At the same time, the churches were failing to engage the resources of their historic tradition with the evolving religious market.[4]

The response was a call to return to communitarian, Christian practices such as prayer, hospitality, forgiveness, and caring for the sick and the poor, and to discover the shaping role of these practices for the everyday Christian life. The hope was that this would lead to a rediscovery of the vitality of the church in a post-modern context, where bare words seemed to have lost their power.

This concern has also influenced the way the traditional churches do—and think about—youth ministry. Kenda Creasy Dean has developed a practical theology for youth ministry based on rediscovering the historical practices of the church.[5] For Dean, Christian practices are tools for the church to communicate with and shape the identity of a generation of passionate young people. According to Dean, the present younger generation in the US has been betrayed by the Mainline Protestant churches, which have failed to offer young people relevant Christian practices that meet their desire and longing for authenticity, fidelity, transcendence, and communion, that could give them "something to die for," as Dean puts it.[6] Dean finds that Christ "Jesus enters the world in these

---

2. I will refer to this as the "Christian practices paradigm" or the "Christian practices conversation." My particular emphasis will be on the works of Dorothy C. Bass, Craig R. Dykstra, and Kenda Creasy Dean. Cf. also how this is referred to as a "practices paradigm" in Dean and Martinson, *OMG*, 74.

3. Along with the term Mainline Protestant Churches, the term Mainline Protestantism is also used. The Roman Catholic Church is often included as one of the Mainline Churches in the US, albeit not Protestant.

4. Dykstra, *Growing in the Life of Faith*, 3–13.

5. Dean, *Practicing Passion*.

6. According to Dean, Mainline Protestantism has proven unable to connect with the real passion of the younger generation. She claims that the mortal sin of the youth ministry of the Mainline Protestant churches is a lack of passion and a fear of moving out of the shallow end of the "theological pool," cf. Dean, *Practicing Passion*, 162–63.

practices again and again . . . through us."⁷ But exactly how the presence of Christ in Christian practices should be understood has been subject to controversy.

Christian Practices and the Presence of Christ in the Light of Lutheran Theology

Interpreting the presence of Christ is a key issue for theological reflection and for ministry as it is key to understand the formation of the Christian self. For every part of Christian ministry, it is crucial to ask:

- How is Jesus Christ present in the world?
- How is Jesus Christ present in the practices of the Christian community?
- What constitutes this presence?

Starting and ending in ministry, this book takes as its point of departure the need to investigate further how the presence of Christ in Christian practices should be interpreted in the light of Lutheran theology. The question of how the presence of Christ in Christian practices should be interpreted is largely "unanswered" within the Christian practices paradigm. But this question is crucial for a church, which wants to rethink and reshape its catechetical practices in a rapidly changing context.

My focus in this book is not to investigate practices in general. This book does therefore not attempt to discuss every possible practice that may occur in the context of ministry theologically, but it is an attempt to develop some basic theological principles on how to understand the presence of Christ in Christian practices. Through this it is my aim to enable systematic and critical reflection on the role of Christian practices in the context of ministry.

It is my intention, that the reflections and discussion in this study will offer helpful theological insights for other theological traditions than just the Lutheran tradition. Lutheran ecclesiology is in its scope and intention fundamentally ecumenical. The logical structure of the *Confessio Augustana* (1530) is one example of this understanding, where the first twenty-one articles of the confession are presented as catholic, common,

---

7. Dean, *Practicing Passion*, 15.

for the one church.[8] Ultimately, the scope of this book is therefore to contribute to the outlining of an ecumenical theology of Christian practices in the context of ministry based on a Lutheran interpretation of the doctrine of the presence of Christ.

In the light of Lutheran theology, the question of how to interpret the presence of Christ is fundamentally a soteriological question. In the Lutheran tradition the question of salvation is closely related to the doctrine of the present Christ, *Christus Praesens*. One example of this is found in Article III and Article VI of the Confessio Augustana, CA III and IV, where CA IV on justification by faith relies on CA III on Christology. Also by looking at Luther's main treatises, soteriology and Christology are intrinsically connected.

For Luther this soteriology is fundamentally connected to ministry and everyday life, and it finds its practical expression in the "practice" trajectory of the Small and Large Catechisms, which both outline the everyday life of the new self, born in baptism.[9] Here the life of the Christian is outlined as an everyday life shaped by a set of "practices": using or practicing the Creed, one's baptism, the Lord's Supper, the Ten Commandments and prayer.

Many of Luther's treatises take as their point of departure the liturgical practice of the church—like the Lord's Supper, baptism, or the creed.[10] Luther even develops the notion of the marks of the church—the *notae ecclesiae*—when he speaks about these practices. These marks of the church run as a binding ecclesiological theme through all the main documents of the reformers. Rather than being peripheral to Lutheran theology, the marks of the church arise from the very center of it, from

---

8. Wengert, along with many others, argues for a strict distinction between the first twenty-one articles (which in the original document were unnumbered) and the last seven, which described the few practices which Melanchthon and Luther and the Saxon court sought permission to change. Therefore the statements of the first twenty-one articles were thought of as non-negotiable, as, according to the reformers, they reflected the faith of the church of all ages. Lathrop and Wengert, *Marks of the Church*, 55. For further elaboration on how doing (Lutheran) theology (ecclesiology) is fundamentally something ecumenical, and in that sense universal, cf. Hegstad, *The Real Church*, 8–11.

9. For an account of this, cf. Wengert, *Martin Luther's Catechisms*.

10. In many ways Luther's approach is fundamentally different from a classical Reformed perspective, as expressed, for instance, in the Leuenberg Concord, where theological abstractions are made from liturgical practice.

justification by faith alone.[11] The question of how the presence of Christ should be interpreted, and how it relates to certain "practices" is therefore central to theological discourse in general and to Lutheran theological discourse in particular.

So although the Lutheran account serves as a sort of confessional filter or confessional hermeneutics, it is not an arbitrary theological perspective, but a strategic "perspective" developed by a systematical-theological interpretation of how Lutheran theology—theology in an Evangelical-Lutheran tradition and for an Evangelical-Lutheran church—should interpret the topic of this study—the presence of Christ in Christian practices for the whole church and for theological and ecclesiological discourse in general.[12]

There is a "gap" of several centuries between Luther and the current engagement in Christian practices. Luther wrote his treatises during the first half of the sixteenth century, whereas the engagement in Christian practices has been developing during the last part of the twentieth century and the beginning of the twenty-first century. My reading of the texts is a systematic-theological reading, not a historical reading. This means that I will focus on how these texts address the contemporary theological debate on Christian practices. Hermeneutically, this also resembles how Gadamer distinguishes between historical and philosophical hermeneutics.[13] The interpretation of selected Luther texts is meant to serve as a resource in developing an interpretation based on the "problem" of this study—how to interpret the presence of Christ in Christian practices. It is

---

11. Wengert claims, by examining the role of the marks of the church in *The Book of Concord* that it is not just an arbitrary or strategic selection which came about at the establishment phase of the Reformation in the late 1530s, cf. Lathrop and Wengert, *Marks of the Church in a Pluralistic Age*, 55, 60.

12. Jenson formulates this task in a similar way: "The church, we may say, is the community that speaks Christianese, and theology formulates the syntax and semantics of this language. Doctrinal statements function as accepted rules of proper usage; theological opinions of individual theologians or schools are attempts to point out such rules." Jenson further describes Christian theology as *"prescriptive grammar."* Jenson here distinguishes himself clearly from Lindbeck. Jenson therefore maintains, that "all sentences of Christian doctrine could not be stripped of first-level sentences, and that therefore does any considerable body of theology never in practice appear as pure second-level discourse." Jenson further distinguishes two strands in normative theology, pastoral and systematic theology. Jenson, *Systematic Theology*, 1:18, 20, 19, 22.

13. Cf. here how Gadamer finds that (philosophical) hermeneutics is the methodological basis of the human sciences, but also a universal aspect of philosophy, Gadamer, *Wahrheit und Methode*, 479.

therefore the contemporary, interpretative use of these texts—for formal and strategic reasons—that is the hermeneutical focus here. The texts are used to "produce" meaning in order to further a better understanding of an interpretative problem.[14]

The most in-depth engagement of Lutheran theology with the MacIntyrian approach to practices, has been offered by German theologian (now US-based), Reinhard Hütter. In his book, *Suffering Divine Things. Theology as Church Practice* (2000), he elaborates a theology that examines and criticizes Macintyre's use of the Neo-Arisotelian practice(s) approach.[15] Hütter elaborates extensively on how his notion of "practice" is related to Macintyre's definition of (social) practices. Hütter's theological ambition is profoundly ecclesiological, and he advocates that the freedom and identity of theology as a church practice can only be realized in relation to the salvific-economic *telos* of the public of the Holy Spirit, e.g., the church.

Hütter's particular contribution to the practices conversation is his application of Luther's notion of the seven "marks of the church" (the *notae ecclesiae*) from Luther's treatise *On the Councils and the Church* (1539). Hütter claims, that from a certain perspective, these marks may be understood as practices, and he calls them "the church's core practices."[16] These are practices which "at once both constitute and characterize the church" because of their soteriological *telos*, namely that Christ himself is present in the practices.[17]

To develop a Lutheran understanding of the presence of Christ in Christian practices in critical dialogue with contemporary Lutheran

---

14. Cf. here how Gadamer insists on the importance of the continuous interpretation of (old) texts: "Der Text, ob Gesetz oder Heilsbotschaft, wenn er angemessen verstanden werden soll, d.h. dem Anspruch, den der Text erhebt, entsprechend, in jedem Augenblick, d.h. in jeder konkreten Situation, neu und anders verstanden werden muss. Verstehen ist hier immer schon Anwenden" (Gadamer, *Wahrheit und Methode*, 314).

15. Hütter, *Suffering Divine Things*. Hütter develops his perspective on the church as a public and the role of the church's core practices further in his book written in 2004, cf. Hütter, *Bound to be Free*.

16. Hütter, *Suffering Divine Things*, 129. In Hütter's listing, the seven core church practices are named: 1. The external, orally preached word of God (which includes believing, confessing, and acting in accordance with it); 2. baptism; 3. the Lord's Supper; 4. the office of the keys as church discipline; 5. ordination and offices; 6. public prayer, praise, thanksgiving, instruction; and 7. discipleship in suffering.

17. Hütter, *Suffering Divine Things*, 133.

engagements in the practices conversation and a systematical-theological interpretation I will focus mainly on the following works of Luther:

The Small Catechism and *The Large Catechism* (1529)

On the Councils and the Church (1539) *(mainly the third part)*

Confession Concerning Christ's Supper (1528) *(mainly the third part)*

There are both *formal* and *material* reasons for choosing these treatises:

Formally, the Catechisms are part of the confessional basis in most Evangelical-Lutheran churches. The Confession Concerning Christ's Supper is not an official confessional document, but the third part of this treatise is quoted frequently in the Book of Concord. *Formally*, these treatises represent the work of the mature Luther. They take the form of positive confessions of the theology of the reformer. The Catechisms are in many ways the closest one can come to a comprehensive Lutheran theology.

Both *formally* and *materially*, these treatises are important, as those who have tried to engage Lutheran perspectives in the discussion on Christian practices have used both *On the Councils and the Church* and the Catechisms.[18] But most importantly, *materially*, I believe that a systematical-theological reading of these texts will serve as an important resource in addressing the problem that this book works with– how to interpret the presence of Christ in Christian practices, as all these treatises focus on the link between practices and the presence of Christ, and I believe that this will enable me to criticize and challenge the theology of the Christian practices paradigm.

After Aristotle—After MacIntyre

Craig R. Dykstra's 1991 article "Reconceiving Practice" marked the starting point for a certain theological engagement with practices.[19] In this article Dykstra discusses how theology, and in particular theological

---

18. In the *Small* and *Large Catechism* Luther develops the theological foundations of a Christian everyday life, a life shaped by some of the same gifts or "practices" he later outlines in *On the Councils and the Church*. The catechisms are also important from a historical-contextual youth ministry perspective. Their role as textbooks for ministry over the centuries cannot be underestimated. For a broader discussion of the "Lutheran" research front on the theme of Christian practices, see the beginning of chapter 3.

19. Dykstra, "Reconceiving Practice."

education, should engage with Alasdair MacIntyre's Neo-Aristotelian interpretation of virtue ethics through his concept of social practices. At the beginning of the practices conversation the main focus was on how theological education should be informed or re-structured by a practice approach to theology.[20] During the 1990s Dykstra and other theologians, such as Dorothy C. Bass, started to engage Christian practices in a wider context, not only focusing on theological education, but also by elaborating on the role of Christian practices in the life of a Christian and in the life of Christian communities.[21]

Rethinking theological education through Christian practices also expanded the focus of theological education and theology beyond the academy. In the book *Practicing Theology* (2002) theologians from different theological and ecclesial traditions elaborated on what it means to do theology departing from an engagement in Christian practices.[22] The main point for the authors in this book is that reconceiving the importance of practices ultimately reorders the way one should think about and do theology.

Fundamentally, the engagement in Christian practices is also a quest to rethink the construction of the Christian self. It has to do with identity. Kenda Creasy Dean roots her theological project in the claim that it is really the identity of adolescents which is at stake. Drawing upon and criticizing the work of developmental psychologist Erik H. Erikson, Dean argues that youth ministry has for too long been sold to psychology and social science. Dean's alternative is to let the post-modern adolescent patchwork self be transformed and shaped through passionate Christian practices, which convey the cruciform pattern of self-giving love.[23]

The term "Christian practices" is a term coined by Dorothy C. Bass and Craig Dykstra. Dean's use of the term "practice" is inspired by Bass and Dykstra. By "Christian practices" Bass and Dykstra mean "things Christian people do together over time to address fundamental human needs in response to and in the light of God's active presence for the life of the world."[24] They have developed their understanding of this term

---

20. Cf. also Kelsey, *To Understand God Truly*, 118–24.

21. For a better overview of the different contributions, cf. www.practicingourfaith.org.

22. Volf and Bass, *Practicing Theology*.

23. Dean, *Practicing Passion*, 234.

24. Dykstra and Bass, "A Theological Understanding of Christian Practices," 18. Bass and Dykstra add that "we think that the definition of practices quoted here would

mainly in dialogue with moral philosopher Alasdair MacIntyre's Neo-Aristotelian use of the term "social practices" as a way to rediscover communitarian virtue ethics.

Alasdair MacIntyre's focus on virtues and practices as a way forward for (communtarian) ethics in a shifting culture has given birth to a whole discussion, including in theological circles, on how "practice" and "praxis" should be understood. Reinhard Hütter addresses this discussion when he seeks to develop an understanding of theology as a church practice. Hütter discusses both Plato's and Aristotle's distinctions between *poiesis, theory, practice* and *praxis*. Hütter underlines that Aristotle's understanding of practice, or *poiesis*, is linked to his idea that every meaningful action is oriented towards a goal, where the goal of *poiesis* resides outside *poiesis* itself.[25] Hütter refers to MacIntyre's application of Aristotle's distinction between praxis and practice. Fundamentally, MacIntyre understands practices as "social practices," which are complex social activities that pursue certain goods internal to the practice themselves. MacIntyre develops his understanding of (social) practice as:

> Any coherent and complex form of socially established cooperative human activity through which goods internal to that form of activity are realized in the course of trying to achieve those standards of excellence which are appropriated to, and partially definitive of, that form of activity, with the result that human powers to achieve excellence, and human conceptions of the ends and goods involved, are systematically extended.[26]

The theological reflection on practice is a contested field. Needless to say, there are several approaches to the term "practice."[27] Some, like

---

be strengthened by the addition of the words 'in Jesus Christ' at the end, which would clarify the character and content of the active divine presence that is so central to our understanding of practices." For another overview of different definitions of Christian practices, cf. D. B. Bass, *The Practicing Congregation*, 65.

25. Hütter, *Suffering Divine Things*, 32–33.

26. MacIntyre, *After Virtue*, 187. MacIntyre's definition of virtue builds on his definition of practice: "A virtue is an acquired human quality the possession and exercise of which tends to enable us to achieve those goods which are internal to practices and the lack of which effectively prevents us from achieving any such goods" (MacIntyre, *After Virtue*, 191).

27. Cf. here, for instance, Bourdieu's use of the term "practice" in *The Logic of Practice*, 16; and Bourdieu, *Outline of a Theory of Practice*, where practice is defined as "systems of durable transposable *dispositions*" (72), and "subjective but not individual systems" (86). Cf. also Certeau's use of the term "practice" in *The Practice of Everyday*

Kathryn Tanner, following Bourdieu, stress the improvisational character of practices. Others focus on practices as a form of spiritual discipline. Others, following MacIntyre, understand practices in the light of moral philosophy.[28] Some find that Bourdieu and MacIntyre do not necessarily represent mutually exclusive definitions of practices, as they speak in different registers. They find that MacIntyre's register is most useful for framing questions about the *telos* of a whole whereas Bourdieu's helps to see the ways most practices are congeries of practices, each with a *telos* of its own.[29]

METHOD AND RESEARCH DESIGN

The Structure of the Study

This study takes Bass and Dykstra's understanding of Christian practices as its point of departure, but also engages other theological approaches to (Christian) practices, in particular that of Reinhard Hütter. The intention is to criticize and develop the understanding of "Christian practices," focusing on how the presence of Christ in Christian practices should be interpreted. This book is not first and foremost an investigation into the epistemological meaning of the term practice, but a systematic- theological discussion on some of the more important theological issues that the engagement in "Christian practices" raises. This theological focus is also in line with how Bass and Dykstra underline that their approach to practices is fundamentally theological.[30]

In chapter 2 I will largely be interested in how Bass, Dykstra, Dean et al. develop their own (immanent) understanding(s) of "Christian

---

Life and *The Practice of Everyday Life*, vol. 2. For a broad account of different practical theological approaches to the term "practice," cf. Cahalan and Nieman, "Mapping the Field of Practical Theology," 68–69. Hütter reflects on the interest in "practices" in retrospect in an article from 2007 (Hütter, "The Christian Life," 296–97). For yet another, and early, approach to practices, cf. Hauerwas and Willimon, *Resident Aliens* and *Where Resident Aliens live*.

28. In the introduction to *Practical Theology* Bass claims that "Macintyre's virtue ethics emphasizes that practices pursue the good in a coherent, traditioned way, while social scientists influenced by Marxist thought stress the constant negotiations over power that give particular shape to practices in specific social situations." Dykstra and Bass, "A Theological Understanding of Christian Practices," 20.

29. Daniels III and Smith, "History, Practice and Theological Education," 217.

30. Dykstra, *Growing in the Life of Faith*, 23.

practices."[31] In chapters 3 and 4 these understandings and definitions of (Christian) "practices" will be challenged and criticized by other interpretations of the term, for instance, the definitions offered by Hütter.

Discussing Christian practices does not only include discussing the nature of the practice itself, but it also implies focusing on the role of the practicing subject in Christian practices and the role of the context in which these practices take place. The interest and engagement in Christian practices has come out of an analysis of the context. Likewise, an inherent claim in the Christian practices paradigm is that practices may develop and possibly transform the lives of the practitioners. It is therefore crucial to interpret and discuss Christian practices as something that takes place in a triangle between *practice, practitioner* and *context*. This should be interpreted as a "hermeneutic triangle," not as three separate ends: I aim to analyze and discuss the presence of Christ in Christian practices in the interconnectedness of *practice-practitioner-context*. In terms of "context," the focus in this book is clearly selective, as the investigation here focuses mainly on the ecclesiological context or the eccleciological implications of the Christian practices paradigm.

My three research questions, set out below, are structured by this triangle. They arise from the central doctrinal questions—the "unanswered questions"—concerning the presence of Christ in Christian practices. There is a certain "hierarchy" between them, however. The point of departure is Christology—investigating the presence of Christ in Christian practices. This is the starting point of the book. Based on this Christological investigation, I go on to analyze and discuss the anthropological, soteriological, and ecclesiological "implications" of the problem.

The term "implications" may be misleading if it is taken to signal a one-way movement. The point here is rather to signal that from the primary point of departure—discussing how to interpret the presence of Christ in Christian practices—a circular movement starts, which implies analyzing and discussing the anthropological and soteriological implications and how they influence the analysis and discussion of the ecclesiological implications. This finally leads back to the primary point of departure—trying to develop an understanding of the presence of Christ in Christian practice—and discussing this problem related to practice-practitioner-context.

31. As we will see in chapter 2, Dean makes use of both Edward Farley's idea of ecclesial activities and Dykstra and Bass's definition of Christian practices; cf. Dean, *Practicing Passion*, 155–57.

The three research questions are therefore as follows:

(Practice)
1. How should the presence of Christ in Christian practices be understood, and what constitutes the presence of Christ in a practice? (*Christology*)

(Practitioner)
2. What are the anthropological and soteriological implications of this understanding?
(*Anthropology and Soteriology*)

(Context)
3. What are the ecclesiological implications of this understanding? (*Ecclesiology*)

Method and Aim of the Study

With this set-up, I lean on the work of Reinhard Hütter, who understands theology as a church practice, which participates in and is defined by the work of the Holy Spirit in the world. Doing theology is participating in a sending to the world, which is revealed in the interplay between the doctrine of the church (theory—or *doctrina evangelii*) and the church's core practices (practice). With this definition of theology Hütter gives a helpful contribution to the problem of whether theology as a science defines itself or is defined from the outside. Hütter claims that: "Only in the Holy Spirit and its genuine poiesis of communion does theology as church practice participate in God's liberum arbitrium. Only by remaining bound to God's economy of salvation does it step into the "freedom of the children of God."[32]

From this perspective, ministry should be understood as a part of the theological enterprise, in line with how Hütter understands theology as a church practice.[33] This ties ministry, and youth ministry for that matter, closely to the ecclesiological discourse. This does not mean that ecclesiological discourse should not engage in dialogue with insights from

---

32. Hütter, *Suffering Divine Things*, 157.

33. Similarly Rasmusson argues that "it is the church, as a set of specific discourse-practices, that makes theology as social theory possible and therefore also gives theology the perspective from which it can interact with and christianly interpret the societies in which the church exits." Cf. Rasmusson, *The Church as Polis*, 378.

other sciences—such as cultural sciences, sociology (of religion), social anthropology, history of ideas, ethnography, psychology (of religion) etc. As the church is doing ministry and employing ministers, theology and particularly ecclesiology is forced to reflect upon this practice.

Don Browning points out that "our concrete practices are theory-laden; a change in these rules implies a change in our view of the fundamental structure of our narratives, deep metaphors, and world views."[34] This book takes a change in practice rules—the introduction of the Christian practices paradigm to ministry—as its point of departure, and analyzes and discusses this change and its theological implications, with a particular focus on how it understands the construction or formation of the Christian self in relation to baptism.

This book is therefore a study in *practical theology*, insofar as it takes as its point of departure the "practical" context of ministry and also aims at returning to address this context. By starting and ending in practical ministry this study has practical theological reflection as its "outer framework." If the "outer framework" is practical theology, however, the "inner framework" of the book is *systematic theology*, as discussing the presence of Christ in Christian practices is profoundly a systematic theological enterprise.[35]

The emerging interest in Christian practices represents in many ways "new" language. I have chosen to analyze this language with the help of "old" classical language—dogmatic analysis.[36] I do this by discussing the theology of Christian practices, looking particularly at their Christological, soteriological, anthropological and ecclesiological implications. The reason for doing this is that the Christian practices paradigm explicitly and implicitly makes normative, dogmatic claims, and it is therefore worth analyzing dogmatically.

---

34. Browning, *A Fundamental Practical Theology*, 281. For a critique of Browning's methodological scheme, cf. Graham, *Transforming Practice*, 208–10.

35. As Webster points out, there is no firmly established usage of the term systematic theology, but the adjective "systematic" suggests that systematic theology is "especially interested in the scope, unity, and coherence of Christian teaching." Cf. Webster "Introduction: Systematic Theology," 1. Webster further pinpoints that "the subject matter which is engaged in systematic theological inquiry is Christian teaching, that is, Christian claims about reality." Therefore, systematic theology "attempts conceptual articulation of Christian claims about God and everything else in relation to God, characterized by comprehensiveness and coherence." Ibid., 2.

36. One may call this the *etic* language of this book, whereas the practice-talk is the *emic* language.

In its inner framework this book therefore works mostly with what John Webster calls "the internal orientation of systematic theology." According to Webster, systematic theology has both an external and an internal orientation. The more internal orientation—what Webster calls the dogmatic-analytic element—is where systematic theology "concerns itself with ordered exposition of Christian claims about reality."[37] This is also the focus in this study.

More precisely, the interpretative methods used in the main chapters may be schematically outlined in the following way: In chapter 2 the analysis may be labeled *analytic dogmatics*. In various ways, the analysis in chapters 3, 4 makes use of what may be labeled *discursive dogmatics*, as the dissertation here sets out to interpret different texts dogmatically (cf. the research questions) and bring them into critical dialogue with each other in order to develop answers to the problem addressed in the dissertation. But the ultimate aim of the book is *normative*, as it seeks to give an answer to how the presence of Christ in Christian practices *should* be interpreted. Therefore the final interpretive method used is *normative dogmatics*, which I have often used in the concluding paragraphs. It is also important to underline, however, that the borders between these three ways of doing dogmatics should not be distinguished too sharply.[38]

Don Browning outlines the concept of "fundamental practical theology," consisting of four sub-movements; *descriptive theology, historical theology, systematic theology,* and *strategic practical theology*.[39] The research design of this dissertation, with its use of various interpretative methods, relates to this concept. But in this study the emphasis is mainly on one of the sub-movements, namely the third—systematic theological analysis, and discussion on a particular theme—here, how to understand the presence of Christ in Christian practices. This is a deliberate

---

37. Webster further finds that "in its external orientation—what might be called the apologetic-hermeneutical element of the task—systematic theology concerns itself with the explication and defence of Christian claims about reality in order to bring to light their justification, relevance, and value." Cf. ibid., 7. Webster argues that Barth is a typical example of the internal orientation, whereas Pannenberg is a typical example of the external orientation.

38. Austad, *Tolkning av kristen tro*, 46–49. But it is also important to underline that the borders between these three ways of doing dogmatics should not be distinguished too sharply.

39. Browning also relates his project to MacIntyre and the Neo-Aristotelian turn and interest in *phronesis*—practical reason, cf. Browning, *A Fundamental Practical Theology*, 8, 11.

and selective move in the book—to attempt to pause on the systematic theological questions that the Christian practices conversation raises. By doing this, the book offers theological reflection on a particular theme emerging from a particular practice conversation within a particular context, the context of ministry. It is an attempt to answer questions, which are crucial to any context of Christian ministry, where people are called to follow Jesus:

- How is Jesus Christ present in the world?
- How is Jesus Christ present in the practices of Christian community?
- What constitutes this presence?

Fundamentally, the study aims at discerning the shape of Christian discipleship[40] in the light of Lutheran Christology and Lutheran baptismal theology in an era of heightened personal autonomy.

---

40. *Discipleship* is made the point of departure and orientation in many contemporary attempts to map practical theology. Christian discipleship is described as "being called by Jesus to follow." There is a strong, and explicit, normative energy in these attempts, which is another argument for analyzing and discussing the more dogmatic implications of the engagement in Christian practices. Cf. for instance, Cahalan and Nieman, "Mapping the Field of Practical Theology," 66–67. Cahalan and Nieman also critique models of practical theology coming from liberation theology: "Other views of practical theology have proposed three or four distinct stages of operation, such as 'see-judge-act' or 'describe-interpret-evaluate-strategize.' Besides being needlessly complicated and unidirectional, these models do not fully appreciate what counts as theological work. On the one hand, they treat certain moments in the process as relatively value-free, especially efforts to describe the context. Yet if the very reason for practical theology is to promote discipleship, then we approach any situation interested in what Christian faithfulness entails" (Cahalan and Nieman, "Mapping the Field of Practical Theology," 84).

2

The Engagement in Christian Practices

A NEW PARADIGM FOR MINISTRY

The Emergence of a Paradigm

THE CHRISTIAN PRACTICES PARADIGM has evolved in a context where more and more theologians argue that church and society exist in a post-Christendom climate. Craig Dykstra argues for the use of Christian practices from this perspective and claims that consumer society has made the church unable to recognize and meet the (spiritual) hunger for meaning. In other words, consumer society has made the construction of the Christian self something dubious and ambivalent. The other problem—and here Dykstra leans on his teacher Edward Farley—is that contemporary theology is plagued by insecurity on the most fundamental issue—knowledge of God.[1] Therefore church and theology is ridden

---

1. Cf. here also how Dykstra roots the concepts "knowledge of God" and "faith" in Calvinistic theology: "Faith, for Calvin, is not a blind leap into the utterly unknowable, much less speculation. No, it is *knowledge*. It is a deep, profound, existential knowledge that infuses not only our minds, but also our hearts and even our bodies. It is knowledge that, as we come to know it more and more deeply, over many years, will give form and substance to our entire imagination, to our whole way of being in the world, to our very existence. It is knowledge of the overflowing abundance of the grace and mercy and love of God" (Dykstra, "Pastoral and Ecclesial Imagination," 56).

by a kind of "practical atheism," where "we are not really sure that all the things we do in church and as church count for much."[2]

As the interest in Christian practices started with an interest to reform education in general, and education of clergy in particular,[3] Dykstra claims that theology, and theological education in particular, is troubled with an idea of practice that is harmfully individualistic, technological, ahistorical, and abstract. Departing from Edward Farley's critique of the clerical paradigm Dykstra argues for a communal rather than an individual understanding of practice. Dykstra finds that too often we leave out the larger social and historical context and instead focus on the practicing individual, often perceived as the practicing expert.[4]

The roots in Aristotelian ethics and modern social theory are fundamental for the engagement in Christian practices.[5] Craig Dykstra's understanding of Christian practices was developed in the late 1980s and the early 1990s, but the most profound presentation of Dykstra's theology on Christian practices is presented in his book *Growing in the Life of Faith: Education and Christian Practices* (1999/2005). Craig Dykstra here makes an effort to combine, discuss and critique the insights of theologians and philosophers such as Lindbeck, Hauerwas and MacIntyre.[6]

In his examination of MacIntyre's definition of social practices, Dykstra concludes that "practices are those cooperative human activities through which we, as individuals and as communities, grow and develop in moral character and substance."[7] In this book Dykstra also defines "practice" as "an ongoing, shared activity of a community of

---

2. Dykstra, *Growing in the Life of Faith*, 8–9. Other theologians influencing Bass, Dykstra, Dean, et al. are Robert W. Jenson and Jürgen Moltmann.

3. Dykstra, "Reconceiving Practice," 53–54, 58. Hauerwas and Willimon's approach to practices differs from that of Dyktra and Bass, and I (purposely) do not engage with the work of Hauerwas and Willimon in this analysis.

4. Ibid., 35–37.

5. Bass and Dykstra here explicitly refer to the philosophers Ludwig Wittgenstein, Charles Taylor, and Alasdair MacIntyre and social theorists Pierre Bourdieu and Michel de Certeau; cf. Bass and Dykstra, *For Life Abundant*, 2, 5. For this, cf. also the lengthy footnote on page 7 in the same book. Aristotelian language is implicit in much of their thinking on Christian practices, and in particular their use of the word "telos," cf. for instance p. 8 in the same book. The whole idea of a "life-giving way of life" also evokes Aristotelian connotations.

6. Dykstra, *Growing in the Life of Faith*, xii.

7. Ibid., 68–70.

people that partly defines and partly makes them who they are."[8] Dykstra wants to learn from Alasdair MacIntyre's definition of social practices and focus on practice as something cooperative, understanding "practice" mainly not as people doing things *to* each other, but people doing things *with* each other.[9]

Dykstra also discusses whether a practice demands that the practicing subjects are within physical proximity, but he argues that the cooperation in a practice does not come primarily through persons interacting physically. Rather the cooperative element in practices comes through persons engaging in activities that gain their meaning from the *form*. Further, this form emerges through a complex tradition of interactions among many people sustained over a long period of time. Therefore Dykstra also defines a practice as "participation in a cooperatively formed pattern of activity that emerges out of a complex tradition of interactions among many people sustained over a long period of time." Dykstra also underlines that a practice cannot be abstracted from its past, as the past is embedded in the practice itself.[10]

Dorothy C. Bass, in her first book on practices, *Practicing Our Faith* (1997), underlines that the book originated in Dykstra's insight that the idea of "practices" provides a fruitful way of addressing what Bass labels the yearning of contemporary people for deeper understanding of and involvement in the redemptive practice of God in the world.[11] Related to this, Bass therefore argues that practices are shared activities that address fundamental human needs, and which woven together, form a way of life.[12]

Together Bass and Dykstra underline several important components in practices:

---

8. Ibid., 48. Related to MacIntyre's definition Dykstra underlines that "the idea of excellence in a practice makes most sense when the point of a practice is the achievement of mastery." Ibid., 75.

9. Dykstra, "Reconceiving Practice," 42.

10. Ibid., 43–44.

11. Bass, *Practicing our Faith*, xiii. Here she writes about the yearning for a way of life that is "whole, and touched by the presence of God." Bass also finds that human beings "yearn for a richer and deeper understanding of what it means to live as Christian in a time when basic patterns of human relationships are changing all around us."

12. Ibid., xi.

> Practices address fundamental human needs and conditions through concrete human acts. Practices are done together and over time. Practices possess standards of excellence.[13]

In later contributions on Christian practices Bass and Dykstra still relate their understanding of practices to MacIntyre, but also underline that their account of practices differs from MacIntyre on certain points in that their account is theological and normed not only internally but also through the responsive relationship of Christian practices to God.[14]

Bass also points out four distinct components, which characterize practices in general:

> Practices resist the separation of thinking from acting. Practices are social, belonging to groups of people across generations. Practices are rooted in the past but are also constantly adapting to changing circumstances. Practices articulate wisdom that is in the keeping of practitioners who do not think of themselves as theologians.[15]

Concluding on what defines a practice, Bass therefore highlights the following:

> Practices are borne by social groups over time and are constantly negotiated in the midst of changing circumstances: Practices are clusters of activities within which meaning and doing are inextricably interwoven. Therefore practices shape behavior, but they also foster practice-specific knowledge, capacities, dispositions, and virtues. Finally, those who participate in practices are formed in particular ways of thinking about and living in the world.[16]

As I have already pointed out, other theologians in the US have also engaged in defining and interpreting Christian practices. One of them is Kathryn Tanner, who gives a distinct contribution to the understanding of Christian practices. She underlines that the meaning of Christian practices is not internal to them, but rather this meaning is established *in relationships*. This happens by what is done or not done in church about

---

13. Dykstra and Bass, "Times of Yearning," 6–7. They here also admit that their use of the term practices is "loosely based on the work of the moral philosopher Alasdair MacIntyre," by making and explicit reference to MacIntyre's definition of social practices. Cf. Bass and Dykstra, "Growing in the Practices of Faith," 205.

14. Dykstra and Bass, "A Theological Understanding of Practices," 21.

15. Volf and Bass, *Practicing Theology*, 6.

16. Bass, "Ways of Life Abundant," 29.

the practices of the wider society, by what Christian practices do or don't do *to* them.[17] Amy Plantinga Pauw, on the other hand, underlines the importance of keeping the focus on a theology of grace in understanding practices. In regard to this, Pauw points out there may be exemplary cases of discipleship, where the coherence of belief and practice is so impressive that it masks the extent to which beliefs and practices undermine each other. More often, however, the ordinary struggles of religious people tend to lay bare the ligaments that hold beliefs and practices together.[18]

Diana Butler Bass suggests a grouping of three different categories of practices:

1. *moral* practices, like hospitality and healing (Bass and Dykstra inspired by MacIntyre)
2. *ascetical* practices, like contemplation and silence (Sarah Coakley inspired by the mystics)
3. *anthropological* practices, negotiating the faith in relation to the larger culture (Kathryn Tanner inspired by Bourdieu and de Certeau).[19]

Bass and Dykstra have been criticized for not paying enough attention to the standards of excellence in practices, that it is not enough to have a set of practices that shape us, we must also have a set of Christian practices that shape us *in a particular way*: The definition of Christian practices should have a specific reference to internal goods, that acknowledges that kingdom of God is internal to Christian practices.[20]

Miroslav Volf also gives his distinct definition of beliefs and practices. Volf defines "practices" as "cooperative and meaningful human endeavors that seek to satisfy fundamental human needs and conditions and that people do together over time." Based on this, Volf argues that what he calls "core Christian beliefs" are "*by definition normatively inscribed in sacraments*" but not in "practices." Hence sacraments ritually enact normative patterns for practices.[21] Therefore Volf claims that "Christian

---

17. Tanner, "Theological Reflection and Christian Practices," 242.

18. Pauw, "Attending to the Gap between Beliefs and Practices," 36. Pauw is also one of the many who conclude that "practices shape beliefs, but religious beliefs also shape practices." Ibid.

19. D. B. Bass, *The Practicing Congregation*, 65–68.

20. Muthiah, "Christian Practices," 174–75.

21. Volf, "Theology for a Way of Life," 248.

beliefs are indispensable for the creation of the Christian moral space in which alone engagement in Christian practices makes sense."[22]

Volf also claims, however, that "basic Christian beliefs *as beliefs* entail practical commitments," therefore "Christian beliefs are not simply statements about what was, is, and will be the case; they are statements about what *should* be the case and what human beings should do about that."[23] Based on this, Volf advocates that it is Christian beliefs that normatively shape Christian practices. Therefore engaging in practices can lead to acceptance and deeper understanding of these beliefs. Further Volf argues, drawing on Pierre Bourdieu's idea of the socially informed body, that people make Christian beliefs their own and understand them in particular ways partly because of the practices to which they have been introduced—in which their souls and bodies have been trained—in the course of their lives. Volf finally points out that "we engage in practices for the sake of God; we don't construe a picture of God so as to justify engagement in a particular set of practices."[24]

With their focus on Christian practices and their social setting (Tanner), Christian practices and a theology of grace (Pauw), Christian practices and how it relates to the work of the Spirit (Muthiah), and Christian practices and their relationship to normative, core Christian beliefs and sacraments (Volf), Bass and Dykstra's approach to Christian practices is both complemented and challenged. This short overview of the variety of approaches to practices also shows the need to reflect further theologically on Christian practices.

Much of Bass and Dykstra's explicit theological reflection on Christian practices is found in the introduction chapters to the books on Christian practices.[25] In *For Life Abundant* (2008) Bass and Dykstra start with a lengthy theological and programmatic vision:

> God in Christ promises abundant life for all creation. By the power of the Holy Spirit, the church receives this promise through faith and takes up a way of life that embodies Christ's abundant life in and for the world. The church's ministers are called to embrace this way of life and also to lead particular

22. Ibid., 251.
23. Ibid., 253–54.
24. Ibid., 256–60.
25. Cf. for instance, Bass and Dykstra, *For Life* Abundant, 12. On the same page Bass and Dykstra give a good historical overview of the different books and publications of the project.

communities of faith to live it in their own situations. To do this, pastors and other ecclesial ministers must be educated and formed in ways of knowing, perceiving, relating, and acting that enable such leadership.[26]

Although Bass and Dykstra in this vision offer some new perspectives and approaches, their main theological features have been pretty much the same over the last ten to fifteen years. Signal words are "way of life" and "in and for the world."[27] What is "new" in *For Life Abundant* is an expanded focus on and deepened articulation of the particular communities of faith.

Bass points out that for her and Dykstra Christian practices are clusters of meaningful action, which includes thinking and representation, and that are sizable and significant enough to address certain basic human needs and conditions. The basic needs might be "relationship with one another, creation and God; for physical care in illness for injury; for certain material goods," and the conditions might be "finitude, mortality, and physical and psychological vulnerability."[28]

In concluding their work on Christian practices and practical theology, Bass and Dykstra underline that what they seek to develop is a practical theology that takes as its *telos* a life-giving way of life in and for the world. This way of life is necessarily open-ended, as it emerges in specific times and places which are constantly in flux. For Bass and Dykstra there is therefore a potentially unlimited range of actual situations and communities within which abundant life can emerge.[29] Ultimately, Bass and Dykstra's project is all about reclaiming Christian faith as a way of life. Therefore they also argue that the shape of practical theology should fit the way of life it tries to describe, critique, sustain, and embody.[30]

Altogether, Bass and Dykstra claim that their engagement in Christian practices is profoundly a "theological movement."[31] They describe this

---

26. Ibid., 1.

27. Cf. also the first question on the list of questions congregations should ask: "How can the church best foster a way of life that truly is life-giving in and for the sake of the world?" (ibid., 11).

28. Bass, "Ways of Life Abundant," 30.

29. Bass and Dykstra, *For Life Abundant*, 355.

30. Ibid., 356.

31. Dykstra, *Growing in the Life of Faith*, 23. For an overview of Bass and Dykstra's engagement in Christian practices, see Bass' foreword to the second edition of Dykstra's *Growing in the Life of Faith*, xii–xvi. Bass explains that her work with Dykstra on

movement as being guided by two main questions: What does it mean to live the Christian life faithfully and well, and how can we help one another to do so?[32] This theological understanding takes as its point of departure that Christian practices are the constituent elements in a way of life. Such a way of life becomes incarnate when human beings live in the light of and in response to God's gift of the life abundant. When Bass and Dykstra refer to Christian practices, they therefore have something theologically normative in mind, which once again underline the importance of a more profound dogmatic engagement with Christian practices.[33]

Christian Practices in the Context of Youth Ministry

The interest in rediscovering Christian practices as a curriculum for youth ministry grows out of the same uneasiness about the development of religious faith and practice in the US. In *Practicing Passion* (2004), Kenda Creasy Dean takes the increased interest in spirituality among young people in North America as her point of departure. She explains this interest by pointing at paradigm acts or events, like the terrorist attacks on September 11, 2001, and the shooting tragedy at Columbine High School in 1999. For Dean, both these events are events where passionate religious faith has been displayed.[34] Dean advocates that the

---

practices started with engaging in Alasdair MacIntyre's account of social practices. But Bass also points out that "the theological turn we have taken marks a significant break with the concepts developed there." The break that Bass and Dykstra claim to have made is that "the 'goods' that concern us are not 'internal' to a practice but are oriented to God and God's intentions for all creation." Bass, "Ways of Life Abundant," 30.

32. Dykstra, *Growing in the Life of Faith*, xii. The two main questions for Bass and Dykstra in *For Life Abundant* are: 1. What is the shape of a contemporary way of life that is truly life-giving in and for the sake of world? 2. How can the church foster such a way of life, for the good of all creation? Bass, "Ways of Life Abundant," 23.

33. Dykstra and Bass, "A Theological Understanding of Christian Practices," 21. Bass even writes that "Dykstra and I have probed theological and normative dimensions that are not necessarily in the foreground for other theorists" (Bass, "Ways of Life Abundant," 30).

34. Dean extends this motif in *Practicing Passion*, where the opening chapter points to how these events and acts have shown American teenagers what it means to be passionate about what you believe in—for better and for worse. It is against this background of what Dean interprets as teenage martyrdom that she develops her notion of passion as the leading motif for youth ministry. The story of the young American John Walker Lindh, who converted to Islam at the age of sixteen and after a while joined the Taliban, is used by Dean as a "critical" example of how important

church has to respond to this increased interest in spirituality by rediscovering a curriculum of Christian practices.

In *Almost Christian* (2010), however, Dean is less sure about *how* passionate American teenagers are about religion. Based on the findings of the National Study of Youth and Religion, Dean here argues that American young people are being formed into an imposter faith that poses as Christianity.[35] Ultimately, Dean finds that this faith lacks the holy desire and missional clarity necessary for Christian discipleship.[36] Dean's predicament is an echo of Craig Dykstra's self-critical reflection on behalf of the traditional churches that Christians do not know the language of faith because they simply do not live the form of life out of which such language grows. According to Dykstra, to foster such a connection is particularly crucial for youth ministry, as the care and education of the young demands the recovery of a lively, vital, usable religious language.[37] This focus on recovering religious language is something Dean and Dykstra have in common.

In *Almost Christian* (2010) Dean takes as her point of departure the dominant religious faith in America—Moralistic Therapeutic Deism, according to the National Study of Youth and Religion. According to Dean, this is a religion, which helps people to be nice, to feel good, and which leaves God in the background. In this book, even more strongly than in her previous books, Dean advocates why youth ministry could not be done (well) when separated from the larger faith community. As a response to this, she proposes three Christian practices that can help to refocus what she labels self-indulgent Christianity in the direction of missional faith, namely; translation, testimony and detachment.[38] Once again, the need to develop a new-old religious (body) language is emphasized.

The focus on historical Christian practices which Dean and others promote is designed to as a counterpart and in juxtaposition to the previous paradigm in youth ministry—the program and entertainment model. In different ways, *The Godbearing Life* (1998), *Practicing Passion* (2004) and *Almost Christian* (2010) are theological attempts to relate adolescent identity and the passion of Christ. Here Dean proposes a strong

---

it is to approach youth ministry and teenagers with the passion they deserve. Dean, *Practicing Passion*, 3, 30–31.

35. Smith and Denton, *Soul Searching*.
36. Dean, *Almost Christian*, 6.
37. Dykstra, *Growing in the Life of Faith*, 124–25.
38. Dean, *Almost Christian*, 21, 23.

interconnectedness: Adolescents *need* to be incorporated in the Passion of Christ through passionate practices to develop an authentic identity, and the church *needs* adolescent passion to rediscover its true identity.

In these books Dean criticizes how the church and the para-church movements alike have focused on programs instead of people. Due to this, youth ministry has often operated as a satellite apart from the center of congregational life. Dean finds that this program-driven youth ministry has served, consciously or unconsciously, as part of a strategy from the grown-up church to tame the passion of the youths in the church basement. As a result of this, young people have started to search for passion and identity outside the church walls.

In addition to Dean's books, there are numerous other books and authors engaging with Christian practices in youth ministry.[39] Many engagements in Christian practices in youth ministry have grown out of projects sponsored by the Lilly Endowment Inc.[40] In two books Mark Yaconelli draws on his experiences from co-directing the Youth Ministry and Spirituality Project (YMSP), which was launched in 1997 at San Francisco Theological Seminary and sponsored by the Lilly Endowment.[41] Yaconelli shares many of the same theological ambitions and motifs as Dean, and through this project he has served as a mentor for youth ministry within a wide range of denominations and churches in the US. Yaconelli quite explicitly addresses how contemplative Christian practice is a way to depart from a result- and program-based youth ministry to a youth ministry focused on discerning how Christ may be present in the lives of young people. Yaconelli also claims, that those in the church have forgotten how to be in relationships. Yaconelli sees contemplative youth ministry and Christian practices as a way to overcome this fallacy by "courageously beholding the reality of our own lives, the reality (whether

---

39. Cf. among others White, *Practicing Discernment with Youth*; and Edie, *Book, Bath, Table and Time*; and finally Jones, *Postmodern Youth Ministry*.

40. The Lilly Endowment Inc. is a large, private, family-owned philanthropic foundation, based in Indianapolis. It was founded by J. K. Lilly Sr. and his sons Eli and J. K. Jr., three members of the Presbyterian family who owned the Eli Lilly pharmaceutical company (founded in 1876), with gifts of stocks in the company. The Lilly Endowment Inc. largely focuses on three different "areas": religion, education, and charitable organizations operating within the state of Indiana. Craig R. Dykstra is Vice President for Religion at the Lilly Endowment Inc. See www.lillyendowment.org.

41. Yaconelli, *Contemplative Youth Ministry*, 26.

it be joy or suffering) of the young people we serve, and the reality of God's love beneath it all."[42]

Another example of a Lilly Endowment-sponsored research project in youth ministry is the Study of Exemplary Congregations in Youth Ministry. This project tried to examine the characteristics of a committed, maturing Christian youth, departing from seven essential characteristics of vital faith in young people, based on prior research studies.[43] Yet another example of a Lilly Endowment-sponsored project focusing on Christian practices is the Project on Congregations of Intentional Practices, focusing on "the role of Christian practices in fostering congregational vitality as experienced in churches of the historic mainline."[44]

In another Lilly-sponsored project, published in the book *Way to Live*, eighteen teenagers and eighteen adults share their reflections after exploring eighteen different Christian practices together.[45] Here Craig Dykstra is also credited with having taught those participating in the project "to think about a way of life that takes shape as we participate in Christian practices."[46]

Altogether, the appeal to a paradigm shift by rediscovering Christian practices in ministry is motivated by the cultural shift in the Western world, and it is theologically grounded, and didactically focused in its tactical strategy.

---

42. Ibid., 24.

43. The study combined quantitative and qualitative methods of research and worked with 131 congregations (nominated from among the seven participating denominations—Assemblies of God, Evangelical Covenant, Evangelical Lutheran Church in America [ELCA], Presbyterian Church [USA], Roman Catholic, Southern Baptist, and United Methodist Church). The twenty-one congregations with the highest score on the surveys were studied in more detail. The research project was based upon two previous studies, Effective Christian Education and Five Cries for Youth, and on the basis of these two studies identified seven key characteristics of a mature faith. The seven characteristics were "seeking spiritual growth," "possessing a vital faith," "practicing faith in community," "making faith a way of life," "living a life of service," "exercising moral responsibility," and "possessing a positive spirit." Cf. Martinson, Black, and Roberto, *The Spirit and Culture of Youth Ministry*, 19–27.

44. D. B. Bass, *The Practicing Congregation*, xi.

45. Richter and Bass, *Way to Live*.

46. Ibid., 309.

CHRISTIAN PRACTICES AND THE PRESENCE OF CHRIST

What Makes a Practice Christian?

Bass and Dykstra's understanding of what makes a practice Christian is quite complex and multi-faceted. First of all, Bass and Dykstra emphasize that every activity is not to be considered a practice. Dykstra underlines that the "form" of a practice is related to its value. Therefore, activities, which lack the "coherence and complexity necessary for generating value internal to the activity itself" are not to be considered as practices.[47]

Secondly, Dykstra, trying to move beyond MacIntyre, underlines that practices bear more than moral weight. They also bear epistemological weight in the sense that through practices we may become aware of certain *realities*, which outside of these practices are beyond our ken. Dykstra even argues that certain practices are in fact conditions for the possibility for us to recognize the risen Lord. Based on this he claims that "the engagement in the practice of service is a *condition* for the knowledge of a reality absolutely central to faith—the reality of the resurrection presence."[48] He also offers criteriological reflections on the term "practice," rather than Christological reflections. Dykstra does however argue that theology has to get involved in the discussion of which practices are constitutive for the Christian life.[49]

Thirdly, Bass and Dykstra further claim that each Christian practice "also has distinctive roots in Scripture."[50] But they also believe that each Christian practice incorporates both critical and self-critical perspectives, although it is the normative and theological understanding of practices, which does lead us to see each Christian practice as a whole as a good. Therefore Bass warns against the temptation to idealize Christian practices and the way of life they comprise, by making Christian practices seem more smooth and coherent than they actually are as they are intertwined with what they refer to as "the realities of everyday life."[51]

Fourthly, Bass and Dykstra underline the important role of the Christian community. At some points it seems that Bass (and Dykstra)

---

47. Dykstra, "Reconceiving Practice," 44.
48. Ibid., 45–46.
49. Ibid., 48, 52.
50. Bass, "Ways of Life Abundant," 31.
51. Ibid., 30, 34.

think that what really constitutes a practice as Christian, is Christian people. But later Bass explicitly points out that this is not the case: "To be called 'Christian' a practice must pursue a good beyond itself, responding to and embodying the self-giving dynamics of God's own creating, redeeming, and sustaining grace."[52] Therefore a practice is not Christian just because it is performed by Christians. Finally, and fifthly, Bass and Dykstra believe that engaging in Christian practices is a way of participating in the activity of God's Spirit in the world.

So what really makes a practice Christian according to Bass and Dykstra? The two offer several lists of criteria. Craig Dykstra has made a list of fourteen practices, which he finds, "appear consistently throughout the tradition and that are particularly significant for Christians today." The practices listed are practices Dykstra claims constitute being the church. He even claims that these practices make it possible for the Christian community "to continue their experience with God made present in the Word, in sacrament, in prayer, and in the community's life in obedience to its vocation in the world."[53]

The practices Dykstra lists are:

> Worshiping God together—praising God, giving thanks for God's creative and redemptive work in the world, hearing God's word preached, and receiving the sacraments given to us in Christ.
>
> Telling the Christian story to one another—reading and hearing the Scriptures and also the stories of the church's experience throughout its history.
>
> Interpreting together the Scriptures and the history of the church's experience, particularly in relation to their meaning for our own lives in the world.
>
> Praying—together and by ourselves, not only in formal services of worship but in all times and all places.
>
> Confessing our sin to one another, and forgiving and becoming reconciled with one another.
>
> Tolerating one another's failures and encouraging one another in the work each must do and the vocation each must live.
>
> Carrying out specific faithful acts of service and witness together.

---

52. Ibid., 30.
53. Dykstra, *Growing in the Life of Faith*, 42–43.

Giving generously of one's means and receiving gratefully the gifts others have to give.

Suffering with and for one another and all whom Jesus showed us to be our neighbors.

Providing hospitality and care, not only to one another but to strangers and even enemies.

Listening and talking attentively to one another about our particular experiences of life.

Struggling together to become conscious of and to understand the nature of the context in which we live.

Criticizing and resisting all those powers and patterns (both within the church and in the world as a whole) that destroy human beings, corrode human community, and injure God's creation.

Working together to maintain and create social structures and institutions that will sustain life in the world in ways that accord with God's will.[54]

This list is the only "hierarchical list" proposed by Dykstra (and Bass). Dykstra argues that worship comes first on the list because it is the "central and orienting practice of the Christian life." He calls these practices "and disciplines," as "discipline" for Dykstra is "virtually synonymous with practice."[55] He also underlines that they are "means of grace."[56] And furthermore, knit together in a way of life, these practices have the "power to place us where we can receive a sense of the presence of God."[57]

Bass and Dykstra see Christian practices as forms of a way of life, that "seeks to respond to God's presence."[58] This way of life shaped by

---

54. Ibid. In *For Life Abundant* there is an explicit focus on the practice of vocation "as a crucial dimension of the Christian life." Cf. Bass and Dykstra, *For Life Abundant*, 9. Dykstra later also focuses on the practice "imagination" understood as seeing and interpreting through the eyes of faith. Dykstra claims that "imagination is what makes human life meaningful and engagement with the world possible." This imagination is the capacity to perceive the "more" in what is already before us and the capacity to see beneath the surface of things, to get beyond the obvious and the merely conventional, to note the many aspects of any particular situation, to attend to the deep meanings of things. Cf. Dykstra "'Pastoral and Ecclesial Imagination,'" 41, 48.

55. Dykstra, *Growing in the Life of Faith*, 48–49.

56. Ibid., 45.

57. Ibid., 63.

58. Bass, "Ways of Life Abundant," 32.

Christian practices—to live "abundantly"—is also understood as participating in "the true life that comes from God, the Life first and most fully known to this community in the resurrection of Jesus from the dead."[59] Therefore, Bass and Dykstra have high hopes for what Christian practices may accomplish. When practices are done faithfully, they might teach us "surprising things about God, our neighbors, and the world."[60] Moreover, by participating in them we might increase our knowledge of the Triune God. The rationale behind this, that Christian practices are attuned to the active presence of God, for the life of the world is not elaborated on theologically: How and on what theological basis the triune God is actually present in practices is often described in rather vague terms. Bass and Dykstra write about "God, who is present and active in certain ways."[61]

Altogether, the presence of Christ in Christian practices is described in rather mystical terms. Those who participate in Christian practices may "be surprised along the way by the living God and recognize and know that Christ is present—to us, in our own lives."[62] Dykstra also makes faith the focal "place" of encountering the presence of Christ. In what he calls, "the situation of faith," the practitioner might encounter the *presence* of God in Jesus Christ.[63]

The engagement in Christian practices offers a rich, and sometimes confusingly rich, metaphorical language to describe the way of life stemming from Christian practices. Bass finds that it may be a way to navigate by the light of Christ.[64] Christian practices are described as "vessels." As every practice is a place of mystery, it may also serve as "a gracious vessel" where people might participate in God's activity. At the same time this vessel can be broken by "loveless acts."[65]

So, what makes a practice Christian? Are some Christian practices *more* Christian than others for Bass and Dykstra? They underline that two practices are fundamental for all Christian practices, namely prayer and reading the Bible.[66] They also claim, that there are specific practices

---

59. Ibid., 35.
60. Bass and Dykstra, "Growing in the Practices of Faith," 200.
61. Dykstra and Bass, "A Theological Understanding of Christian Practices," 25.
62. Dykstra, *Growing in the Life of Faith*, 10.
63. Ibid., 21.
64. Bass, "Ways of Life Abundant," 40.
65. Bass and Dykstra, "Growing in the Practices of Faith," 198.
66. Ibid.

by which we respond to God's grace. These are practices such as prayer, forgiveness, and hospitality. These practices bear knowledge of God, the world and human beings. According to Bass and Dykstra, this knowledge cannot be reduced to words, "even though words are often indispensable in helping us to learn and participate faithfully in them."[67]

Miroslav Volf complements and challenges the approach of Dykstra and Bass and adds clarity to the criteria for what makes a practice Christian. Volf finds that Christian practices share a structure similar to that revealed in Romans 15:7: "Accept one another, then, just as Christ accepted you, in order to bring praise to God." Volf also asks whether we first accept Christian beliefs and then engage in practices, or whether it is the other way around. Usually, Volf claims, practices come first: You get engaged in practices and then you make Christian beliefs your own on the background of the practices you have been engaged in.[68]

But for Volf the relationship between belief and practices is more complex and nuanced. Volf sees them as part of a mutually interpretive pattern, in the way that Christian belief(s) normatively shape Christian practice(s), but also in the sense that by participating in Christian practice(s) one may gain a deeper understanding of Christian beliefs. Volf therefore chooses to speak about "belief-shaped practices" and "practice-shaping beliefs."[69] In turn this also influences the way theology is understood.[70] Ultimately, what makes a practices Christian for Volf is expressed in the criterion that a practice is Christian "only insofar as Christ serve as the model for its practitioners, and Christ is available as model only through such beliefs."[71]

Altogether then, what constitutes the presence of Christ in Christian practices for Bass and Dykstra? The picture is quite complex, as Bass and Dykstra are mainly interested in how basic social practices, in which

---

67. Bass and Dykstra, *For Life Abundant*, 358.

68. Volf, "Theology for a Way of Life," 256, points to Bourdieu's idea of the socially informed body; cf. Bourdieu, *Outline of a Theory of Practice*, 124.

69. Volf also makes a distinction between practices and sacraments, because he finds faith understood as *belief* relates differently to practices than to sacraments: "Core Christian beliefs are by definition normatively inscribed in sacraments but not in 'practices.' Hence sacraments ritually enact normative patterns for practices (sacraments)" (Volf, "Theology for a Way of Life," 250–51, 248).

70. "At the heart of every good theology lies not simply a plausible intellectual vision but more importantly a compelling account of a way of life, and that theology is therefore best done within the pursuit of this way of life" (ibid., 247).

71. Ibid., 250.

all humans engage, Christian or not, based on their humanness, may be transformed by the Holy Spirit to form a way of discipleship.[72]

Above all, the constituting role of the Christian fellowship, based on Matthew 18:20, is emphasized. Dykstra seems to advocate that the real presence of God today is found in the way the congregation embodies Christ's love in the world.[73] But Dykstra also stresses the importance of the Word of God.[74]

Christian Practices and the Passion of Christ

According to Kenda Creasy Dean, Christian practices are the "means of grace by which God strengthens individuals and the church to live faithfully."[75] Dean mentions several examples of such practices—prayer, preaching, tolerance, living simply, tithing, and conferencing with other Christians, studying Scripture and serving others. According to Dean, these practices corporate the suffering love of Christ, and they are designed to help young people discover God in their midst. The most important practice within this new rhetoric, she stresses, is the passion for worship.

For Dean, Christian practices shape a way of life empowered by the Holy Spirit that enables Christians to love and serve God and their neighbor in accordance with the original intention. In *The Godbearing Life* it is underlined that the curriculum of practices represents a counter-cultural lifestyle in an achievement-oriented post-modern society. Dean also underlines negatively what will happen if these practices are not practiced: "If we are not shaped by practices that point to the God who is perfect, then we will be shaped by practices that point to imperfect gods instead."[76]

At the same time Christian practices are distinguished from "wholesome activities." Such activities are "valuable ways you and your youth spend time with one another (like picnics, cleanup projects, and fundraisers)." But in regard to this, it is underlined that if youth ministry

---

72. Bass, "Ways of Life Abundant," 31.

73. Dykstra, "Pastoral and Ecclesial Imagination," 44–45.

74. Ibid., 52. In line with Dykstra, Daniels makes an important point, namely that "the practices of Christian faith point towards and even embody a grace with which they are not identical." Daniels and Smith, "History, Practice, and Theological Education," 239.

75. Dean and Foster, *The Godbearing Life*, 107.

76. Ibid., 105–6.

is going to foster identity, then it must do more than involve youth in wholesome activities. The practices of faith invite us into "the life, death, and resurrection of Jesus Christ every time we participate in them." It is also underlined that if wholesome activities are to be experienced as Christian practices, they are in need of an interpreter "who can point out the cross in the middle of the moment and explicitly connect the activity with our life in Jesus Christ."[77]

Perhaps the most poignant definition of Christian practices offered by Dean is found in *Almost Christian* (2010). Here Dean summarizes the insights gained in *The Godbearing Life* (1998) and *Practicing Passion* (2004) and defines faith practices as "the on-going human activities of Christian communities by which centuries of people have 'imitated' Christ, enacting and taking part in the mystery of his life, death, and resurrection."[78] What then constitutes the presence of Christ in a practice, for Dean? According to *The Godbearing Life*, the practices of faith "smuggle Jesus into the world." This term is not pursued in *Practicing Passion* and *Almost Christian*. In *Practicing Passion* Dean claims that Christ's passion is made visible in the practices of the Christian community, and that Jesus enters the world again through such practices, through us.[79] Dean also speaks about Christian practices as "vessels of grace."[80] For Dean, Christian practices are crucial for the forming of an adolescent self-identity rooted in the passion of Christ. Altogether, Dean seems to think that the main theological premise constituting the presence of Christ in such practices is Jesus' promise in Matthew 18:20. The notion of Christian practices, which makes Christ's passion present "again and again," is a returning phrase in Dean's theological elaborations.[81]

To sum it up: Dykstra and Bass find that practices are Christian because they have "distinctive roots in Scripture," and Christ is present in Christian practices as Christian practices "pursue a good beyond itself, responding to and embodying the self-giving dynamics of God's

---

77. Ibid., 110.

78. Dean, *Almost Christian*, 70.

79. Dean, *Practicing Passion*, 15.

80. It is interesting and worth noticing that Dean (and Bass and Dykstra to some extent) generally applies the term "vessels of grace," which has a stronger connotation of "transportation," instead of the more common classical Protestant expression "means of grace," although she sometimes seems to think that they are synonymous. Ibid., 151.

81. Ibid., 173–74.

own creating, redeeming, and sustaining grace."[82] Craig Dykstra makes a "hierarchical list" of Christian practices, starting with worship as the first and constitutive practice. Dean, in particular, seems to avoid listing Christian practices in hierarchical ways. Her approach to Christian practices is more "egalitarian" and pragmatic. Altogether, it is therefore difficult to make an extensive and hierarchical list of Christian practices based on the different lists, as the practices presented are merely examples of how religious language may be recovered through different Christian practices. None of these "lists" is presented as extensive or hierarchical, except for Dykstra's one list. The relationship between sacraments and Christian practices also needs to be further discussed and developed.

ANTHROPOLOGICAL AND SOTERIOLOGICAL IMPLICATIONS

The Self-Securing Way of Life Versus the Life-Giving Way of Life

Foundational for Bass and Dykstra's anthropological and soteriological concept is how they oppose the self-securing life with the life-giving life. The programmatic slogan for Christian practices is that they impose a pattern of "self-giving love." This "self-giving love" is opposed to the "human tendency to grasp more control than is rightly ours."[83]

The inherent soteriological language in the Christian practices paradigm is a "soft" language where practitioners engaging in Christian practices "enter more fully into the receptivity and responsiveness, to others and to God, that characterize Christ and all who share in the new creation."[84] This soft soteriological language is also evident in the way Bass and Dykstra write about baptism: Baptism "involves the pouring of actual water on a unique human body, as a specific individual is honored and received in his or her embodied integrity."[85] There is little focus on baptism as dying to sin, and the radical hamartiological drama traditionally ascribed to

---

82. Bass, "Ways of Life Abundant," 30–31.

83. Dykstra and Bass, "A Theological Understanding of Christian Practices," 28. Also in Dykstra's book *Growing in the Life of Faith* sin is described as self-securing. Subversively, salvation is "freedom from compulsive self-securing." Dykstra, *Growing in the Life of Faith: Education and Christian Practices*, 95.

84. Dykstra and Bass, "A Theological Understanding of Christian Practices," 28.

85. Ibid., 30.

baptism.[86] Rather the focus is on how practitioners through Christian practices "can live into the promises made at their baptism,"[87] and how baptism *presents* us with an alternative to self-securing:

> Under water, we cannot secure our own lives, but we can know, in a knowing beyond words, that God's creativity overcame the darkness that covered the face of the deep at earth's beginning, and that water flowed from Jesus' side on the cross, and that the new creation [to] which we now belong anticipates a city where the river of the water of life nourishes the roots of the tree whose leaves are for the healing of the nations.[88]

The closest Bass and Dykstra come to describing what is accomplished through baptism is underlining that in baptism human needs are not just met; they are transformed. In a reference to Luther's *The Freedom of a Christian* they claim that Martin Luther learned as a monk that practices can become self-securing, and an effort to win one's own salvation apart from God. What Luther managed in *The Freedom of a Christian* was to see the Christian life as a response to God's grace.[89]

Bass and Dykstra argue that what differentiates their concept of practices from MacIntyre's concept of social practices, and from social scientific concepts of practice, is a theological anthropology that posits the existence of certain fundamental needs and conditions as belonging to human existence as such. In other words, Bass and Dykstra believe that Christian practices address and are capable of fulfilling human needs, as God addresses and is capable of fulfilling human needs. Fundamentally this means that human beings need God to fulfill (the highest) meaning in life. Bass and Dykstra understand Christian practices as "responses to fundamental needs and conditions that exist in every culture."[90] This fundamental conviction is crucial for their anthropology.

All in all, the anthropology that Bass and Dykstra elaborate is rather complex. On the one hand, Bass and Dykstra take positive anthropology as their anthropological starting point in the sense that they claim that a fundamental human condition is that we all have bodies, and that we

---

86. Bass and Dykstra do at one point quote St. Francis's saying, "In baptism we have already died the only death that matters." Ibid., 31.
87. Ibid., 28.
88 Ibid., 31.
89. Ibid., 23–24.
90. Bass, "Ways of Life Abundant," 31.

are made in the image of God. This starting point in a positive creation-based anthropology also comes to the fore when they state that Christian practices are "congruent with the necessities of human existence as such, as seen from a Christian perspective on the character of human flourishing."[91] But when Bass and Dykstra write about what Christian practices may accomplish the focus is on the redeemed self, rather than the self made in the image of God: "Selves made new by God can respond to God's grace by extending it to others."[92]

Bass and Dykstra seldom relate their anthropological elaborations to the doctrine of sin, but they do address sin as a fundamental condition. Sin is described as to fall short of God's invitation to a way of life.[93] They further write on sin and Christian practices that "a full understanding of a set of Christian practices includes both a profound knowledge of humankind in its most fundamental and orienting need and capacities, including its capacity to sin, and a profound knowledge of God's purposes for all creation."[94]

The hamartiology presented here is tentative, rather then radical, in the sense that sin is a "capacity" and a set of (possible) misdeeds, but not as much a determining condition, or even corruption in the relationship between God and humans. Bass and Dykstra underline that when talking about Christian practices, we "must also take account of the problem of sin and evil."[95] But the focus is more on how sin may distort and corrupt a practice, not so much on further elaborating on human beings' capacity to sin. Therefore, any given practice—including any practice that is historically Christian—may become so distorted that its pursuit and outcome are evil rather than good, according to Dykstra and Bass.

Maybe the hesitation to elaborate fully on how Christian practices address sin and the sinner has to do with the inherent focus on *telos* in practices, that by participating in practices one is set on a path to pursue a higher end or good? At one hand, Bass and Dykstra do claim that "the normative and theological concept of Christian practices that we propose situates Christian practices themselves within the mystery of fall *and* redemption, of sin *and* grace, that informs Christian reflection on

---

91. Dykstra and Bass "A Theological Understanding of Christian Practices," 22.
92. Ibid., 28.
93. Ibid., 16.
94. Ibid., 24.
95. Ibid., 27.

the problem of evil."⁹⁶ But how exactly this *simul*-structure informs the thinking on Christian practices is not fully developed.

Another example of this *telos*-focus is found in the role Dykstra ascribes to discipline in relation to faith and Christian practices. Dykstra underlines that the life of faith is not "immune to the devastations that evil can bring or to the powers of destruction and death than other kinds of life.⁹⁷ Therefore Dykstra argues that the life of faith has to be disciplined. Dykstra understands obedience as "a response of gratitude of love to a gracious and loving God whose requirements are for the sake of creation."⁹⁸ But still Dykstra is optimistic on behalf of what faith and the life of faith may accomplish as both faith itself and the life of faith have the power to transform and shape human development and the life journeys of individuals and communities. Therefore Dykstra argues, that "every aspect of one's human development and historical existence may be transformed by and employed in faith and in the life of faith."⁹⁹

Bass concludes, that "the freedom granted by God's grace, in sum, has a shape."¹⁰⁰ She claims that the source of this way of life is "not our own righteousness but that of Jesus Christ, who was given to and for the world out of God's deep and inexplicable love."¹⁰¹ Bass claims that faith in Christ gives us a new kind of freedom, unthinkable apart from God's grace. This freedom is the source and point of orientation for the way of life shaped by Christian practices.

Here Bass also makes a connection to Luther, as she claims—quoting Luther's Preface to the Epistle to the Romans (1522)—that "faith, as Martin Luther portrayed it at an early and dangerous point in his struggle to reform the church, 'is a lively, daring confidence in God's grace, so sure and certain that the believer would stake his life on it a thousand times.'" Interestingly enough, Bass also uses this to connect Luther with Calvin, claiming that "Luther and Calvin clearly shared an emphasis on the embodied knowledge of God's grace that is at the heart of Christian life."¹⁰² This claim also raises the question as to whether Christian practices in

---

96. Ibid., 27.
97. Dykstra, *Growing in the Life of Faith*, 29.
98. Ibid., 28.
99. Ibid., 37.
100. Bass, "Ways of Life Abundant," 33.
101. Ibid., 27.
102. Ibid, 27.

general are "embodied knowledge of God's grace." The question remains, however, how to distinguish between different Christian practices. Or if all Christian practices—more or less—offer or embody the saving presence of Christ.

For Bass and Dykstra Christian practices discipline and shape people in such a way that the self-securing life is challenged and replaced by a life-giving way of life. In these two contrasting metaphors the main emphasis in their inherent anthropology and soteriology is found. In the article *Reconceiving Practice* (1991) Dykstra underlines that "as people participate in practices they are involved in their ongoing history and may in the process significantly reshape them."[103] The liberating grace offered by God in Jesus Christ is, according to Dykstra, something which not only frees us *from*, but it also frees us *for* a new life.[104]

Generally, Bass and Dykstra present a rather optimistic anthropology of practices: It is possible to shape and discipline people into a different life through Christian practices. But they also offer hints of a more pessimistic anthropology, underlining that "we hear our greed named as sin."[105] But when we look at the features of the inherent soteriology in the Christian practices theology, which focuses on how being disciplined in Christian practices fosters growth,[106] these hints at a more pessimistic or complex anthropology do not seem to play an important role in the theological reasoning. The main emphasis is on how the new way of life shaped by Christian practices may unleash a potential in human beings and communities through practice. Therefore Bass and Dykstra write that through Christian practices human beings grow in a "way of life that is informed by the wisdom of the Christian tradition, alert to the needs of our time, and responsive to the gracious presence and startling promises of God."[107]

Restoring and Transforming the Passionate Self

For Kenda Creasy Dean the main focus is on how Christian practices support and nurture Christian identity formation, which takes place as new patterns of relating to God and to others emerges on the basis of

103. Dykstra, "Reconceiving Practice," 44.
104. Dykstra, *Growing in the Life of Faith*, 25.
105. Bass and Dykstra, *For Life Abundant*, 359.
106. Bass and Dykstra, "Growing in the Practices of Faith," 196.
107. Dykstra and Bass, "Times of Yearning, Practices of Faith," 12.

passion.[108] By making passion the key to the developing of an authentic (Christian) identity—a true self—identity is first and foremost a theological category, not a developmental-psychological one, for Dean. She therefore claims that: "true identity is ours by redemption, not by development.[109] According to Dean, post-modern teens are longing for the presence of "an Other who will be there to create a we."[110]

Dean does not discuss postmodernity as such in any width, but she elaborates on the notion of "the plural self," when she criticizes Erik H. Erikson's theories on identity formation. This theory was developed during a time when Western society was a more coherent place.[111] In addition to this, the framework of Erikson's theory relied on an ingredient, which is no longer widely available to North American young people, namely grown-ups.[112]

The plural self is therefore the result of young people adapting like chameleons to the multiple roles demanded by postmodern culture. But Dean is generally critical of using the notion of "the plural self" theologically to advocate a principled pluralism in young people, as does the German practical theologian Friedrich Schweitzer. Once again, Dean's conviction that young people and humanity as a whole has a "God-given identity as homo religious" forms the basis of her argument, and she concludes that "although Christian tradition supports the plural self's contextuality, brokenness, and even a normative partialness, it does not support its relativism: when everything matters, nothing matters most."[113] Dean juxtaposes this by developing theologically a Trinitarian and perichoretic view on the (plural) self, based on the theology of Jürgen Moltmann. Following Moltmann's theology of the Trinity and salvation as an act of re-creation, Dean underlines that viewing identity through a perichoretic lens, makes the adolescent's "plural selves" cohere around the cross. For the adolescent developing a perichoretic self this is both something relational and dynamic. It is differentiated around a unifying

---

108. Dean, *Practicing Passion*, 148.
109. Ibid., 84.
110. Ibid., 129.
111. Ibid., 85.
112. Ibid., 78. This view on the relationship between teenagers and grown-ups in North American society is shared with other US youth ministry scholars, such as Chap Clark; cf. Clark, *Hurt*.
113. Dean, *Practicing Passion*, 85–87.

center, but still open to others while maintaining integrity, flexible but fixed around the fidelity of Jesus Christ.

Dean places her perichoretic-Trinitarian view of the self in relation to the *imitatio Christi* motif, and the art of divine love parallel to the human longing for fidelity. Young people can take part in God's 'being there' for them whenever they are 'there' for others. This is a way of making Christ's fidelity visible in the practices of suffering love.[114]

The crux of Dean's argument seems to be that by participating in passionate Christian practices young people, and ultimately all human beings, gain a true and authentic (Christian) identity. The attaining of this identity is labeled as a "new birth":

> The Christ in whose image we were made becomes visible in us through the practices of faith. In these practices, we are literally given "new birth" as we are incorporated into the life of God, and as Christ's identity becomes our own. To put it simply, in the practices of the Christian community Christ recreates us by restoring our "true self" made in the image of God.[115]

Altogether, Dean finds that passion is the DNA of adolescents and grown-ups alike, and incorporated in the passion of Christ; this DNA finds its right place.[116] To Dean the adolescent longing for personal experience is something the church has to take into account in a postmodern climate. In such a climate, Dean finds that the "degree to which Jesus 'moves' us when we practice faith, teenagers believe, is the degree to which Christianity is valid."[117]

Christian Practices—Human Or Divine Agency?

Maybe one reason for the tendency towards a "soft soteriology," as opposed to a more radical soteriology, has to do with Bass and Dykstra's less developed interest in the relation between sacramental theology and Christian practices. One way to investigate this further is to analyze and discuss the distinction between human and divine agency in Christian

---

114. Ibid., 87–89. Dean uses Moltmann's Christology on several occasions throughout her book; cf. also ibid., 156.

115. Ibid., 159. But Dean also underlines that "conforming to a community's practices, even Christian ones, does not necessarily create Christians." Ibid., 146.

116. Ibid., 122.

117. Ibid., 100.

practices. Looking at the distinction between human and divine agency in Christian practices, it is noteworthy that Dorothy C. Bass at one point discusses what she refers to as "the persistent tension between justification and sanctification in the Christian life."[118] But are justification and sanctification just two parts of the unified reality of God's love for us, describing the twofold character of the grace that saves in the way that it both *frees us* and *forms us*? What role does the Calvinist idea of sanctifying grace play in this scheme, where being "disciplined into certain patterns of living, to become a person disposed toward certain kinds of actions and thoughts," is fundamental to understanding Christian life?[119]

As a Reformed theologian, Craig Dykstra finds that in relation to Christian practices faith as a human activity is not denied, but fundamentally this activity is set in the context of a relationship, which depends on God's prior activity. In other words, it is God, "who takes an initiative in making the divine nature and presence known and accessible to human beings."[120] Therefore Dykstra argues for the character of faith as gift,[121] but at the same time this gift of faith shapes a way of life. Dykstra underlines that "faith is primarily a response to a gift, an activity of recognizing and accepting God's grace, which gives rise to a way of life—a way of believing, trusting, committing, and orienting all one's thoughts and actions."[122] Dykstra even speaks about "the way of living that is organized by faith," and he claims that "faith is possible only because the life of faith surrounds it and provides its context."[123]

In his elaborations on faith Dykstra makes use of Calvin and the Reformed tradition, like the Heidelberg Catechism and the Westminster Confession. Dykstra defines sanctification as "participation in Christ's living work."[124] Ultimately, Dykstra's understanding of sanctification is heavily influenced by Calvin as Dykstra underlines with Calvin that one cannot attain justification without at the same time attaining sanctification.[125]

---

118. Bass, "Ways of Life Abundant," 33.
119. Jones, "Graced Practices," 58–59.
120. Dykstra, *Growing in the Life of Faith*, 17.
121. Ibid., 75.
122. Ibid., 17–18.
123. Ibid., 19.
124. Ibid., 27.
125. Ibid., 31–32.

The role of human agency is made even more explicit in Dykstra's view of growth in faith in relation to Christian practices. Here Dykstra underlines that "coming to faith means coming to recognize that the context of all our growing and living is the world in which, over which, and through which the Spirit of God known in Jesus Christ reigns."[126] Still, Dykstra also admits that it is misleading to say that faith grows.

Faith, according to Dykstra, does not grow in the sense that it changes in form, complexity and structure. Rather "faith—understood as the recognition and acceptance of God's enduring, saving presence—may grow in power, significance, richness, and depth as more and more dimensions of our individual and corporate lives are touched by and conformed to it."[127] Dykstra also underlines that practices after a while may become arenas in which something is done to us, rather than by us.[128] But the way Dykstra seems to understand that agency in practices becomes even more complex, or even confusing, when he describes practices as "habitations of the Spirit."[129]

In relation to this, it could also be questioned how the term "excellence," which is a crucial term in a MacIntyre'ian definition of practices, should be defined when a practice is to be understood as Christian—whether it is human agency or God's grace, which fulfills any excellence in a Christian practice..[130] Altogether, the distinction between human and divine agency in Christian practices needs to be further analyzed and discussed. This also means discussing this theme in the light of how to distinguish between different types or groups of Christian practices based on an understanding of the presence of Christ in Christian practices.

ECCLESIOLOGICAL IMPLICATIONS

The Practicing Community As a Means of Grace

Right from the beginning, the engagement in Christian practices has been shaped by a rather culture-critical approach, describing the present

---

126. Ibid., 37.
127. Ibid., 39.
128. Ibid., 56.
129. Ibid., 78.
130. Pauw, "Attending to the Gap between Beliefs and Practices," 48.

state of things as "culturally and socially fragmented."¹³¹ There is also in Bass and Dykstra a fairly explicit counter-cultural element. Bass advocates that one important part of this counter-cultural drive in practices has to do with imagining a way of life that prizes an abundance of life rather than an abundance of things to do and things to possess, which is deeply counter-cultural in middle-class North America.¹³²

Diana Butler Bass, Dorothy C. Bass' sister-in-law, interprets Bass' project as an attempt to place congregations in the "center of a reflexive cultural task of fluid retraditioning—urging Christians to see themselves not only as 'receivers' of tradition but as *makers* of future tradition."¹³³ She links this with Bass and Dykstra's vision that congregations are "like monastic communities with 'porous' borders that present life as a 'way of life' instead of a Christian 'life style.'"¹³⁴ In such congregations, people move from being tourists to becoming pilgrims. Diana Butler Bass frames this congregational type from the 1990s to the present as "intentional congregations." The primary orientations for these congregations is a focus on worship, a way of life, practices, spirituality and formation, and unlike earlier congregational types in the US, the tension between church and society is medium-high to high.¹³⁵ The problem before the change in the 1990s was, according to Butler Bass, that for most of the twentieth century (if not longer) the Mainline Protestant Churches had flattened Christian practices through both lack of attention to them as holy habits and also by depending upon the surrounding culture to teach and support a Christian way of life.¹³⁶

What are then the main ecclesiological features in Bass and Dykstra's work with Christian practices? First of all: There is a strong ecumenical impetus in the Christian practices paradigm that Bass and Dykstra develop. This ecumenical impetus on the one hand focuses on the radically local and contextual character of Christian practices, but on the other hand, Bass and Dykstra focus on how Christian practices unite Christians beyond time and place. This means, Bass and Dykstra argue, that Christian practices are also always oriented towards the future, as

131. Dykstra, "Reconceiving Practice," 51.

132. Bass even speaks of the "heavily-marketed telos of material abundance." Bass, "Ways of Life Abundant," 34–35.

133. D. B. Bass, *The Practicing Congregation*, 52.

134. Ibid., 61.

135. Ibid., 17.

136. Ibid., 62.

communities in the future will have to do just as communities in the past and the present—improvise Christian practices based on the tradition.[137]

At first glance it may seem that Bass and Dykstra are engaged in defining the *particularity* of a Christian community, but they also indicate that their main interest has not been to set Christian practices apart from other human practices or to set Christians apart from non-Christian communities.[138] Bass finds that she and Dykstra have been most interested in basic social practices in which people in every time and place necessarily engage in one way or another, by virtue of their humanness, and then further to ask how the Holy Spirit transforms such practices as communities take up a shared way of life as disciples of Jesus. Therefore they focus on what they understand to be "such basic social practices (and their Christian forms)," like living in time, telling stories, caring for others in injury and illness, and procuring and using material goods.[139]

Bass and Dykstra make an obvious universal claim, but they seem to be most interested in how the Holy Spirit makes Christian forms out of basic social practices.[140] Bass and Dykstra believe that their relatively expansive understanding of Christian practices should resist parochialism, but at the same it insists on the irreducibly local quality of each practice within a given setting. Their definition of Christian practices, therefore aims to honor God's active presence as a gift to the whole world. It is not just to, for, or in the church, "and it tries to show how the many different things that people actually do might add up to a coherent and meaningful whole that gets embodied in a shared way of life."[141]

Craig Dykstra unfolds what may be called a linear, continuous ecclesiology. Asking rhetorically whether the church is a tomb or a path, Dykstra points out that "if the church is a path, a place to walk and to practice the faith, we may be surprised along the way by the living God and recognize and know that Christ is present—to us, in our

---

137. Dykstra and Bass, "A Theological Understanding of Christian Practices," 27.

138. Bass claims with Bonhoeffer that "Christian community embodies God's just and merciful presence to the faithful and, through them, to the world." With the explicit focus on "particular communities" in the opening theological vision it is no surprise that Bass starts of her contribution with a reference to Bonhoeffer's *Life Together*. Bass, "Ways of Life Abundant," 21.

139. Ibid., 31.

140. Dykstra and Bass, "Times of Yearning: Practices of Faith," 5.

141. Bass, "Ways of Life Abundant," 31–32.

own lives."[142] But at the same time Dykstra asserts, that congregations are deeply caught up in strong patterns of sin and alienation.[143]

Although Dykstra points out that the Christian community is a sent community, and that Christian nurture and education are for the sake of mission, such a missional perspective does not perpetuate his thinking on Christian practices.[144] It functions more as an appendix. It is also the very short last chapter of his book, *Growing in the Life of Faith*. Here Dykstra underlines that "the educational mission of the church is to teach people that Christ sends them into all the foreign places of this world and of our lives." Being sent, we become vulnerable, Dykstra argues, and we "begin to need the presence of God."[145]

As a paradigm, the Christian practices paradigm obviously challenges the clerical paradigm, making "Christian people" and the ordinary life of all Christians the point of departure for theological work and reflection. In the light of this paradigm, discipleship—understood as "joining the way of Jesus"—is egalitarian. Some advocates that this links with how Martin Luther preached that all the baptized are members of the priesthood of all believers and are lifted up daily work as a holy calling.[146]

Altogether, the focus on the communal character of a Christian way of life is fundamental to Bass and Dykstra's work with Christian practices and is launched as a critique on the tendency to individualism in Western Christianity. Craig Dykstra emphasizes that the presence of Christ is a communal presence. He argues, that "the presence of Jesus Christ is a presence in, to, and through the community of Jesus Christ."[147] Dykstra even writes that "God uses community as a 'means of grace.'"[148] Drawing on Calvin and Moltmann, Dykstra claims that as the church is a community in the power of the Spirit, its whole life in the world becomes a means of grace.

---

142. Dykstra, *Growing in the Life of Faith*, 10.
143. Ibid., 84.
144. Ibid., 159.
145. Ibid., 160.
146. Rasmussen, "Shaping Communities," 125, 128.
147. Dykstra, *Growing in the Life of Faith*, 40.
148. Ibid., 83.

Passionate Practices—Passionate Church?

To redefine youth ministry is to redefine the church, Kenda Creasy Dean argues. Dean claims that the Mainline Protestant Churches have forgotten to participate in the passion of young people by inviting them into the great narrative of passion—the story of the incarnated and suffering son of God. Dean underlines that the identity the church offers young people has to be a theologically based identity founded in the passion of Christ. Dean's vision of a reformation of youth ministry and the church focuses on Christian practices which make Christ "visible."

Against the entertainment and program-based model of youth ministry, Dean therefore proposes the medieval monastic community as an ideal for the church. This probably relates to her counter-cultural perspective on what it means to be church.[149] However, it may also be because a practicing community, according to Dean's interpretation of the Benedictine rule, can "re-modulate beliefs, (. . . causing) us to find Christ . . . in new and unexpected places."[150] All in all, Dean's relationship to the institutional church is somewhat ambiguous. On one hand, she is skeptical of a pubertal development of youth ministry, where youth ministry operates solo. On the other hand, Dean's focus on the cruciform pattern of self-giving love, which participation in Christian practices brings about, seems to be motivated by a strong counter-cultural motif.

Dean finds that, *all* popular culture today is in some way youth culture. Vice versa, *all* age groups participate in it. On the other hand, this is forcing youth to turn to more and more marginal and dangerous alternatives in order to distinguish from other adults. As we can see, Dean's approach to consumer culture is by large fairly critical. She resents consumer society's manipulative nature, but she is optimistic as to how the new rhetoric of youth ministry—and ultimately the church—may develop a healthy spirituality and new-old ways of being in dialogue with the current culture. Dean underlines that it is not because popular culture is potent with Christology, but because faith enables us to baptize the culture to Christ. Dean also finds that the fate of youth ministry is closely knit with the fate of the church, and that a potential renewal of one part inevitably will lead to a renewal of the other part.[151] Dean finds that

---

149. Dean, *Practicing Passion*, 185.
150. Ibid., 167.
151. Dean, "The New Rhetoric of Youth Ministry," 14.

the Christian community is the guarantee for the presence of Christ in Christian practices—according to the promise given in Matthew 18:20.[152]

Christian Practices—Church Against Or Church Above Culture?

What kind of ecclesiology does the Christian practices paradigm promote? One way to investigate this is to ask which "Christ and Culture" model describes the ecclesiology inherent in the Christian practices paradigm in the most accurate way.[153]

For Bass and Dykstra their inherent ecclesiology is complex. On one hand, they focus on the particularity of the Christian community. On the other hand, the life-giving way of life may very well occur outside church walls. Similarly, Dykstra also underlines that he does not think it is possible to make a complete list of Christian practices, but on the other hand he finds it crucial for the church to be specific about which practices are essential to the life of faith.[154] Therefore Dykstra underlines that Christian discipleship is a vocation to live life in a peculiar way. By this, Christians are a covenant people, a people of "God's new promises, made known in the life, death, and resurrection of Jesus Christ."[155] Here the counter-cultural approach is more evident. Dykstra confirms this by claiming that "a radically secular culture is one in which no adequate context and grounds are provided for the visibility, significance, and meaning of promise-making."[156]

At first glance, one notices a strong counter-cultural motif in Kenda Creasy Dean's theology. Dean's approach seems in part "Christ above culture," and in part "Christ against culture." According to Dean, Christian practices may smuggle Christ into the world and Christian practices are ways of the sacred making space in a way which breaks the rhythm of the ordinary and punctuates it with moments of God-consciousness."

---

152. Dean, *Practicing Passion*, 244–45.

153. The five different types or models are: 1. Christ against culture; 2. Christ of culture; 3. Christ above culture; 4. Christ and culture in paradox; 5. Christ transforming culture. These five types were published in H. R. Niebuhr's famous *Christ and Culture*. For a longer discussion on what it may imply to read H. Richard Niebuhr's Christ and Culture-types in a post-Christendom situation, cf. Carter, *Rethinking Christ and Culture*; or Stassen, Yeager, and Yoder, *Authentic Transformation*.

154. Dykstra, *Growing in the Life of Faith*, 70.

155. Ibid., 106.

156. Ibid., 102.

This seems to indicate a "Christ above culture" perspective, but there are also indications in the direction of a "Christ of culture" approach.[157] But ultimately, Dean distances herself from a "Christ of culture" approach.[158]

What all those engaged in promoting Christian practices have in common is the counter-cultural approach to consumer culture, and the tendency to contrast this by developing a somewhat idealistic ecclesiology as an alternative. Whether this ecclesiological idealism is a part of a larger tendency within North American Protestant ecclesiology[159] or something inherent in the Aristotelian/MacIntyre-ian system will not be discussed here, but questions have been raised as to whether Macintyre's idea of social practices, and his emphatic appeal, at the end of *After Virtue*, to the Benedictine rule is a proof that the whole concept of practices and communitarianism is some sort of utopia.[160]

Altogether, the ecclesiology of the Christian practices paradigm may best be grasped through the model "Christ transforming culture." This is particularly fitting for Bass and Dykstra, who are much concerned with how Christian practices as a divine possibility may renew the present culture through Christian practices. It is a model a little less fitting for Dean, who tends to emphasize the counter-cultural element of Christian practices to an extent that moves in the direction of the model "Christ against culture."

---

157. Dean and Foster, *The Godbearing Life*, 186.

158. Ward and Dean, "Practicing Passionate Theology," 106, 110.

159. American Lutheran theologian, Robert W. Jenson, in his ecclesiology, identifies the church with the body of Christ: "The church *is* the body of Christ for the world and for her members, in that she is constituted a community by the verbal and "visible" presence *to* her of that same body of Christ." Therefore "the body of Christ is at once his sacramental presence within the church's assembly, to make that assembly a community, and is the church-community herself for the world and her members." Jenson, *Systematic Theology*, 1:168. This ecclesiology is largely inspired by the French Roman Catholic, and ecumenical theologian, Henri de Lubac; cf. Jenson, *Systematic Theology*, 2:66, 67, 282.

160. But this may also not be the case. As Boss points out, "MacIntyre has always explicitly refused to provide any large-scale alternative to the governmental institutions of liberal democracy" (Boss, "What's Wrong with Communitarianism," 140).

CHRISTIAN PRACTICES AND THE ROLE OF BAPTISM

Concluding Analysis of the Engagement in Christian Practices

This chapter has offered a theological analysis of the engagement in Christian practices. My main focus has been on the works of Kenda Creasy Dean, Dorothy C. Bass and Craig R. Dykstra. There are, of course, differences between the three: One obvious difference is that Dean is a Methodist, Bass a Lutheran and Dykstra a Presbyterian. Sometimes, as I have tried to point out throughout my analysis, this confessional background implicitly or explicitly shapes how they approach different themes related to the practices conversation. Another difference is that Dean, more than Bass and Dykstra, emphasizes how participating in Christian practices contributes in the shaping of a distinct Christian identity. This difference seems to be related to Dean's particular focus on youth ministry and on adolescence as an important transition period in life.

What constitutes the presence of Christ in Christian practices for Dean, Dykstra and Bass is Jesus' promise in Matthew 18:20. Here Jesus promises that whenever two or three are gathered in his name he is there in the midst of them. But apart from this focal point, a more nuanced criteriology on how to understand the presence of Christ in Christian practices is lacking.

Based on the Christological analysis of the engagement in Christian practices in the first part of this chapter, I analyzed and discussed the soteriological, anthropological and ecclesiological implications. I have tried to conclude on these implications by suggesting the terms "optimistic anthropology," "soft soteriology," and "idealistic ecclesiology." I relate the "optimistic anthropology" to the fact that Bass, Dykstra and Dean seldom, and not very extensively, elaborate on the radicalness of sin as fundamental to the human condition before God. Rather they focus on the inherent opportunities in a life formatted by Christian practices to infuse a life-giving way of life.

I relate the term "soft soteriology" to the fact that Bass, Dykstra and Dean in general picture or describe salvation in semantically soft terms, avoiding terms like "conversion" or "repentance" or "atonement." Subsequently, the inherent soteriology in the Christian practices paradigm tends to focus on how practices foster growth in humans and human communities, rather than on how the gift of salvation transforms the life of humans before God. As I have already pointed out, one of the crucial unanswered questions emerging from such an optimistic anthropology and a soft soteriology is how to discern human and divine agency in Christian practices.

An example of the "soft soteriology" is found in how Bass and Dykstra write that baptism "involves the pouring of actual water on a unique human body, as a specific individual is honored and received in his or her embodied integrity." There is little focus on baptism as dying to sin and the radical hamartiological drama traditionally ascribed to baptism. Rather, as we have seen above, the focus is on how baptism *presents* us with an alternative to self-securing. The closest Bass and Dykstra come to describing what is accomplished through baptism is saying that "when a new Christian rises from the baptismal water, human needs are not just met; they are transformed."[161]

I relate the term "idealistic ecclesiology" to the way the practicing Christian community is often described in positive terms and identified with the Body of Christ, whereas contemporary consumer culture is valued in equally negative terms. The practicing community is pictured by Bass and Dykstra as a potential means of grace, and there are few elaborations on the complexity and ambiguity of a practicing community.

The terms "optimistic anthropology" and "idealistic ecclesiology" also relate to the inherent focus on *telos* in the Christian practices paradigm: By living a self-giving way of life, the community of believers may release their God-given potential and "enter more fully into the receptivity and responsiveness, to others and to God, that characterize Christ and all who share in the new creation."[162]

After Baptism

For Dean, Bass and Dykstra the idea that Christian practices make Christ visible is central, but what is less clear is the relationship between Christian practices and baptism. Baptism may be a point of entry for a theology of Christian practices, but what is missing is an extensive elaboration on the way baptism may continue to influence a life shaped by Christian practices.

Although the first page of Craig Dykstra's book *Growing in the Life of Faith* has a strong reference to baptism, baptismal theology is not really

---

161. Dykstra and Bass, "A Theological Understanding of Christian Practices," 30–31.

162. Ibid., 28.

foundational in Dykstra's elaborations on Christian practices. What Dykstra does is to discuss baptism by departing from the baptismal liturgy in the Presbyterian church, and under the framework of "promise-making," as Christian faith holds a promissory structure. Dykstra claims that such a promissory structure is made particularly evident and is also enacted anew for each new Christian in baptism. Dykstra focuses on three partners making promises in the covenant of baptism; God, the individual and the congregation. The baptismal promises are promises made in response to God's promise. Dykstra also links baptism to discipleship and underlines that the most fundamental promise made in the liturgy of baptism is the promise to be a disciple.[163]

As Dykstra and Bass develop their theological understanding of Christian practices, they intend to explore the abundant way of life entered in baptism. Key here is that baptism marks the baptized with self-giving love.[164] Bass and Dykstra also claim that engagement in Christian practices may provide situations in which "practitioners can live into the promises made at their baptism."[165] The focus is on the promises made by the baptized or the sponsors or the parents, and not so much on what the triune God does in baptism and how that shapes the Christian life. Further Bass and Dykstra maintain that baptism is the liturgical summation of all the Christian practices, not so much a distinct practice. According to Bass and Dykstra, therefore, the grace to which the Christian life is a response is fully and finally presented, visibly, tangibly, and in words in the rite of baptism. Based on this, they find that baptism, unlike other practices, does not address a particular need. It sketches out the framework of a new life, "within which all human needs can be perceived in a different way."[166]

Kenda Creasy Dean also, in some passages, advocates for reserving a special role for baptism: "While every practice incorporates us into the suffering love of Jesus, baptism and communion in this regard, incorporating us into Christ's Passion quite explicitly."[167] Apart from this quotation Dean does not write very much on the role of baptism, except that baptism and communion offers a "pattern" for the venture toward

---

163. Dykstra, *Growing in the Life of Faith*, 97–111.
164. Dykstra and Bass, "A Theological Undestanding of Christian Practices," 7, 13.
165. Ibid., 28.
166. Ibid., 30–31.
167. Dean, *Practicing Passion*, 155–56.

union with God.[168] In *Almost Christian*, Dean quite explicitly claims that baptism is only the first of many immersions into the Christian life that Christian growth proceeds from by joining the baptismal pattern of 'going under' with Christ, and joining Christ in resurrection. Therefore baptism "dramatizes the dying-and-rising grammar of Christian liturgy, seeding a Christian vocabulary in the church."[169]

All in all, although baptism is interpreted as the point of entry for a life shaped by Christian practices, the actual baptism is not described in terms of being formative for the Christian life on a daily basis. Rather it is pictured as a *model* or dramatized ideal type for the Christian life, rather than something constantly and effectively *modeling* the Christian.

The What of Baptism

Finally, Dykstra and Bass also critically discuss what really and effectively happens in the act of baptism. They argue that the baptismal rite does not automatically—*ex opere operato*—bestow new life or solidarity. Rather they question the *what* of baptism. They do this by making reference to the scene in the movie *The Godfather* where the infant godson of Michael Corleone is baptized at the same time as several murders ordered by Don Corleone are taking place. For Bass and Dykstra this is an abuse of baptism, which neglects that "this basic act of initiation into the Christian community means to give life, not death—indeed, abundant life, life that is joined to the life and love of Christ."[170]

Bass and Dykstra even make the radical claim, drawing on Romans 6:3–4, that when baptism is "detached from a way of life abundant, as in the Corleone baptism, *the pouring of water accomplishes nothing.*" Although they add that "we cannot be sure what becomes of the little godson," they are quite skeptical about his prospects, as "it is clear that the godfather himself has only a life-style of abundance, not a way of life abundant, however impressive the riches and might he secures for himself."[171] In other words, it seems that for Bass and Dykstra "the what of baptism" may be jeopardized if it is detached from a way of life abundant.

---

168. Dean, *Practicing Passion*, 172.
169. Dean, *Almost Christian*, 153–54.
170. Dykstra and Bass, "A Theological Understanding of Christian Practices," 15.
171. Ibid., 30.

All in all, it is praiseworthy how Dykstra and Bass through this, and Dean through her references to the Columbine shooting and September 11, confront the theology of the Christian practices paradigm with the problem of radical evil. However, in relation to baptismal theology in particular, but also in relation to Christology, anthropology, soteriology, and ecclesiology, this confrontation needs to be discussed theologically in more detail. That is one of my aims in the following chapters.

The recent interest in Christian practices has grown out of an emerging uneasiness about how the church and theology in the West has been interpreting the nature and shape of the Christian life in a context often understood as a post-Christendom context. The interest in Christian practices originally started as a project to rethink the formative character of theological education. Focusing on ministry, my particular interest in this study is on how to interpret the presence of Christ in Christian practices in a post-Christendom era, and through the analysis in this chapter I have identified some fundamental questions for further investigation:

1. (*Practice*) What constitutes the presence of Christ in Christian practices?

2. (*Practitioner*) What is the role of human and divine agency in Christian practices and how does this relate to baptismal theology?

3. (*Context*) Where is the church to be found, and what kind of ecclesiology should be developed in a context described as post-Christendom in relation to the Christian practices paradigm?

3

Christian Practices in the Light of Lutheran Theology

TOWARDS A LUTHERAN UNDERSTANDING OF CHRISTIAN PRACTICES

Engaging Lutheran Theology in the Christian Practices Conversation

How should a life shaped by so-called Christian practices be interpreted in the light of Lutheran Christology and baptismal theology? Few theologians have so far engaged Luther and Lutheran theology in the discussion on Christian practices. The distinct Lutheran understanding I intend to develop in this chapter is focusing on how the presence of Christ in the so-called Christian practices should be interpreted theologically. The focus is on developing theological reflection for Christian ministry in a post-Christendom era. I have no intention of doing primary historical research on Luther. My aim is to bring Lutheran theology into critical dialogue with the Christian practices paradigm. This means that I will be looking for approaches within contemporary Luther research and Lutheran theology, which already engage in the Christian practices-conversation, or theology and research, which I believe may have the potential to enter into critical dialogue with the Christian practices conversation.

The current appeal to re-introduce Aristotelian virtue ethics in Lutheran theology started with ethics. In the book *The Promise of Lutheran Ethics* (1998) Reinhard Hütter unfolds the ethical implications of his attempt to launch a conversation between Aristotle and Luther. Hütter tries to free Lutheran ethics from being pre-determined by the doctrine of justification by faith. By using Luther's catechismal approach to the life of a Christian—a life formed and shaped by the Ten Commandments—Hütter challenges how Lutheran ethics has been shaped by "the Luther renaissance" and neo-Kantian ethics. According to Hütter, the neo-Kantian ethics of the Luther renaissance has made the doctrine of justification a ceiling, which covers everything.

In Hütter's alternative proposal he makes use of the so-called New Finnish research on Luther, which underlines that justification should not be understood in merely forensic terms, but also as the very real presence of Christ in faith. By doing so Hütter hopes to avoid Christian freedom being understood merely as negative freedom (freedom from the law), but also as *dilectio legis* (delight in the law). Hütter therefore finds that God's commandment is nothing else than the concrete guidance, or what may be called the concrete social practice that allows believers to embody communion with God in concrete creaturely ways. Hütter underlines that such a social practice is ethical, as it always includes God's other creatures. Therefore God's commandment enables and guides that way of life for which human beings, created in God's image, are destined.[1]

In his book *Suffering Divine Things. Theology as Church Practice* (2000), Hütter elaborates further on the role of Aristotelian virtue ethics for theology. He examines and critiques moral philosopher Alasdair MacIntyre's use of the Neo-Arisotelian practice(s) approach. Hütter and the evangelical Catholic engagement with (Christian) practices joins the Reformed engagement with Christian practices, like Dean, Dykstra and Bass, in a shared interpretation of the context: The Western church and Western theology, as either "Post-Christendom" or "Post-Constantinian,"

---

1. Hütter, "The Twofold Center of Lutheran Ethics," 43. Other distinct Lutheran engagements in the Christian practices-conversation have been undertaken by American theologians, such as, for instance, Yeago, "The Office of the Keys"; and Yeago, "The Bible." Yeago shares many of the same theological ambitions and convictions as Hütter. Storz and Scharen have also contributed to engaging Lutheran theology in the Christian practices-conversation; cf., for instance, Stortz "Practicing Christians;" Stortz, *A World According to God*; and Scharen and Volf, *Faith as Way of Life*, 3.

are faced with radically new challenges for faith formation and catechetical theology.

Hütter writes, in the introduction to his *Suffering Divine Things*, that the issues at stake which connect both Europe and North America *theologically* are the church not only "'after Constantinianism' but also 'after modernity' and 'after the state,' and, even more important, theology 'after dogma.'"[2] He draws on Bayer's interpretation of the *vita passiva* as a key concept to understand the role of faith and the believer *coram Deo*. Hütter also shares many of the theological dialogue partners with others engaging in Christian practices—MacIntyre, Hauerwas, Lindbeck, Moltmann, and Volf.

Hütter's theological ambition is profoundly ecclesiological. He applies Luther's teaching of the seven "marks of the church" in *On the Councils and the Church* (1539), and Hütter argues that these marks must be understood as the seven "core practices" of the church:

1. The external, orally preached word of God (which includes believing, confessing, and acting in accordance with it)
2. baptism
3. the Lord's Supper
4. the office of the keys as church discipline
5. ordination and offices
6. public prayer, praise, thanksgiving, instruction
7. discipleship in suffering.[3]

Hütter claims that these practices are the nexus that at once both characterize and constitute the church, as Christ himself has promised to be present in these practices. Hütter also discusses theologically the relationship between human agency in practice(s) and the Trinitarian God. To Hütter it is important that the Holy Spirit is the real subject of the church core practices. Therefore the seven marks of the church are only "practices" in a pneumatological sense. Likewise, the human being, although

---

2. Hütter, *Suffering Divine Things*, xiii. This book is an English translation of Hütter, *Theologie als kirchliche Praktik*. Hütter develops his perspective on the church as public and the role of church core practices further in his book written in 2004, Hütter, *Bound to Be Free*.

3. Hütter, *Suffering Divine Things*, 129.

actively present in the practices, always remains the *recipient*, as it is not human activity that constitutes these practices, according to Hütter.[4]

A Thomistic Turn?

The most intense critique of Hütter's attempt to engage Lutheran theology in the "practices" conversation has come from American Lutheran theologians more or less affiliated with "Radical Lutheranism."[5] Gary Simpson, performs a fundamental critique of Hütter's contribution in *The Promise of Lutheran Ethics*. Simpson interprets Hütter's contribution as a Neo-Aristotelian and Thomistic project which seeks to revivify the so-called "third use of the law" under the guise of an "original and proper" use. This is why, Simpson finds, Hütter would reserve the word "commandment" for this function, using the "law" only when talking about sinners.

According to Simpson, Hütter largely neglects the fact that Luther actually had "much experience with those who toiled to "shape and form" Christian faith and freedom by means of God's law." Simpson on the contrary proposes that it is love that needs the shaping and forming of Christian faith and freedom, because "for Luther the cruciform Christ and his Spirit are the full, historical shape and form of Christian freedom; that's why it is Christian freedom."[6] Simpson's alternative is to opt for a Christology and an equivalent pneumatology and ecclesiology, which maximize Christ in Christian freedom.

Mark Mattes performs an even more radical critique of Hütter's take on practices. His critique is more closely related to Radical Lutheranism, but it also makes use of the theology of Oswald Bayer, whose theology Hütter also makes use of and critiques in *Suffering Divine Things*. Mattes claims that Hütter and his theological ally David S. Yeago represent a Thomistic turn in Evangelical (-Lutheran) theology. To a certain extent Mattes draws on Simpson's critique, but his focus is not merely ethical. He stages his article as a regular "boxing match" between what Mattes labels the (Neo-Aristotelian) Thomistic Turn and Radical Lutheranism,

---

4. Ibid., 131–32.

5. "Radical Lutheranism" is a term coined by Gerhard Forde, former Professor of Systematic Theology at Luther Seminary, St. Paul, Minnesota, Cf. Forde, *A More Radical Gospel*.

6. Simpson, "Daunting Indeed," 192–93. Simpson also suspects that Hütter has been (too) influenced by his work with *Veritatis Splendor*, the 1993 encyclical of Pope John Paul II. Simpson is Professor of Systematic Theology at Luther Seminary, St Paul.

where Radical Lutheranism wins by a technical knock-out somewhere in the third round.[7]

But what are really the most crucial differences between Hütter's approach to the Christian life and the approach of Radical Lutheranism? One obvious difference comes to the fore in the discussion on whether the Christian life should be described in linear or cyclic terms. For Mattes, Hütter's appeal to a more peregrinational view on Christian life, where faith in Christ is the start and center of a journey towards God and the end of times (*telos*) and ultimate good, endangers the central Lutheran doctrine of justification by grace. Closely related to this critique of the Thomistic turn is Mattes' claim that the Thomistic Turners are using Aristotle and Aquinas to introduce (Christian) freedom and life as an ability "to exercise one's potential to participate in the good."[8] Inevitably, for Mattes, such an understanding of the nature and shape of Christian life has to lean on merits, not grace:

> The crux of the disagreement between the Thomistic Turn and Radical Lutheranism between freedom and order is the role of justification by faith alone in theology. As noted, for the Thomistic Turn, justification by faith alone is a floor upon which all other doctrines can be built. However, their structures might be guided by a different plan than that of justification. For Radical Lutheranism, justification by faith is not the floor but the hub that centers and frames all other doctrines. Similar to the centrality that the Thomistic Turn gives "participation," "justification" in its forensic, imputative form has a central, all-encompassing focus. However, and this is crucial to the debate, if justification by faith alone is the hub for all Christian teachings and life, then the Christian life cannot be construed as one's progress toward one's own telos (even if is alleged to be one's highest good), but conversely as the kingdom of God's progress toward us.[9]

Another, but more indirect, difference between Radical Lutheranism and the attempt to combine Neo-Aristotelian virtue ethics and Lutheran theology becomes evident when the topic of Christian practices is discussed in the light of the logic of faith in a sacramental promise.

---

7. Mattes, "The Thomistic Turn in Evangelical Catholic Ethics," 87. "With regard to Luther's ethics, it would seem at every point that Luther harmonizes better with Radical Lutheranism and not the Thomistic Turn." Mattes is a former student of Gerhard Forde.

8. Ibid., 72.

9. Ibid., 74–75.

This has to do with whether the Aristotelian *potentialis-actualis* scheme should shape the view on Christian life. Philip Cary, another American-Lutheran theologian, claims that for Luther formal righteousness cannot be a quality or habit of the soul. In this it differs distinctly from an Aristotelian virtue or skill acquired by repeated practice. But Cary is not fully content with a mere imputative approach to justification, and calls for rediscovering a faith that receives "nothing less than Christ himself, and therefore his righteousness as well."[10]

The attempt to merge Lutheran theology and Aristotelian virtue ethics has also been met with critical appreciation from the Roman Catholic theologian Nicholas M. Healy. Healy examines and critiques, but generally approves of, the practice(s) approach. However, he challenges the movement to engage further in a more profound ecclesiological debate, clarifying the definitions of practice(s)—which according to Healy are unnecessarily discordant—in order to take the dogmatic implications into full account. Healy himself offers a supplementary interpretation of practice(s) by engaging the ecclesiology of Thomas Aquinas. For Aquinas, his view of the church is governed by his view of the world as taking shape between *exitus* and *reditus*—"All that is not God comes forth from (*exitus*) and is sustained by God; all is brought to completion as it returns (*reditus*) to the triune God."[11]

The new Finnish interpretation of Luther has over the last twenty years gained international attention for its insistence on a more dynamic-ontological, rather than a forensic, approach to Luther's soteriology, focusing on how Christ himself, according to Luther, is present in faith.[12] This research, which grew out of the context of an Orthodox–Lutheran dialogue, has also been interested in Luther's concept of love and passion. The new Finnish interpretation of Luther has not engaged directly in the practices discussion. Reinhard Hütter, however, engages this new Finnish interpretation of Luther in his theological engagement with practices, but he does not explicitly make use of the Finnish Luther research to discuss how the presence of Christ in Christian practices should be understood.

The Finnish Luther research has been accused of introducing the notion "participation" in such a way that it endangers the doctrine of

---

10. Cary, "Why Luther is not Quite Protestant," 469.

11. Healy, "Misplaced Concreteness," 303.

12. For an English introduction to this research, see Braaten and Jenson, eds., *Union with Christ*; and Mannermaa, *Christ Present in Faith*. Cf. also Heubach, ed., *Luther und Theosis*; and Kärkkäinen, *One with God*.

justification by faith alone. Criticism has been voiced on both sides of the Atlantic, mainly focusing on what is perceived as a participatory approach to salvation. The Finnish Luther research has also been criticized for over-systematizing Luther and for overstating one part of Luther's theology, and finally for focusing too narrowly on parts of his writings, in particular the letter to the Galatians. But I believe that parts of this research is valuable in trying to develop a Lutheran understanding of how Christ is present in Christian practices, particularly in outlining the soteriological and anthropological implications.

Engaging Luther's Theology in the Christian Practices Conversation

In which way, then, should Lutheran theology, and even Luther's theology, be engaged in the Christian practices conversation, when the aim is to develop a more nuanced and comprehensive understanding of the presence of Christ in Christian practices? Probably Reinhard Hütter's most important contribution to the (Christian) practices conversation has been his focus on why some practices are more important than others, and how agency in practices should be understood theologically. By elaborating on how what Luther calls the *notae ecclesiae*—the marks of the church—should be understood as the "church's core practices," Hütter attempts to create both a hierarchy of (Christian) practices and a theological hermeneutics to discern human and divine agency in practices. According to Hütter, the core practices are constitutive for the church, because they are Christological practices.

Church historian Timothy Wengert has convincingly shown that the *notae ecclesiae* is a concept fully developed by Martin Luther himself. Wengert claims that Luther was the original creator of the content of this term, along with Melanchthon, and that it arose within a very specific ecclesiological polemic, where Luther had to re-formulate his gospel-based ecclesiology. Wengert therefore claims that the "marks of the church" should be considered a part of Luther's Reformation breakthrough. According to Wengert, the list Luther offered in *On the Councils and the Church* (1539) represents one of the most complete lists in the writings of both Melanchthon and Luther. The reason why this is close to a complete list is because although different biblical texts gave rise to different lists, this list focuses on what all these lists seem to have in common—the word and the sacraments (visible words) and their effects on the Christian community (confession of faith and love). Luther's selection of these particular seven marks or holy possessions in this treatise was "prepared" through his earlier writings and treatises. The Word was the primary mark or practice, as according to Luther God created the world through the word, and God re-creates believers through the same word.[13]

The importance of Luther's elaborations in *On the Councils and the Church* also becomes evident when we look at the treatise in its historical context. Martin Luther wrote *On the Councils and the Church* as a kind of follow-up to the Smalcald Articles. It was written in the aftermath of the political and religious turmoil following the diet of Augsburg in 1530, with the peace of Nuremberg in 1532 as a step on the way—peace that made it clear that the Protestant side would not receive a real hearing by pope and emperor. But those following the *Augsburg Confession* marked their willingness to participate in a general, free and Christian Council. In the mid-1530s papal emissaries appeared in Europe, and soon the Smalcald League had to decide if they wanted to attend a future council.

In this treatise Luther outlines his critique of papal and conciliar authority. The first part of the treatise is a rejection of the humanist hope of a reform based on the teaching of the church fathers. Luther proves the ambivalence of authority in relation to the tradition of the church and how even the church fathers contradict themselves. Therefore Luther claims that the only norm to judge what is church is Scripture. For Luther, therefore, the church cannot be reformed according to the decrees of the church fathers and the councils. In the second part of *On the Councils and the Church* Luther discusses and evaluates the Christology of the councils of the early church, starting with the apostolic council in Jerusalem (Acts 15), going on to the first four ecumenical councils; Nicaea (325), Constantinople (381), Ephesus (431) and Chalcedon (451). Luther maintains that councils may protect the church from error, but they do not have the authority to create new articles of faith. In the third and last part, Luther underlines, partly in the form of confession, what constitutes the church according to Scripture. Luther underlines that this church is not purely spiritual and invisible, but is known by its outward and objective marks—*the notae ecclesiae*. The point for Luther—which he made already in the Leipzig Debate in 1519—is that popes and councils should be made subject to the authority of the Word. A list of the marks

---

13. Lathrop and Wengert, *Christian Assembly*, 19, 83–84.

of the church, similar to that in *On the Councils and the Church*, can be found in *Against Hanswurst* (1541).[14]

Luther's interest in the marks of the church can also be traced back to his work with the Catechisms. Although Luther does not mention the marks of the church explicitly in the Catechisms, he links the marks of the church to the Catechisms, for instance in a Sermon on John 16 from May the 9th, 1535, which is just one example of the importance of biblical theology in the whole elaboration of this concept.[15] Wengert thinks that the non-polemical setting of the Catechisms made it unnecessary for Luther to defend the role of the marks of the church. He simply assumed them and used them, as the concept of the marks of the church permeated everything Luther wrote.

In both the Catechisms, there are indirect references to the marks of the church—particularly in Luther's explanations of the Creed, and in particular the third article of the Creed. In the Small Catechism there is also an obvious reference to baptism, the Lord's Supper and confession/the office of the keys: "Daily in this Christian church the Holy Spirit abundantly forgives all sins—mine and those of all believers."[16] Wengert therefore claims that in the creed the phrase 'forgiveness of sins' includes baptism, the Lord's Supper, and confession, which where understood as the signs of a living church.[17] Luther's focus on the marks of the church in the catechisms is an attempt to try to bring the marks of the church into each Wittenberg household, "putting in each person's hand the word, sacraments, and prayer."[18]

---

14. Luther's main enemy in this treatise is the pope and his church, but towards the end of the treatise he also attacks the spiritualists. The treatise was addressed to Duke Henry of Braunschweig-Wolfenbüttel, who since 1514 was the ruler of a duchy frequently divided by family feuds. Henry was a bitter enemy of the Reformation, in addition to being a personal friend of the Emperor Charles V. He was also the first to oppose the German peasants when they revolted in 1525. In 1531 he joined the Catholic Union opposing the Smalcald League, but the duke was unable to prevent the Reformation from spreading even into his duchy. John Bugenhagen, the chief pastor of Wittenberg, managed to persuade most of the magistrates of Braunschweig-Wolfenbüttel to introduce the Reformation into their territories in 1528, when the duke was absent in Italy participating in imperial wars against the Venetian aristocrats. At first Luther took no part in these controversies but, being challenged by the duke, he decided to reply. The treatise was written sometime between February 19 and April 4, 1541. Cf. LW 41:xi–8.

15. Lathrop and Wengert, *Christian Assembly*, 85.

16. BC, 356.

17. Lathrop and Wengert, *Christian Assembly*, 73–74.

18. Ibid., 85. German theologian Peters points to this relation between the marks of the church and catechismal instruction as he underlines in his Introduction to his

Wengert finds that Luther approaches the catechism and the marks of the church with a common purpose, both basic catechesis and preaching and administering the sacraments marks the church.

Church historian David Steinmetz draws the conclusion that the "new" Reformation theology required new practices appropriate to the theology developed. Therefore writing new catechisms to explain both theology and practice to lay people who were formed in the old habits of thought and action was a natural step forward, where affirming the creed, denying the Ave Maria and reinterpreting the keys became important. The role of Luther's catechism should also be interpreted in the context of other catechisms of that time and in the contemporary media and communications situation. Steinmetz points out that more than 100 000 copies were printed and sold over the forty years following the first edition of Luther's catechism.[19]

Luther probably started writing the Small Catechism in late 1528 or early 1529. At this time the chief pastor of Wittenberg, John Bugenhagen, was away helping reform the city of Braunschweig, and Luther was responsible for the catechetical teaching. Luther's experiences during his official visitations in the Electorates of Saxony and Meissen during late 1528 and early 1529 represent a direct motivation for his writings on the catechisms, as Luther concludes that "the ordinary person, especially in the villages, knows absolutely nothing about the Christian faith, and unfortunately many pastors are completely unskilled impotent teachers. Yet supposedly they all bear the name Christian, are baptized, and receive the holy sacrament, even though they do not know the Lord's Prayer, the Creed, or the Ten Commandments!"[20]

The Large Catechism originates in Luther's catechetical sermons in Wittenberg, while Bugenhagen was away helping the Reformation in Braunschweig.[21] The Large Catechism focused, along with the so-

---

commentaries to Luther's catechisms that the catechisms aim at offering the fundamentals of Christian belief and Christian life, For this purpose the catechisms are not mere dogmatic and catechetical handbooks, but even more (practice-oriented) books for prayer and consolation. Cf. Peters, *Kommentar zu Luthers Katechismen*, 1:18–19. He finds that the catechisms are handbooks to help Christians to exercise and keep faith in love. For an overview of how Luther's work with the catechisms served as a prelude to later conceptions of didactical approaches to religious education; cf., for instance, Kalloch, Leimgruber, and Schwab, *Lehrbuch der Religionsdidaktik*, 33–54.

19. Steinmetz, *Luther in Context*, 139, 135–36.
20. BC, 347.
21. BC, 377.

called *Visitation Articles* (1528), on the often poorly trained clergy. The Catechism, then named the German Catechism, appeared by mid-April 1529, but Luther started revising it shortly after that, and a more complete version appeared in 1530. The catechisms were supposed to function as Bibles for the laity, offering material, which was necessary for each Christian to know.

Just previous to writing the catechisms, Luther was engaged in a heated debate with the radical wing of the Reformation on the presence of Christ in the Lord's Supper. During the 1520s a large number of theologians involved in the Reformation engaged in discussions on the nature and practice of the Lord's Supper. Luther's confession on the Lord's Supper in 1528 came as his final response in the controversy between Luther and those on the Reformed side who championed a figurative or spiritualistic interpretation of the biblical texts on the Lord's Supper and therefore also a figurative interpretation of the presence of Christ in the celebration of the Lord's Supper. Luther's main opponent was Zwingli, at that point the leading figure in the Swiss Reformation. Luther finished his treatise in the winter of 1528, and it appeared in print in February 1528. But Luther's discussion with Zwingli, which for Luther reached its climax in this treatise, had started earlier. In the spring of 1527 both Zwingli and Luther had published treatises on the Christology of the Lord's Supper. Luther considered the 1528 treatise to be his final word in the controversy, and he did not respond to later attempts by Zwingli and others to rebuke his theology on the Lord's Supper.

The Confession offers the most detailed and profound treatment by Luther on the Lord's Supper.[22] It is also the most often and most extensively quoted treatise of Luther in the formula of the Concord. Luther's treatise is made up of three parts. In part I Luther refutes the arguments of the spiritualists and develops his chief doctrinal points and arguments on the presence of Christ in the Lord's Supper. In part II Luther examines the four biblical texts on the Lord's Supper, and concludes that they require a literal rather than a figurative exegesis. Finally, in part III Luther relates the controversy on the Sacrament(s) to the articles of faith. By doing so, he hopes to refute the arguments of the fanatics for good.

Based on the scope of this study, where the focus is on developing an interpretation of the presence of Christ in Christian practices, I have argued for engaging a selection of Luther texts. In the forthcoming analysis and discussion a particular emphasis will be given to:

22. LW 37:158.

- *The Catechisms* and in part the *Visitation Articles*
- *On the Councils and the Church* and in part *Against Hanswurst*
- *Confession concerning the Lord's Supper* and in part *The Freedom of a Christian*

THE PRESENCE OF CHRIST

Towards a Lutheran Understanding of "Practice(s)"

Discussing how (Christian) practices should shape the life of a Christian has to do with how "the Christian self" is understood and how the term "practice" is defined theologically. In *Suffering Divine Things* Reinhard Hütter defines "practice," in opposition to "praxis" and "process,"[23] but in close relation to a distinct understanding of the bios of faith: "Faith is to be understood rather as *vita passiva*, as a *bios* grounded in God's salvific activity, a *bios* that rather than appearing in an abstract sense is grounded in and bound to specific activities of actualization."[24]

It is important to state the semantically and historically obvious, that Luther does not talk directly about "practices" in the way MacIntyre and other contemporary moral philosophers use the term. Luther does use the verb "practice," with the German equivalents "treiben" or "üben" on several occasions, however. In the closing of his explication on baptism in the Large Catechism, Luther writes:

> Therefore let all Christians regard their baptism as the daily garment that they are to wear all the time. Every day they should be found in faith and with its fruits, suppressing the old creature and growing up in the new. If we want to be Christians, we must practice the work that makes us Christians.[25]

The German original here says "*treiben*," which may very well be translated "practice" in English, but which does not necessarily include all the connotations given to the Aristotelian concept of "practice."

---

23. "Practices are not processes since the latter are an inherent constituent part of *poeitic logic*, according to which any given process is evaluated from the perspective of the specific result it produces" (Hütter, *Suffering Divine Things*, 211).

24. Ibid., 37.

25. BC, 466.

In *On the Councils and the Church* Luther makes an interesting comment, which is also relevant for the development of a Lutheran understanding of the term "practice." Here Luther juxtaposes five different verbs, including "practice": "Wherever God's word is, there the church must be; likewise, wherever baptism and the sacraments are, God's people must be, and vice versa. No others *have, give, practice, use, and confess* these holy possessions save God's people alone."[26] The German original says: "*hat, gibt, übt, braucht und bekennet.*"[27]

"Practice" and "use" are here used as synonymous verbs, and the meaning of these more "technical" verbs is fulfilled by the three others; "have," "give," and "confess." Luther also uses another verb or concept, which is helpful for developing a Lutheran understanding of the term "practice." Luther writes "so that they *exercise themselves in faith* and openly confess that they are Christian, just as they do with the word and with baptism."[28] To "practice" baptism is therefore a way of exercising oneself in faith. For Luther, the point is that the marks of the church are given freely to the believer to be used. The baptized is called to *use* his baptism. When Luther writes on the office of the keys he speaks about the "use of the keys."[29]

Hütter critically uses MacIntyre's definition to develop his own understanding of what a practice is. Hütter defines practices generally as "distinct, describable, and meaningful contexts of action that are cooperatively implicitly ordered and regulated."[30] Hütter concludes that this definition serves his development of theology as a core church practice. The most crucial point for Hütter, though, is to apply the terms "poiesis"

---

26. LW 41:152.

27. "/ hat / gibt / vbet / braucht / bekennet /." StA 5:593.

28. LW 41:152. The German original is once again üben: " / damit es sich auch vbet vnd o(e)ffentlich bekennet / das es Christen sey / wie es thut mit dem Wort vnd mit der Tauffe." StA 5:593.

29. LW 41:153. The German original has "*Brauch*," StA 5:594. Luther also speaks about using one's baptism as an equivalent to what here is referred to through the concept *practicing baptism*. Lohse points out in relation to baptism that "Luther intended to say not that faith is the presupposition for baptism, but that faith is its only proper use." Cf. Lohse, *Martin Luther's Theology*, 303.

30. Hütter, *Suffering Divine Things*, 35–36: "MacIntyre articulates this pointed definition of 'practice' with a distinct goal in mind, a goal that *cannot* be of concern in what follows, namely, the establishment of the necessity of virtues in a teleologically structured theory of action not directly dependent on Aristotelian biology and ontology."

and "praxis" as counter concepts to the term "pathos," because for Hütter the church's core practices are antithetical to Aristotelian practices. According to Hütter, the core church practices are practices with a considerably different logic, as the true subject of these practices is the Holy Spirit. Human beings "suffer" (*passio*) or undergo these practices, as these practices are teleological only from a soteriological perspective. Through these practices the Holy Spirit performs the work of the triune God in the person.[31] By his critical use of the Aristotelian practice tradition, Hütter hopes to safeguard the *vita passiva* motif in soteriology; that human beings receive God's grace as an alien grace, as a *verbum externum*.

In the book *Knowing the Triune God* (2001) theologians from different confessional traditions elaborate on the work of the Spirit in the practices of the Christian church. Reinhard Hütter is one of the contributors and writes about the church. In the introduction to this book the editors, David S. Yeago and James J. Buckley, claim that although MacIntyre's definition of practices is fruitful for many purposes, it does not radically include how Reinhard Hütter has redefined practice by speaking about the *pathos* of the church, which is the practice it takes to endure, "the compassion it takes to be a passionate people, the way that *passio* is genuine *actio*."[32]

What kinds of practices are then most important for the construction of a "Christian self"? In Bass and Dykstra's engagement with Christian practices many of the so-called Christian practices are quite close to cultural practices outside the church, in a way that makes the boundary between Christian and non-Christian practices quite fuzzy. This reveals how the engagement in practices has, from a cultural anthropological perspective (with some affinity to Bourdieu's idea of the ongoing dialectic between the *habitus* of a culture and the embodiment of this *habitus* in cultural practices), tried to critique a one-way movement from beliefs to practices. On the other hand, Hütter, differing from Bass and Dykstra, focuses particularly on the importance of the core church practices as they are constitutive for the church and as their *telos* is *soteriological*. Hütter's core practices "are distinguished *primarily* by the way the Holy Spirit is present in those practices, *not* by their outward form."[33]

---

31. Ibid., 132.
32. Buckley and Yeago, eds., *Knowing the Triune God*, 13.
33. Stubbs, "Practices, Core Practices and the Work of the Holy Spirit," 17–20.

The problem in Lutheran theology is how to situate the role of practices in the construction of a Christian self, as this self through grace is freed from meriting grace through works: Does this mean that practices are just ways to exercise the second use of the law—humbling the Christian self to recognize the need for grace again and again? Or may (certain) practices compose the (social) contours and construct of a Christian self? In *The Freedom of a Christian* (1520) Luther refers to Matthew 7:18 on the good fruit and Luther points out that "good works do not make a good man, but a good man does good works; evil works do not make a wicked man, but a wicked man does evil works."[34] This resonates well with Luther's foundational axiom in the treatise that a Christian is a perfectly free lord of all, subject to none, and that a Christian is a perfectly dutiful servant of all, subject to all.[35]

Here Luther also famously states, that "our faith in Christ does not free us from works but from false opinions concerning works, that is, from the foolish presumption that justification is acquired by works."[36] This in turn leads to the radical focus for Luther that good works is for the neighbor: "I will therefore give myself as a Christ to my neighbor, just as Christ offered himself to me."[37] Luther here outlines the direction and shape of the Christian life rooted in the union between Christ and man, which takes place through the Word of promise in baptism: "Surely we are named after Christ, not because he is absent from us, but because he dwells in us, that, because we believe in him and are Christs one to another and do to our neighbors as Christ does to us."[38]

If a Christian life is not a life freed from works, but a life freed from "false opinions concerning works," in which way may the commandments be seen as Christian practices? Hütter claims, that "in Christian catechesis, the Decalogue circumscribes the practices in which creaturely

---

34. LW 31:361.
35. LW 31:344.
36. LW 31:372–73.
37. LW 31:367.

38. LW 31:368. Therefore Luther claims that, "although the Christian is thus free from all works, he ought in this liberty to empty himself, take upon himself the form of a servant, be made in the likeness of man, be found in human form, and to serve, help, and in every way deal with his neighbour as he sees that God through Christ has dealt and still deals with him. This he should do freely, having regard for nothing but divine approval." LW 31:366. Luther concludes, that "works, being inanimate things, cannot glorify God, although they can, if faith is present, be done to the glory of God." LW 31:353.

freedom is genuinely received and therefore continuously practiced, and continuously practiced and therefore genuinely received."[39] Luther seems to think of the Commandments as a sort of "practices" of their own. He writes enthusiastically about how the First and Second Commandments may constantly be practiced.[40]

At the same time there is an obvious ambivalence here. According to Luther, the first-tablet commandments, and particularly the first four, are all about coming under the rule of God. These commandments "take a man captive, rule him, and bring him into subjection so that he does not rule himself, does not think himself good or hold himself in esteem, but rather he humbly recognizes himself for what he is and allows himself to be led so that he may resist pride." The second-tablet commandments, on the other hand, "deal with men's passions and lusts in order to kill them."[41]

Still, for Luther The Commandments are "the true fountain from which all good works must spring, the true channel through which all good works must flow."[42] Like in *On the Councils and the Church* Luther here uses different verbs to describe a life formatted by the practices of the catechisms—Christians should "üben" and "*treiben*"[43] the contents of the catechism, which literally means to "practice" the "practices" of the catechism—prayer, the Creed, the Ten Commandments, baptism and the Lord's Supper. Luther also uses a multitude of active verbs to describe the different ways to practice—read, teach, learn, meditate and ponder.

It is important to note that the Commandments are "practices" only because they are "versions" of the basic "practice" in Luther's theological system—the Word of God.[44] The Word of God is namely the "treasure that makes everything holy."[45] But not only the Commandments are thought of as "practices," even the Creed and the Lord's Prayer are "practices" in this sense. Luther even talks about the first article of the Creed as a "practice," as he writes: "We ought to daily practice this article."[46] Luther qualifies this

39. Hütter, *Bound to be Free*, 143.
40. BC, 396. Cf. German "Übung," in BELK, 578.
41. LW 44:100
42. BC, 428. Luther even claims that "now I hold that a young man could be more easily trained and encouraged by the fear of God and by his commandments than by any other means." LW 44:44.
43. BELK, 553.
44. Cf., for instance BC, 398: "practice God's Word."
45. BC, 399.
46. BC, 433, cf. also BELK, 645: "sollen wir diesen Artikel täglich üben."

further, by stating that to "practice" (the first article of) faith is to "impress it upon our minds, and remember it in everything we see and in every blessing that comes our way."[47] In the Large Catechism Luther relates the practice of the Creed to the practice of the Ten Commandments. The Creed is therefore given to help do what the Ten Commandments require. This implies that the evangelical function of the Creed is to set forth "all that we must expect and receive from God."[48]

Luther further underlines that if human beings were able to keep the Ten Commandments by their own strength, they would not need the Creed, or the Lord's Prayer. When investigating Luther's explanation of the Creed, once again, the importance of the First Commandment becomes evident: Luther claims that the Creed is nothing other than a response and confession of Christians based on the First Commandment.[49] Luther claims that if we "practice" these "practices" of the Catechism, we "regulate our entire life and being in accordance with God's Word."[50]

At the same time, the nature of the new life in Christ is tentative, and not definite or determinative, as the Small Catechism also witnesses. But does this relativize any claim to speak about how the Christian self is constructed socially through practices? In the first and original preface to the Large Catechism Luther ends by underlining that all who wish to be Christians in fact as well as in name, both young and old, may well be "trained" and become "familiar" with the contents of the catechism—here Luther refers to the three original parts: The Ten Commandments, The Creed and the Lord's Prayer.[51] As in the Small Catechism the verbs "trained" and "become familiar" (*sich übe und läufig werde*) are in the subjunctive tense of the verb.

Altogether, for Luther a (Christian) "practice" is not mainly something "outward." It is intimately connected with the heart and what it gazes upon or what it seeks help from. For Luther, a life before God, and then in the next instance before the world, is a life formatted by the First Commandment. It is a life which is to shape "the walk of life" of the Christian, according to God's order."[52]

---

47. BC, 433.
48. BC, 431.
49. BC, 432.
50. BC, 398.
51. BC, 384.
52. BC, 394. "Walk of life" is *Stand* in German; cf. BELK, 572.

The Lutheran engagement in "practices" has been successfully advanced by Reinhard Hütter's attempt to interpret the term *"notae ecclesiae"* as soteriologically and ecclesiologically constitutive core church practices. Understanding "practices" in the light of Lutheran theology, the following points are of particular importance: On one hand, the Christian life has a tentative shape and the fundamental soteriological *vita passiva* motif in Lutheran theology is opposed to the inherent idea in Aristotelian practices of growth and standards of excellence. On the other hand, even in the light of Lutheran theology, the Christian self is constructed socially through practices. The gift-aspect of faith and life is particularly important to Luther, and subsequently to a Lutheran view of practices. To practice (the first article of) faith is to "recognize how God gives and does all of this so that we may sense and see in this his fatherly heart and his boundless love toward us."[53]

Christian Practices and the Three Modes of Presence

If "practices," as defined above, may play a role in the shaping of "the walk of life" of the Christian, it is important to ask, how this relates to different understandings of the presence of Christ. Practices are always practiced in a context, in a historical setting. From a theological perspective this radical context-bound approach to practices corresponds with Luther's radical focus on how and where to locate the presence of Christ. It is crucial to evaluate Luther's understanding of the presence of Christ in relationship to his understanding of the Incarnation and Luther's broader (Christ)ontological vision.[54] I will now look at the presence of Christ in Christian practices in the light of Luther's larger Incarnation theology and his teaching on the three modes of Christ's presence in particular.

It is important to note that, Luther holds a fundamentally different view on the ascension than that of the Reformed tradition and Zwingli: When Christ has come to us in the Incarnation; he does not go away, but remains in our space and time. What the ascension changes is not Christ's presence as a fact, but the mode of that presence. Prior to the

---

53. BC, 433.

54. Cf. here for instance Haga, *Was There a Lutheran Metaphysics*, where Haga outlines Luther's Christ(onto)logy. Haga takes Luther's sacramental theology and Christology as his point of departure and focuses on the reception of the term *communicatio idiomatum* after Luther.

ascension Christ was accessible in a very graspable way to the sight, after the ascension he is accessible invisibly through the means of grace.[55]

In the *Confession concerning Christ's Supper* (1528), Luther makes a radical assumption, which has a strong influence on how a Lutheran approach to the context in which Christian practices take place should be understood. Luther rejects Zwingli's concept that the risen Christ is located (only) at the right hand of God. Rather Luther argues that Christ's body is everywhere because the right hand of God is everywhere.[56] For Luther, according to Scripture, God's "right hand" to which Christ ascended is not merely a location in heaven. Rather it is the manifestation of God's power. The implication of Christ's being at the right hand of God means that wherever the triune God is *now* at work, there the divine-human Christ is at work as well. Another fundamental point seems to be that the "logic" of the nature, essence and work of the persons in the Trinity transcends the logic of human nature. Luther therefore questions severely the attempt to confine Christ to a particular place.[57]

According to Luther, there are three modes known to us in which Christ is present. The teaching of these three modes is helpful in developing further the understanding of the presence of Christ in Christian practices. Luther develops these modes both based on the interpretation of Scripture, more precisely the Jesus narrative, and in critical dialogue with medieval philosophy.[58] *The first mode of presence*, the local or circumscriptive mode, is the mode when Christ walked bodily on earth, the mode when he occupied and yielded space according to his size. *The second mode*, or the diffinitive, uncircumscribed, spiritual mode of presence, is the mode of presence where Christ neither "occupies nor yields

---

55. Steinmetz, *Luther in Context*, 81.

56. LW 37:207 Luther made this assumption already in his treatise "This Is My Body" (1527); cf. Steinmetz, *Luther in* Context, 47, 55. In reality this is also a rejection of Calvin's notion of the *locus circumscriptum*.

57. LW 37:281.

58. LW 37:214–31. Cf. in particular: "My grounds on which I rest this matter, are as follows: The first is this article of our faith, that Jesus Christ is essential, natural, true, complete God and man in one person, undivided and separable. The second, that the right hand of God is everywhere. The third, that the Word of God is not false or deceitful. The fourth, that God has and knows various ways to be present at a certain place, not only the single one of which the fanatics prattle, which the philosophers call 'local.' Of this the sophists (Occamist Scholastics) properly say: There are three modes of being present in a given place: locally or circumscriptively, definitively, repletively" (LW 37:214–15).

space but passes through everything created as he wills."[59] This is the mode of presence, which Luther generally applies to the Risen Christ, and also the mode, which he ascribes to the presence of Christ in the Lord's Supper.[60] *The third mode*, the repletive mode, or the divine or heavenly mode, is a mode of presence ascribed to the exalted Christ seated at the right hand of the Father. In this mode created things "cannot measure or circumscribe him but they are present to him so that he measures and circumscribes them."[61]

Luther finds that the diffinitive, uncircumscribed mode of presence was the mode "in which the body of Christ was present when he came out of the closed grave, and came to the disciples through a closed door, as the gospels show." But Luther also underlines that Christ "was able, when he wished, to let himself be seen circumscribed in given places where he occupied space and his size could be measured." Therefore

---

59. Luther illustrates this mode of presence with vision, light, heat, or a sound or a tone, which "passes through and exists in air or water or a board and a wall and neither occupies nor yields space." Cf. LW 37:222-23.

60. "For as the sealed stone and the closed door remained unaltered and unchanged, though his body at the same time was in the space entirely occupied by stone and wood, so he is also at the same time in the sacrament and where the bread and wine are, though the bread and wine in themselves remain unaltered and unchanged." (LW 37:216)

61. LW 37:223. Luther here makes use of late medieval philosophy, and spells them out in accordance with the Ockhamist tradition he knew well through his own teachers, such as Gabriel Biel. The three modes are translated into German as: *begreiflich*, *unbegreiflich*, and *übernatürlich*; cf. StA 4:88-89. The first mode is the mode where space and object correspond exactly. In the second mode of presence "the object or body is not palpably in one place and is not measurable according to the dimensions of the place where it is, but can occupy either more room or less." Luther call this an uncircumscribed presence in a given place, "since we cannot circumscribe or measure it as we measure a body, and yet it is obviously present in the place." Luther writes about the third mode, the repletive mode of presence, that this is the mode where "an object occupies places repletively, i.e., supernaturally, if it is simultaneously present in all places whole and entire, and fills all places, yet without being measured or circumscribed by any place, in terms of the space which it occupies." Luther points out that this mode of existence belongs to God alone, and Luther quotes Jeremiah 23:23 as a proof of this: "I am a God at hand and not afar off. I fill heaven and earth." Luther is eager to underline that this mode is altogether incomprehensible, "beyond our reason, and can be maintained only with faith, in the Word." LW 37:215-16. Luther also underlines that: "You must place this existence of Christ, which constitutes him one person with God, far, far beyond things created, as far as God transcends them; and on the other hand, place it as deep in and as near to all created things as God is in them. For he is one indivisible person with God, and wherever God is, he must be also, otherwise our faith is false" (LW 37:223).

Luther maintains, that "Christ can be and is in the bread, even though he can also show himself in circumscribed and visible form wherever he wills."[62] But Luther also underlines the freedom of God when it comes to the presence of Christ:

> Our faith maintains that Christ is God and man, and the two natures are one person, so that this person may not be divided in two; therefore, he can surely show himself in a corporeal, circumscribed manner at whatever place he will, as he did after the resurrection and will do on the Last Day. But above and beyond this mode he can also use the second, uncircumscribed mode, as we have proved from the gospel that he did at the grave and the closed door.[63]

Therefore Luther argues—in line with his idea that the right hand of God is everywhere—that Jesus Christ according to the third, supernatural, mode is and can be wherever God is and that therefore "everything is full of Christ through and through." Or as Luther poignantly puts it: "If you can say, 'Here is God,' then you must also say, 'Christ the man is present too.'"[64]

Luther's creation theology, his Incarnation theology, and finally his sacramental theology meet at an important crux—Luther's understanding of the right hand of God. These three strands of his theology are interconnected in the understanding of the three modes of Christ's presence. This presence was a concrete and historical presence through the Incarnation changing the conditions for how human beings may relate to God and the world. This presence is now both a presence for the world, upholding creation (creation theology), and it is a saving presence through the Word and the sacraments (sacramental theology).

But how may this teaching help us to discern how Christ is present in Christian practices? Luther claims that although the right hand of God is everywhere, it is false religion to look for God in such a way that one despises "the places of God's choice and [to] manufacture signs and places of their own."[65] Luther underlines that human beings are not to "run back and forth throughout all creation," rather, the salvific presence of Christ is found where Christ is there for you—*pro me*:

---

62. LW 37:216.
63. LW 37:218.
64. Ibid.
65. Trigg, *Baptism in the Theology of Martin Luther*, 24.

... the right hand of God, although this is everywhere ... you can actually grasp it nowhere, unless for your benefit it binds itself to you and summons you to a definite place. This God's right hand does, however, when it enters into the humanity of Christ dwells there. There you will surely find it, otherwise you will run back and forth throughout all creation, grasping here and yet never finding, even though it is actually there; for it is not there for you.[66]

In order to develop a Lutheran understanding of how Christ is present in Christian practices, Luther's Incarnation theology, and his theology of the sacraments and the marks of the church need to be engaged. For Luther a realistic understanding of the Incarnation and an equally realistic doctrine of the Eucharist imply and demand each other. Therefore Luther celebrates both the universal presence of Christ (the repletive mode) and the particular presence of Christ (the diffinitive mode) to the fullest. On one hand, Christ is in the midst of all human experience—in, with and under it. On the other hand, Christ is there for you and me in a particular way in the places to which he has promised his saving presence, like the Eucharist.[67]

What Constitutes the Presence of Christ in Christian Practices?

In his work with practices Reinhard Hütter distinguishes between different clusters of practices. Most important for Hütter are the already mentioned "church's core practices," which are "complex and quite distinct contexts of action constituting and characterizing the church." Whereas these core practices are grounded in a distinct *bios*, Hütter maintains that there are also practices which are "necessary without being constitutive," and still others which are "either necessary or constitutive.'"[68]

What then constitutes the presence of Christ in (Christian) practices? Reinhard Hütter does not discuss this theme in any length, but roots much of his theological work on practices on the works of German Lutheran theologian Oswald Bayer. Bayer claims that the gospel—the preached, bodily Word—is Jesus Christ himself, and "therewith the undivided presence of

---

66. LW 37:68–69.
67. Steinmetz, *Luther in Context*, 82–83; and Lohse, *Martin Luther's Theology*, 231.
68. Hütter, *Suffering Divine Things*, 37. For an example of these categories, cf. ibid., 211.

the triune God."[69] This Word holds the form and structure of a *promise*.[70] Bayer points out that what is most important for Luther is the presence of Jesus Christ as the justifying Word of God, which comes to human beings in the promises at penance, baptism, and the Lord's Supper. Therefore the term "promise" (*promissio*) is the center of Luther's theology.[71]

This means that when Luther says or writes that God promises, this is not a reference to something in the future that we may anticipate. Rather, the promise is a valid and powerful promise and pledge that takes immediate and present effect, not just an announcement that will only be fulfilled in the future. Therefore, when Luther in the Large Catechism speaks of the word, which embraces the water of baptism, his concentration is upon the divine *command*.[72] In the Small Catechism Luther emphasizes how baptism gives the believer part in the saving works of Christ: According to Luther, baptism brings about forgiveness of sins, it redeems from death and the devil, and it also gives eternal salvation to all who believe it, as the words and promise of God declare. In the third article on baptism Luther elaborates on the content of the first article and underlines that "without the Word of God the water is plain water and not a baptism, but with the Word of God it is a baptism, that is a grace-filled water of life and a 'bath of the new birth in the Holy Spirit.'"[73]

The same approach is evident in Luther's outlining of the Lord's Supper in the Small Catechism. Here Luther underlines that it is not the eating and drinking which does it, but rather the words that are recorded: "given for you" and "shed for you for the forgiveness of sins." Ultimately, it is these words, when they are accompanied by the physical eating and drinking, which are the essential thing in the sacrament, and whoever believes these words *has* what they declare and state, namely, forgiveness of sins. Based on this, Luther does not dismiss the practices of fasting and bodily preparation before the Lord's Supper, but they are not compulsory, as they are

---

69. Bayer, *Living by Faith*, 50.

70. Bayer claims that "to speak theologically of sin and grace means to speak of God's promise (*promissio*) and of his law (*lex*), of the accusing and killing law (*Gesetz*) and the comforting and lifegiving gospel (*Evangelium*)." Cf. Bayer, *Theology the Lutheran Way*, 17.

71. Bayer, *Living by Faith*, 51. Spinks underlines that, "ultimately, Luther always falls back to the need to trust in the promise of God." Cf. Spinks, *Reformation and Modern Rituals and Theologies of Baptism*, 8.

72. Trigg, *Baptism in the Theology of Martin Luther*, 69.

73. BC, 359.

not constitutive to the practice. They might be "fine external discipline," but what constitutes the preparation before communion is "faith in these words, 'given for you' and 'shed for you for the forgiveness of sins.'"[74]

If we look further at baptism as a "practice," Luther understands baptism as the "practice" through which the baptized are initially received into the Christian community.[75] Luther also argues that baptism is of divine origin, and that to be baptized in God's name is to be baptized by God himself, and not by human beings. Therefore, baptism as a "practice" holds its power and position as a sacrament because it is commanded and instituted by the Word of God. Again, rooting his argument in Scripture is of ultimate importance for Luther –here he refers in particular to Matthew 28:19 and Mark 16:16.

In this Luther distinguishes between the two sacraments and the other parts of the catechism. Luther underlines that if the Ten Commandments, the Creed and the Lord's Prayer are revealed and given by God himself, baptism is "instituted by God himself."[76] Therefore, "baptism is not a work that we do, but it is a treasure that God gives us and faith grasps, just as the LORD Christ upon the cross is not a work but a treasure placed in the setting for the Word and offered to us in the Word and received by faith."[77]

In the Large Catechism Luther basically repeats his poignant definition of baptism given in the Small Catechism, but he gives it a different wording. Luther writes that baptism is "not simply plain water, but water placed in the setting of God's Word and commandment and made holy by them."[78] This definition offers a hermeneutical key to understand how Luther pictures the presence of Christ in the "practice" of baptism: Christ is the living Word of God. When we are baptized, we are baptized to (the present) Christ. This happens when water and human beings, both the baptismal candidate and the baptizer, are "placed in the setting of God's Word and commandment." Because of this commandment, or promise, the baptized is "made holy," i.e., enrapt in the presence of the living Son of God, Christ. Because of the promise or commandment which is bound

74. BC, 359.
75. BC, 456.
76. BC, 457, cf. BELK, 692: "eingesetzt."
77. BC, 461.
78. BC, 458. Luther also quotes St. Augustine: "*Accedat verbum ad elementum et fit sacramentum*," which he quoted frequently.

to both water and Word, baptism cannot be a mere spiritual matter. Its external character is indispensable, due to God's promise.

Therefore Luther also underlines that faith cannot be separated from its object, baptism, on the grounds that the object is something external. Rather faith should cling to the water and believe it to be baptism, "in which there is sheer salvation and life, not through the water, (. . .), but through its incorporation with God's Word and ordinance and the joining of his name to it."[79] Already in the introduction to his explanation to The Sacrament of the Altar, The Lord's Supper in the Large Catechism, Luther repeats this premise. This premise is fundamental for understanding the presence of Christ in Christian practices. The constitutive elements of the sacrament are "established from the words Christ used to institute it."[80]

Luther points out, as he does with the sacrament of baptism, that it is the Word, which is the voice of Christ. This is also what makes this a sacrament and distinguishes it from ordinary bread and wine. Therefore it is "called and truly is Christ's body and blood."[81] Luther underlines that the fundamental nature of the presence of Christ in the sacrament is not dependent upon the receiver, or on they way it may be handled by human beings. This is the case with the Commandments, the Lord's Prayer and the Creed, but this is also the case with the sacraments: Their nature cannot be violated by unworthily use, because their value is rooted in the promise of Christ's presence in forgiveness of sins.[82]

The same line of argument is used in the *Visitation Articles*. Here Luther outlines more extensively how Christ is present in the Lord's Supper, referring to the texts of the three Evangelists, Matthew, Mark, and Luke, and to 1 Corinthians 11. On this basis those who participate in the Lord's Supper should believe that Christ is truly present in body and blood, "since Christ has so declared." The miracle, which takes place when communion is celebrated, happens "because Christ has ordained that when we commune his body is present."[83]

In this treatise on the Lord's Supper Luther defends and elaborates his theology of the Word, which is constitutive for Christ's presence.

79. BC, 460.
80. BC, 467.
81. BC, 468.
82. BC, 467,
83. LW 40:289. Cf. The German original: "Sondern darumb / das Christus also geordenet hat" or the almost parallel wording in the next part "Denn Christus hat solchs also geordenet" (StA 3:231).

Against Zwingli's attempt to depart from the words of Scripture into several different kinds of words, such as command words, permission words, action words or written words, Luther maintains that the Word of God is "not merely a word of imitation, but a word of power which accomplishes what it expresses (Ps 33:9)."[84] This point is crucial in order to understand Luther's conception of the presence of Christ in the practices, which mark the church, such as the Lord's Supper: Everything that the words declare takes place by the power of the divine imperative ascribed to them.

In my analysis of those engaging Christian practices I showed that there is a tendency to underline the importance of the practicing community—Christian people—to such an extent that this community almost becomes constitutive to making a practice Christian.[85] This is not the case in the light of Lutheran theology. Luther makes it abundantly clear that the effect and validity of the Lord's Supper does not depend upon what he refers to as the "holiness of men."[86] And what more: In his theology of the efficacious Word of the triune God even Luther's soteriological impetus finds its point of departure: Therefore Luther maintains that there is forgiveness of sins in the Supper. This is not because of the eating, nor because Christ merits or achieves forgiveness of sins there, but on account of the word through which Christ "distributes among us this acquired forgiveness, saying: 'This is my body which is given for you.'"[87]

In *On the Councils and the Church* Luther uses different terms to argue why a *notae*—or a "practice," if you like—belongs to list of the marks of the church. First of all he identifies the Word with Christ himself.[88] Speaking about baptism he speaks about Christ's ordinance,[89] when it comes to the Lord's Supper he talks about Christ's institution,[90] and when it comes to the office of the keys he says "as Christ decrees."[91] But as he goes on to elucidate on the last three of the seven marks, the logic of

---

84. LW 37:181.

85. Cf. here also the definition of Christian practices by Bass and Dykstra, which are things *Christian* people do together over time; Dykstra and Bass, "A Theological Understanding of Christian Practices," 18.

86. LW 37:188

87. LW 37:192.

88. LW 41:148–51.

89. LW 41:151. Cf. " / nach Christus Ordnung /"; StA 5:592.

90. LW 41:152. Cf. " / wo es recht nach Christus einsetzung gereicht /"; StA 5:593.

91. LW 41:153. Cf. " / Wie Christus setzt /"; StA 5:594.

the argument shifts and the last three marks are "weighted" differently. They are marks of the church because of the way they relate to the four above-mentioned marks. The sixth mark—prayer, praise or thanksgiving, for instance—is a mark of the church in so far as it is performed "in accordance with the word of God and the true faith."[92] "The true faith," as a parallel expression to the *regula fidei* or the *doctrina evangelii*, is introduced as a regulating principle next to the word of God when it comes to the sixth core practice.[93]

As Luther comes to end of the third part of *On the Councils and the Church* he sums this up by saying that:

> Therefore the *ecclesia*, "the holy Christian people," does not have mere external words, sacraments, or offices, like God's ape Satan has, and in far greater numbers, but it has these as *commanded, instituted*, and *ordained* by God, so that he himself and not any angel will work through them with the Holy Spirit. They are called word, baptism, sacrament and office of forgiveness.[94]

Once again we see that the *notae* derive their power from God's command and institution. We also see that Luther includes the office of forgiveness as a *notae* in line with the word and the sacraments.

Luther also discusses the nature of the presence of Christ in the marks of the church earlier in the treatise: he links a false understanding of the marks of the church to a Nestorian Christology, which subsequently fails to understand the theology of *communicatio idiomatum*—the exchange of human and godly commodities in the Son of God.[95] And finally: the way Luther advocates the importance of baptism as a sacrament in the Small Catechism—that baptism is not simply plain water, rather it is water "enclosed in God's command and connected with God's Word"[96]—is consistent with the way he argues in *On the Councils and the Church*: It is Christ's command and promise, in this case in Matthew 28, which institutes and constitutes baptism as a sacrament.

Altogether, in the light of Lutheran theology the presence of Christ in (Christian) practices is constituted by God's word of command,

---

92. LW 41:164. Cf. " / nach dem wort Gottes vnd rechtem glauben /"; StA 5:604.
93. Cf. Hütter, *Suffering Divine Things*, 134.
94. LW 41:171. Cf. " / geboten / gestifft und geordnet /"; StA 5:610.
95. LW 41:103.
96. BC, 359.

institution or promise.[97] Luther's fundamental understanding of the presence of Christ in practices may probably best be understood through his explication of the holy Word of God, as the primary mark of the church. This Word is Christ, and it is the Holy Spirit which acts through this Word, which is the true subject of the marks of the church. This Word is an external word, and to "practice" this Word is to use—to believe and profess—it.[98] It is based on this premise that Luther finds the seven first-tablet practices outlined in *On the Councils and the Church* to be constitutive for the church. These practices are by necessity Christian practices. Luther poignantly sums up what constitutes the presence of Christ in such practices, by pointing out that:

> Just as water becomes baptism by the power of God, a bath unto eternal life, washing away sin and bringing salvation, a power which is not inherent to water; just as bread and wine become the body and blood of Christ; just as sins are remitted by the laying on of hands in accordance with God's institution.[99]

One striking example of this understanding is how Luther characterizes the practice of prayer in *On the Councils and the Church*. Here he develops theological criteria to measure what makes one practice more important than another. In this argument Luther's notion of the presence of Christ and Christ's promise (*promissio*) of his presence plays a determining role.[100] Luther argues that "God does not regard prayer on account of the person but on account of his Word and the obedience accorded it."[101] Here Luther develops a twofold premise: Firstly, prayer is a Christian practice because it lives from the promise of God in his Word. Secondly, prayer is a Christian practice because to pray is to look at God's promise.[102]

---

97. These terms are largely equivalents. Oswald Bayer gives a poignant description of the presence of Christ in line with this: "God lets himself be grasped, namely, in the Word of his promise. We can hear and taste the promise in a very condensed form in the Lord's Supper" (Bayer, *Living by Faith*, 72).

98. LW 41:149.

99. LW 41:168.

100. Cf. also Peters, *Kommentar zu Luthers Katechismen*, 4:85: "Die Taufe bleibt eingefügt in die Grundordnung: Promissio—Fides. Diese Grundordnung freilich verweist den Glauben nicht an sich selber, sondern an das leibhaft vernommene Wort sowie die noch konkretere Berührung unseres Leibesmenschen mit dem irdischen Element. Der innere Mensch des Herzens dringt gleichsam vor bis in die Aussenhaut seines Leibes, um auch hier seinem Herrn zu begegnen."

101. BC, 442.

102. BC, 456.

Towards a List of Christian Practices

The presence of Christ in the church's core practices, belonging to the first tablet of Moses, is constituted through the divine command and promise of Christ's presence. But on what basis may it be claimed that other practices are "Christian," practices on the economy of creation, belonging to the second tablet of Moses? According to Dykstra, Bass and Dean these practices are crucial in the construction of a Christian identity, a Christian self. This is a question of how to discern between different clusters or categories of practices. Reinhard Hütter speaks about the core practices, and further about necessary but not constitutive practices, and finally about indifferent practices.[103]

Danish Lutheran theologian Anne Marie Aagaard argues that Luther's list in *On the Councils and the Church* should be interpreted as a "7+7" list of the marks of the church, first the seven *notae ecclesiae* and then the second set of commandments from the second tablet of Moses. For Aagard the latter seven are also marks of the true church, because through them the church does the will of God in fighting for justice, peace, and human dignity, rather than fighting or disclosing the realm of justification and sanctification by which the church lives. By this take on the marks of the church, Aagard advocates a thicker ecclesiology, arguing that the church should engage in a broader range of questions that matter for contemporary society.[104]

Hütter, on the other hand, focuses more "narrowly" on the constitutive ecclesiological character of the seven marks. In a way, Hütter argues for a very high view of the church and the core practices through which the Holy Spirit acts. Hütter may be criticized for being too Barthian in his rejection of the more Schleiermacherian, and phenomenological impetus in the "practices" approach, but there is not necessarily a dichotomy here. In other words, a high view of the core practices need not have the effect of "dichotomizing these core practices of the church from the practices of culture or from other Christian practices."[105]

On what premises then should practices on the economy of creation be judged as "Christian" practices? Oswald Bayer claims that "practices"[106] in the realm of worldly righteousness are in a way "secular" or even "athe-

---

103. Hütter, *Suffering Divine Things*, 37.
104. Aagard, *Identifikation af kirken*, 18–19.
105. Stubbs, "Practices, Core Practices and the Work of the Holy Spirit," 28.
106. Bayer, however, does not talk about "practices" in the strict meaning of the term.

istic." Bayer founds his argument in a quotation from Luther in his 1524 exposition to Psalm 127, that in the sphere of worldly righteousness, "we must ourselves do all that we have to do 'as if there was no God.'"[107] This understanding of how the Christian should live within the rule of God in state and household also has some resemblances with Swedish theologian Gustav Wingren's take on Luther's teaching on vocation. The "practices" stemming from the second tablet have nothing to do with the life of troubled soul, and according to Luther they do not constitute the church. They are there for the neighbor and the life of the world.[108]

The basic point for Luther himself in *On the Councils and the Church* seems to be that Christian holiness, which is a life marked by the *notae ecclesiae*, is a life in accordance with the first tablet of Moses.[109] But Luther also discusses "practices" which may flow from the second tablet of Moses—such as to honor your parents, to serve the authorities, and not to steal. They are also the work of the Holy Spirit, who, according to Luther, sanctifies and even awakens the body to such a new life until it is perfected in the life beyond.[110] But they are given a fundamentally different character:

> However these signs cannot be regarded as being as reliable as those noted before since some heathen too practice these works and indeed at times appear holier than Christians; yet their actions do not issue from the heart purely and simply, for the sake of God, but they search for some other end because they lack a real faith in and a true knowledge of God.[111]

At the end of his treatise Luther offers a lengthy but poignant theological explication for other things or items, which could play a role in church life, but which are still clearly to be distinguished both from the *notae*, which constitute the church and the second tablet practices. These

---

107. Bayer, *Living by Faith: Justification and Sanctification*, 37.

108. For yet another approach, cf. *Marks of the Body of Christ*, ed. Braaten and Jenson. Here the ecumenical potential in the seven marks of the church is elaborated as North American authors from different confessional traditions elaborate on the contemporary importance of the teaching of the marks. The authors therefore discuss the theme from a distinct contextual understanding of the role of the church in a rapidly changing culture. Likewise the authors stress the difference between Luther and our time.

109. LW 41:146.

110. LW 41:146, 166.

111. LW 41:167.

are things like certain holidays and certain hours, which are set aside for preaching or praying, or the use of a church building or a house, or an altar, pulpit, baptismal font, candlesticks, candles, bells, priestly vestments, and the like. Such things do not "sanctify and awaken" according to either the first or the second tablet of Moses, but they can be "useful, proper and good."[112]

Luther then goes on to describe what he finds to be the "false" practices of the pope—"the prescription of chasubles, tonsures, cowls, garb, food, festivals, days, monkery, nunning, masses, saint-worship and countless other items of an external, bodily, transitory nature." These practices are false practices because, according to Luther, they presuppose "false trust in works.""[113] Luther also addresses what he understands to be practices that do *not* constitute the church. Criticizing the Roman Church he writes about how the Devil works as God's ape and tries to imitate all God's things and to improve on them. According to Luther, the Devil also tried his luck with external things in order to make man holy—just as he tries with rain-makers, sorcerers, exorcists of devils, etc. But Luther does not fully dismiss all this as he compares it to the way children say God's word over created things such as their food or themselves as they go to bed. But this does not make these things holy possessions, which constitute the church, as Luther points out. Luther's critical comment here may also serve as a criterion to distinguish between distinctly Christian practices, as in the core practices, and more loose practices, which may still be "Christian." Luther writes: "The creature derives no new power from such a practice, but is strengthened in its formal power."[114]

Once again, 1 Timothy 4:5 forms the biblical premise for Luther's argument. The point for Luther seems to be that these things, or "practices,"

---

112. LW 41:173: "These things have no more than their natural effects just as food and drink accomplish no more by virtue of the grace the children say at the table, for the ungodly and rude folk who don't say it, that is, who neither pray to God nor thank him, grow just as fat and strong from food and drink as Christians do. To be sure, Christians could be and remain sanctified even without these items, even if they were to preach on the street, outside a building, without a pulpit, if absolution were pronounced and the sacraments administered without an altar, and if baptism were performed without a font as happens daily that for special reasons sermons are preached and baptisms and sacraments administered in the home. But for the sake of children and simple folk, it is a fine thing and conducive to good order to have a definite time, place and hour to which people can adapt themselves where they may assemble, as St Paul says in I Corinthians 14 (:40), 'All things should be done decently and in order.'"

113. LW 41:147.

114. LW 41:168.

are not capable of forming a firm foundation for faith, and thereby also for the church, as they lack the explicit institution or ordinance by Christ. By using 1 Timothy 4:5 Luther also unfolds an important part of creation theology "Everything created by God is good." And by doing so he also links creation and salvation in the work of the church.

Luther develops different lists of practices—or the *notae ecclesiae*—which may help in further developing a criteriology for Christian practices, even for those practices on the economy of creation. In *Against Hanswurst* (1541) Luther notes ten or eleven signs or marks of the true church similar to those in the list in *On the Councils and the Church*:

1. Baptism
2. The holy sacrament of the altar
3. The true and ancient keys
4. The preaching office and the word of God
5. The Apostles' Creed
6. The Lord's Prayer
7. The honoring of temporal powers
8. The praise and honoring of marriage
9. Experiencing suffering
10. Refraining from revenge and praying for others[115]

Luther explicitly underlines that the first four marks, which coincide with the first four marks of the list in *On the Councils and the Church*, are commanded and instituted by Christ himself. If we compare the eighth and ninth mark here, we may find traces of how Luther distinguishes between practices on the economy of creation, and practices on the economy of salvation. When it comes to the eighth mark, Luther maintains that it is an ordinance of God's creation. Ergo, it is ordained by God, but is not distinctly Christian, in the sense that it is a practice on the economy of salvation, a first-tablet practice. The ninth practice or mark is different—here Luther argues, similarly to the seventh mark in *On the Councils and the Church*, that by experiencing suffering "we (like the same ancient church) are like the Lord Christ himself on the cross."[116] At the end, Luther also discusses whether fasting should be considered

115. LW 41:194–98.
116. LW 41:197.

a mark of the true church. He does not fully dismiss it, but he is very ambivalent. Rather, Luther seems to think that much more important than fasting is feeding the poor and the hungry.[117]

Particularly interesting here is the elaboration concerning the tenth mark, refraining from revenge. We see threads of this logic in the Catechisms. Here Luther links the first and the fifth Commandment by underlining that God "always wants to remind us to recall the First Commandment, that he is our God; that is, that he wishes to help, comfort, and protect us, so that he may restrain our desire for revenge."[118] Luther also underlines in his exposition of the Fifth Commandment the importance of loving one's enemy: "It is God's real intention that we should allow no one to suffer harm but show every kindness and love. And this kindness, as I said, is directed especially toward our enemies. For doing good to our friends is nothing but and ordinary virtue of pagans, as Christ says in Matthew 5 (:46–47)."[119] In other words, the practice of refraining from revenge is a practice on the border between first- and second-tablet practices. It is something the church cannot *not* do, but it is not necessarily constitutive for the church. Rather it marks a negative definition of church: Where there is revenge, there is no church.

How then does Luther distinguish between what are here labeled necessary, indifferent, and false (mal-)practices? Towards the end of the third part of the treatise *Confession concerning Christ's Supper*, Luther discusses other sacraments in the papal church, such as unction, marriage and the office of the priesthood. He does not speak against them as "practices," but he maintains that making sacraments out of them is "nonsense" or not needed, as "these orders are sufficiently holy in themselves."[120] Luther also shortly discusses "images, bells, eucharistic vestments church ornaments, altar lights, and the like." These things he regard as "things indifferent." But Luther underlines that he has "no sympathy with the iconoclasts," and that "images or pictures from the Scriptures and from good histories" may be very useful, but they are still "indifferent" and optional.[121]

A list of what the modern reader may call "Christian practices" is also found in the *Visitation Articles* under the heading "The Human Order

117. LW 41:198–99.

118. BC, 413. Cf. the tenth mark in *Against Hanswurst*.

119. BC, 412.

120. LW 37:370. Cf. " / darynnen vns der heilige geist vergebung der sunden reichlich darbeut gibt vnd vbet." StA 4:255.

121. LW 37:371. Cf. "frey vnd wilko(e)rig," StA 4:255.

of the Church," where the authors of the *Visitation Articles* give a list of "important subjects."[122] This list of "practices" could very well—from a contemporary systematic-theological perspective—be read as a list of important Christian practices. The list is to function as a contrast to the papal church's focus on ecclesiastical order. The list also seems to reflect an internal hierarchy between the listed "practices," where the first to be mentioned are those to be considered as primary. The hierarchy also refers to the first and second tablets of Moses, as in *On the Councils and the Church*. But here only "practice" 1, 2, 5, and 6 (and maybe 4) could be regarded as first tablet practices. The list probably should not be considered complete, however, particularly from the perspective of the second tablet:

1. Christian repentance
2. Faith
3. Good works
4. The fear of God
5. Prayer
6. Honoring God
7. Regard for parents
8. The education of children
9. Respect for government
10. Not to envy
11. Not bear hate
12. Not to injure or kill anyone
13. Chastity
14. Living virtuously in marriage
15. Not to be greedy
16. Not to steal
17. Not to drink intemperately
18. Not to lie
19. Not to slander.[123]

---

122. "/die stu(e)cke die no(e)tig sind/." StA 3:440.
123. LW 40:297–98 The importance of keeping certain festivals and days is also

Even in the Large Catechism, Luther distinguishes between the first and the second tablet of the Decalogue, with respectively the first three commandments, "which are directed toward God" and the next seven commandments, "which relate to our neighbor."[124] Although Luther discerns life before God—*coram Deo*—and life before human beings—*coram hominibus*—the two are never set apart.[125]

For Luther, both true faith and trust and idolatry are "revealed" in "practice." Luther writes that "the world practices nothing but false worship and idolatry."[126] Luther dealt with the question of true or false church, both in the lectures on Genesis and elsewhere. Luther pointed out at least four "marks" of the false church—misuse of God's name, contempt for the things that belong to the true church, being preoccupied with the pleasures and glory of this life and contempt for the promise of God in the lives of believers.[127] Even when he discusses what is anti-church, i.e., the Devil's temple, Luther avoids any puritan definition of the church by stating that the Devil made his church by imitating God. The Devil, according to Luther, "noticed that God utilized outward things, like baptism, word, sacrament, keys, etc. whereby he sanctified his church."[128] By saying this Luther also underlines an important part of his own ecclesiology—God does use outward things to sanctify his church.

In the last part of the treatise *Against Hanswurst* Luther lists what he sees as mal-"practices," "practices" invented by the papal church. By trusting to these practices the papal church has abandoned the heritage

---

discussed. Here it is maintained that each one should keep peacefully to his custom. Therefore not all holy days should be done away with. In general, it is well if there is some uniformity. Therefore—unlike the days of Annunciation, Purification, Visitation of the Virgin Mary, St John the Baptist, Michaelmas, Apostles' Day, and Magdalene, which have already been discarded and could not conveniently be restored—Christmas, Circumcision, Epiphany, Easter, Ascension, and Pentecost should be kept, as these days have been instituted because it is not possible to teach all parts of the gospel at one time. Finally the main point for the authors is that "the people are to be taught that the only reason for keeping these festivals is to learn the Word of God." LW 40:298.

124. BC, 400.

125. "In God's sight it is actually faith that makes a person holy; it alone serves God, while our works serve people. Here you have every blessing, protection, and shelter under the Lord, and, what is more, a joyful conscience and a gracious God will reward you hundredfold" (BC, 406–7).

126. BC, 388. Cf. "wie die Welt falschen Gottesdienst und Abgötterei treibt." BELK, 563.

127. Lathrop and Wengert, *Christian Assembly*, 96.

128. LW 41:167.

of the true ancient church and, most importantly, misinterpreted what it means to live a life shaped by one's baptism, the prime mark of the church. The problem, Luther argues, is that the papal church seems to profess that these practices—like indulgences, holy water and salt, pilgrimages to gain forgiveness of sins, private masses, and worshipping the saints, among others—makes a man become "as pure as if he had baptized by the baptism of Christ."[129] This is the negative counterpart to life in faith as *practicing baptism*. Therefore, according to Luther, it is possible to "fall away from one's baptism"[130] when the baptized starts trusting in his own merits instead of the saving work of Christ.

Altogether, Luther always comes back to the Word as determinative for any list of (Christian) practices, his explanation of the third Article of the Creed in the Large Catechism is a clear proof of the central role assigned to the "practice" of the Word. Luther writes that we "believe in him who daily brings us into this community through the Word, and imparts, increases, and strengthens faith through the same Word and the forgiveness of sins."[131] But next to the Word comes baptism. Parallel to his ranking of baptism as the prime mark of the church in *Against Hanswurst*, in the Large Catechism Luther prizes what a wonderful gift of God baptism is. Baptism is "far more glorious than anything else God has commanded and ordained; in short, it is so full of comfort and grace that heaven and earth cannot comprehend it."[132] Based on the analysis and discussion here, I suggest that practices should be grouped in four different categories:

1. *First-tablet practices*: The church's core practices, practices on the economy of salvation

2. *Second-tablet practices*: (possibly) Christian practices, practices on the economy of creation

3. *Indifferent, but partly helpful practices*

4. *False (mal-)practices.*

Category 4 includes practices, where the church fails to practice second-tablet practices, like telling the truth, fighting for justice, peace and

---

129. LW 41:199.
130. LW 41:207.
131. BC, 439.
132. BC, 461.

human dignity. These are malpractices, which form a negative definition of church—where the church is *not*.

Christian Practices and the Common Order of Christian Love

The aim of this book is to discuss how the presence of Christ in (Christian) practices relates to the shaping of the Christian life and of the Christian self. One particular concept of Luther—*the common order of Christian love*—may be particularly helpful in further understanding the nature of those practices which are potentially Christian, practices belonging to the second tablet of Moses, practices on the economy of creation.

Throughout his writings Luther continued to use a variety of words for the marks of the church, using colors and markings and signs. In a sermon on the footwashing on Maundy Thursday in 1538, Luther, preaching the text of John 13, was "forced" to include love as a fruit of the faith created by the word and the sacraments. This sermon also demonstrates how Luther is deeply committed to the notion of the *notae ecclesiae*. In this case, when Luther was confronted by a clear word of Christ, "by this they shall know you are my disciples, that you love one another," he did not abandon his own definition of the Christian marks or "colors" but simply tacked Jesus' sign (love) onto his previous list of marks of the church.[133] The larger point here, however, is that love is made a guiding principle for discipleship. What are the implications of this?

In *Confession concerning Christ's Supper* Luther makes a reference to what he understands as the three holy orders or institutions established by God, namely, the office of the priest, the estate of marriage, and the civil government. According to Luther, these three orders are holy because they are found in God's word and commandment, as for Luther whatever is contained in God's Word must be holy, and God's Word is holy and sanctifies everything connected with it and involved in it. Luther's argument here is similar to the way he argues the importance of the "practices" or things of the second tablet of Moses in the third part of *On the Councils and the Church*. But superseding all these three institutions is what Luther refers to as "the common order of Christian love." In this

---

133. Later in a disputation a similar discussion about John 13:35 takes place, on love as a sign of the true church. It is claimed on the basis of John 13:35 that the mark of the church is love. Here there is also reference to Matt 28:19 and the argument that love is comprehended in the sacraments themselves. Lathrop and Wengert, *Christian Assembly*, 83, 105.

order one serves "not only the three orders but also every needy person in general with all kinds of benevolent deeds, such as feeding the hungry, giving drink to the thirsty, forgiving enemies, praying for all men on earth, suffering all kinds of evil on earth, etc." The list of "practices" given by Luther here bears similarities to the list of "practices" listed under the second tablet of Moses in *On the Councils and the Church*, but they have what one may call a diaconal focus. For Luther these practices are "Christian" in the sense that by participating in them we exercise "the common order of Christian love"—love for the sake of the neighbor and the world in need. But they are not Christian in the sense that they make those who practice them (any more) Christian. Luther therefore strictly underlines that all these "practices" are "good and holy works," but "none of these orders is a means of salvation."[134]

Reinhard Hütter argues that the relationship between practices and beliefs should be interpreted by distinguishing between God's economy of creation and God's economy of salvation. Hütter finds that the practices which are fundamental to sustaining and enhancing human life across a variety of cultures and throughout times belong to God's economy of creation. The practices belonging to God's economy of salvation are the practices through which God's salvific activity is meditated and communicated. Hütter argues, based on the Lutheran tradition, that it is "the Christian faith that uncovers the inherent interconnectedness of all (of these) practices."[135]

---

134. LW 37:364–65. Cf. the German original: " /Dennoch ist keiner solcher o(e)rden ein weg zur seligkeit/." StA 4:251.

135. Hütter writes: "Here I can only gesture toward the kind of theological taxonomy of practices that I presuppose in my essay. Fundamental to this taxonomy is the distinction (*not* dichotomy) between God's economy of creation and God's economy of salvation. Those fundamental practices that we encounter as central to the sustenance and enhancement of human life across a variety of cultures and throughout time and that we therefore tend to call 'universal' are theologically to be identified as belonging to God's economy of creation—due to their very 'point'; namely the sustenance and enhancement of human life. Practices belonging to God's economy of salvation, on the other hand, are those through which God's salvific activity is communicated and mediated which are crucial embodiments of this communication and mediation. It is, I argue, the Christian faith that uncovers the inherent interconnectedness of all of these practices. To be precise: Practices are not legitimated by the Christian faith, but the very fact that they cannot stand alone but depend decisively on other practices makes sense in the light of the Christian faith. This is true of both 'universal' and 'distinctly Christian' practices that bear witness to God's salvific activity—and of practices which fall in both categories, such as forgiveness. I suggest that what makes these practices possible in the first place, as well as what represents their final fulfilment, is revealed

Discussing practices, a distinction between creation and redemption can be made, but it is not necessarily a dichotomy, as part of redemption is a revelation of the ends and purposes of creation. Therefore Hütter's strict distinction between practices of creation and practices of redemption may be criticized, although it is helpful, as it also raises further questions. The main problem with the distinction comes to the fore in the following critical question: "Is the forgiveness of sin and 'going back to Eden' the only impetus behind the incarnation, life, death, resurrection and ascension of Christ and the sending of the Holy Spirit at Pentecost?"[136]

The distinctions here made may help us to understand the presence of Christ in the large range of practices listed as Christian practices more comprehensively. For Luther all practices stemming from the second tablet of Moses are "Christian" in the sense that they are ways that Christians may exercise "the common order of Christian love." But they are not practices that offer salvation—forgiveness of sins—that Christ offers for, as Luther writes: "To be holy and to be saved are two entirely different things."[137]

For Luther the gift of salvation is given through Christ alone, through the "practices" which are instituted by Christ himself. In *Confession concerning Christ's Supper*, elaborating on the third article of faith, Luther lists three means or methods—identical with the first three "practices" in the list in *On the Councils and the Church*.[138] They are; the gospel, baptism, and the sacrament of the altar. Through these outward "practices," as Luther labels them, the Holy Spirit helps to receive and preserve the grace in Christ. Luther even claims that through these means or methods—i.e. "practices"—the Holy Spirit helps us to use grace in Christ to our advantage "and impart it to others, increase and extend it."[139]

---

through their particular Christian equivalent as this communicates and reflects God's own practice (let us say of forgiveness). This is possible because the enactment of such practices is rooted in the church's core practices. This theological taxonomy also makes sufficiently clear that the use of the term 'practice' for the church's core practices is an ultimately analogical use, since the Holy Spirit is the subject who works his mission through these practices" (Hütter, "Hospitality and Truth," 206–7).

136. Stubbs, "Core Practices and the Work of the Holy Spirit," 26.

137. LW 37:365.

138. Cf. "mittel oder weise." StA 4:252.

139. LW 37:366 Cf. " /So kompt der heilige geist vnd gibt sich auch vns gantz vnd gar / der leret vns solche wolthat Christi vns erzeigt /erkennen / hilfft sie empfahen vnd behalten / nu(e)tzlich brauchen vnd austeilen / mehren vnd foddern /." StA 4:251–52.

By this, Luther does not mean to devaluate becoming holy. This happens both through faith in Christ and the "methods" which strengthen and preserve that faith, and through "these divine foundations and orders"—i.e. the "practices" stemming from "the common order of Christian love" and the "practice" of living in and serving the three institutions." For even Luther claims, as long as he is assured that it has nothing to do with the righteousness of works, that "God wishes us to perform such works to his praise and glory." Luther even, rather optimistically, proclaims that "all who are saved in the faith of Christ surely do these works and maintain these orders."[140]

How do these elaborations relate to Luther's teaching of the three modes of Christ's presence? In Luther's treatise on the Lord's Supper it is particularly the two last modes which are of importance in developing a Lutheran understanding of the presence of Christ in Christian practices. Through the uncircumscribed mode of presence, the *diffinitive* mode, Christ is present for our salvation and for the forgiveness of sins—as in the Lord's Supper and in baptism. But in the divine, *repletive* mode of presence Christ is present as one of the persons of the Trinity, as the one who upholds the world we inhabit.

Finally therefore, the presence of Christ in Christian practices should be discerned by seven interrelated principles—which stem from Luther's idea of the three modes of presence:

First of all, Christ is and has always been present in this world. As one person of the Trinity, Christ took part in creation, and as the right hand of God is everywhere, Christ is still present to uphold the created world until the Last Day. Through practices belonging to the second tablet of Moses, all, both Christians and non-Christians, may practice a life which benefits their neighbor and God's creation. This practice of the common order of Christian love relates to Christ's repletive presence, as the triune God still upholds this world, and because Christ is present for the life of the world.

Secondly, through certain "practices," which are instituted, commanded or ordained by Christ himself in Scripture and promised for salvation through the Word, true, salvific fellowship with God may be found. In these first-tablet practices, the *notae ecclesiae*, the salvific presence of Christ is offered. In these marks of the church instituted by

140. Luther even seems to expect this: "All who are saved in the faith of Christ surely do these works and maintain these orders" (LW 37:365).

Christ, the real presence of Christ according to the uncircumscribed, diffinitive, mode is encountered. Through these practices the practitioner undergoes the work of the Holy Spirit—through which the practitioner, who is fundamentally a receiver, is freed from sin and enrapt in the triune God's eschatological renewal of creation.

Thirdly, according to Luther, Christ may be present in any mode he finds suitable, comprehensible or incomprehensible to us, even the circumscribed mode. This argument is for Luther rooted in the radical freedom of God.

Fourthly, the presence of Christ in practices—or at all—for Luther is centered around the *pro nobis-pro me*. Therefore the repletive presence of the son of God is not a "sign" of God's saving action.

Fifthly, Luther's strong rejection of "running forth and back throughout all creation" should not be interpreted as a rejection of practices on the level of the economy of creation. Luther's point is to underline the fundamental difference in quality between sacramental-salvific practices which offer us God's saving presence—forgiveness of sins—and practices which may be Christian in the sense that through them the common order of Christian love may be exercised for the benefit of the neighbor and all of creation.

Sixthly, in the light of Lutheran theology, this implies that love is made the focal point of all Christian practices: first-tablet practices offer God's saving love in Christ, and second-tablet practices are ways to practice the common order of Christian love.

Seventhly, for the shape of the Christian life this implies that the Incarnation and baptism are not mere models for the practitioner to imitate, but events that model the shape of the Christian life.

THE CONSTRUCTION OF THE CHRISTIAN SELF

Christian Practices and the Doctrine of Sin

The crux of the disagreement within Lutheran engagements in the Christian practices debate has been the relationship between Christian practices and human agency. A Lutheran understanding of sin and the new self born in baptism influence the way human agency in Christian practices and the *telos* of the Christian life should be understood. Like most scholars engaging in the practices conversation, Reinhard Hütter does not address the doctrine of sin in relation to practices directly on many occasions. For Hütter the main focus is the new self-identity, which evolves from baptism and a life formatted by the core practices. Hütter claims that human freedom, which is acquired only in faith through baptism, consists in being able, as a baptized person, to give oneself over to obedience.[141] Therefore a further elaboration on Luther's understanding of sin in relation to the practices conversation is needed.

Looking at Luther's larger cosmological conception, in which his understanding of sin belongs, it is important to take into account how strange this may seem to a modern reader. Luther makes frequent references to the Devil and the impact of evil powers in daily life. For Luther human beings are not mere observers in the battle between God and the Devil, they themselves are ridden by this battle.[142] Luther puts the baptized at the beginning of a lifelong fight with evil, as evil resists being fought and defeated.[143] In the Western hemisphere such a cosmology seems to have a renaissance only in times of major crises, like terror attacks or massacres that display incomprehensible amounts of radically, evil deeds.

Luther's response to the presence of radical evil is to envision a fundamentally theo-centric view on life. Even in the catechisms, there are traces of such a radical and dramatic cosmology. According to Luther, the role of the First Commandment is foundational, as everything proceeds from the power of this commandment.[144] In his explanation Luther outlines the pillars of his theology. First of all, Luther envisions a fundamentally theo-logical cosmology. The relationship to God is the most fundamental relationship in the life of a human. It is what constitutes the world—as "a "god," for Luther, is the term "for that to which we are to look for all good and in which we are to find refuge in all need," and

---

141. Cf. for instance Hütter, *Suffering Divine Things*, 123, 177–78.

142. Lohse, *Martin Luther's Theology*, 254: "With respect to the devil as God's antagonist, Luther wrote that the devil is ultimately involved in everything opposed to God's will, doing injury to the world and humankind."

143. Cf. for instance, Lexutt, "'. . . dass der böse Feind keine Macht and mir finde,'" 329. Cf. also Spinks, who writes in relation to Luther's baptismal theology that, "for Luther the devil was very real, and baptism was about being saved from sin and evil." Spinks, *Reformation and Modern Rituals and Theologies of Baptism*, 11.

144. BC, 430.

"therefore, to have a god is nothing else than to trust and believe in that one with your whole heart."[145]

For Luther this definition of what a god is also makes faith and trust fundamental human categories in the life of human beings. Therefore the intention of the First Commandment is "to require faith and confidence of the heart, which fly straight to the one true God and cling to him alone."[146] Likewise, if the First Commandment is to instruct the heart and teach faith, the Second Commandment also focuses on the relationship to God, it is to lead us forward and direct the lips "into the right relationship with God."[147] On the other hand, the opposite of true faith in the one God, idolatry, is faith, which is not placed in the one God. But this idolatry is not merely about erecting an image and praying to it, but it is primarily a matter of the heart, which gazes upon other things and seeks help and consolation from creatures, saints, or devils. Ultimately, this is the false worship of a "conscience that seeks help, comfort, and salvation in its own works and presumes to wrest heaven from God."[148]

Central to Luther's understanding of man is therefore his holistic, and theo-centric, anthropology, his emphasis on the *totus homo*. Soul, body, mind, spirit and flesh are referring to the whole human being as it is situated in relationship to God, the neighbor, and the self.[149] Luther also radically understands human beings as beggars or receivers before God. Human beings live of and by the gifts of God, and this constitutes all of life and all of its relations with a *gift character*. Moreover, Luther argues, although human beings are able to give and to do much good, man and other creatures are only the hands, channels, and means through which God bestows all kinds of blessings. But it is possible for human beings to fail to rely on this, if they are "unwilling to receive anything as a gift of

---

145. Cf. also "to have a god is to have something in which the heart trusts completely." BC, 386–87.

146. Ibid. Cf. *Glaube* for Latin *fides* and *Vertrauen* for Latin *fiducia*. BELK, 560. Cf. also: "You can easily understand what and how much this commandment requires, namely, that one's whole heart and confidence be placed in God alone, and in no one else" (BC, 388).

147. BC, 392.

148. BC, 388.

149. Steinmetz points out that "Luther reads the anthropological terminology of the New Testament in such a way as to stress the psychosomatic unity of the human person" (Steinmetz, *Luther in Context*, 76).

God, but desiring to earn everything by itself."[150] Only if human beings are "led to it by the Holy Spirit" can they realize and recognize this.[151]

Ultimately, Luther finds that every human is part of the great cosmological drama between God the creator of all things and God's enemy, the Devil. Luther even situates his approach to upbringing within this complex cosmological anthropology, where man is both the first and finest of creation and at the same time, the most fragile and tried creature in God's creation.[152]

In this drama the catechisms play a central role. In the preface to the Small Catechism Luther underlines that the catechisms are tools for the believer's spiritual warfare. A life formatted by the catechisms is a life where the believer practices and nurtures the gift of faith given in baptism. The catechisms are therefore tools to help faith withstand "the constant and furious attacks and assaults of the devil." Therefore Luther claims that through the practices of the catechism God wishes to warn, equip and protect the believer against the Devil's attacks. It is also important to note that these tools are there for the whole life-journey. The catechisms are not just for some particular stage in the life of the believer. Rather, they are the center of the life of the Christian, to which the believer is always called to return.[153]

What then is the role of baptism within this cosmological drama? Fundamentally, baptism is redemption from the power of the Devil. But at the same time the Devil is a like wild beast, stalking the baptized. In the light of this, baptism is also liberation from death, in the sense that even though the baptized in this earthly life are still moving toward death, they are delivered from death.[154]

But how does a Lutheran understanding of sin relate to this? It is important to note that for Luther sin, by its nature, is unbelief. This means that sin is lack of trust in God, and the absence of love for God. From

---

150. Luther writes: "We are to trust in God alone, to look to him alone, and to expect him to give us only good things; for it is he who gives us body, life, food, drink, nourishment, health, protection, peace, and all necessary temporal and eternal blessings. In addition, God protects us from misfortune and rescues and delivers us when any evil befalls us. It is God alone from whom we receive everything good and by whom we are delivered from all evil" (BC, 389).

151. BC, 404.

152. Asheim, *Glaube und Erziehung bei Luther*, 94-95.

153. BC, 382-83.

154. Schlink, *Theology of the Lutheran Confessions*, 148-49.

this perspective sin is the desire to set oneself in place of God, not allowing God to be one's God. Luther therefore calls sin self-love (*amor sui*), and speaks about the *homo incurvatus se*—the person turned in upon the self.[155] Ultimately, sin is rebellion against human beings' creaturely dependence on their Creator, doubting the promise of God to be their Lord.[156] In this scheme, baptism becomes the presupposition for Christian life, as baptism also compensates original sin.[157]

This complex and realistic anthropology, which is evident in Luther's understanding of sin, also comes to the surface in the catechisms. When Luther here elaborates on prayer, he writes: "The human heart is by nature so desperately wicked that it always flees from God, thinking that he neither wants nor cares for our prayer because we are sinners and have merited nothing but wrath."[158] In his elaboration of the Fifth Petition of the Lord's Prayer, Luther's view on humans' role in the cosmological drama is clearly explicated: "For the flesh in which we daily live is of such a nature that it does not trust and believe God and is constantly aroused by evil desires and devices, so that we sin daily in word and deed, in acts of commission and omission."[159] This is in concordance with one of Luther's concluding comments: "God wants us to pray to him for everything that attacks even our bodily welfare so that we seek and expect help from no one but him."[160]

In Luther's vocabulary, therefore, "practice does not make perfect," at least not on this side of the Eschaton. Luther sticks to this realistic or complex, one may even say ambiguous, anthropology, as he is convinced that human beings sin daily with eyes, ears, hands, body, and soul, money and property, and with all that they have. Therefore human beings also have problems believing with their whole heart, or practicing with all

---

155. Therefore ingratitude is the most disgraceful blasphemy and greatest dishonor toward God for Luther; cf. Lohse, *Martin Luther's Theology*, 250–51. Jetter, in his study on baptism in the early Luther, points out that for the young Luther his interest is the Christian life—and in particular how to find help or medicine against sin; Jetter, *Die Taufe beim jungen Luther*, 173.

156. Kolb, *Martin Luther*, 106–9.

157. Jetter, *Die Taufe beim jungen Luther*, 169.

158. BC, 441–42.

159. BC, 452.

160. BC, 456.

their mind, body, and spirit. Luther maintains that if we believed the first article of faith "with our whole heart, we would also act accordingly."[161]

This understanding of sin forms the point of departure for Luther's elaboration on the Second Article of faith. The medicine against the captivation of sin, is for us to be captivated by Christ, to believe that Jesus Christ has become our *Lord*.[162] For Luther this implies that Jesus Christ has redeemed and released us from sin, from the Devil, from death, and from all misfortune. Therefore, Luther sees Jesus Christ as the one who "has brought us back from the devil to God, from death to life, from sin to righteousness, and keeps us there."[163] But this seems to indicate that Luther pictures an enduring presence of Christ in the life of the believer, because Christ is the one who "keeps us there," in the new relationship with God through Christ, freed from the Devil.

Luther's radical cosmology and hamartiology is of great importance for the development of a Lutheran understanding of human agency in Christian practices. For Luther it is unthinkable that *human performance* may in any way improve the position of the human being *coram Deo*. It is impossible, in the light of Lutheran theology, to suggest that any human effort or contribution by Christian practices may in any way improve the practitioner's position before God. But at the same time, the life of the Christian, through the grace of Christ and the gifts of the Holy Spirit, is on a paradoxical journey of change: The paradox here, known in the famous "simul" doctrine (man as *simul iustus et peccator*)—is that Luther presumed that the mystery of the continuation of sin in the baptized could not be solved.[164] The continuous construction and shaping of the new self, the *practitioner*, takes place as a continuous battle, where Christian practices may serve as God's weapons in a spiritual warfare with the Devil: Participating in the first-tablet Christian practices is living by faith, trusting in the triune God only. But this does not make the *practitioner* free from sin. It does not allow for the practitioner to establish self-righteousness. Altogether, there is notable complexity in Luther's doctrine of sin. What is new with Luther's baptismal theology in relation to the great cosmological battle between God and the Devil, is that baptism, in

---

161. BC, 433.
162. Cf. the German "Herr(n)," BELK, 651.
163. BC, 434.
164. Kolb, *Martin Luther*, 108.

its saving power, guides the whole life of the Christian by directing the baptized to the continuous forgiveness of God.

Made a Receiver

> A Christian is a perfectly free lord of all, subject to none.
> A Christian is a perfectly dutiful servant of all, subject to all.[165]

This famous quote from *The Freedom of a Christian* captures the core of Christian existence, according to Luther, where anthropology and soteriology are intimately connected. Soteriologically, Lutheran theology has always radically claimed that, in the act of baptism, the one who is baptized *receives* God's gift of grace. Human beings are therefore at the receiving end when it comes to first-tablet practices, like baptism. Luther underlines that the Christian life comes about through a new birth, which gives the individual something that he or she did not have in advance. Ergo: Christians do not become children of God through merits or through upbringing, although life in Christ may mature and develop, anthropologically speaking, through life. The directing and shaping starting point of Christian life remains: It is not upbringing, but the new birth to live in faith, in Christ, through the gift of baptism. Therefore the Christian is not a fruit of upbringing, but a new creation, who owes his or her existence radically to God.[166]

So what constitutes this new self rising from baptismal waters? What does it look like? And, in which way should this understanding influence the understanding of human agency in Christian practices? Miroslav Volf explores the practices of giving and forgiving as a pattern for the Christian life. Drawing on Luther's treatise *On the Freedom of a Christian* and Romans 15:7, he points out that as a Christian you depend on a giver to whom you cannot offer anything in return. Therefore faith,

---

165. LW 31:344

166. For Luther, from a certain perspective, the *imago Dei* was lost in Paradise, and won back by Christ. The *imago Dei* is not something in human beings, but something by (*am*) them, something, which is restored relationally—through the saving action of Christ. For Luther, Erasmus's pedagogical-teleological approach to upbringing is rooted in an idealistic anthropology, where the defining difference between the two is their concept of sin. For Erasmus sin is something external, in the sense that sin does not relatively affect all of humanity, whereas for Luther sin is radically personal sin, which affects all of humanity. cf. Asheim, *Glaube und Erziehung bei Luther,* 207 and 116–17.

understood as receiving what God has to give, is the most appropriate language before God.[167] We are receivers. All we need to live is given to us by God, and God sets us free to live a life formed by the very same pattern which God in faith gives to us—that of giving and forgiving.

Similarly, Reinhard Hütter elaborates on the role of baptism in the life of the believer. After having referred to Orthodox theologian John D. Zizioulas' idea of baptism making us into (enhypostatical) beings,[168] Hütter goes on to develop a more Lutheran approach to baptismal identity. According to Hütter, baptism is about giving oneself over to obedience. In that obedience is freedom, because the freedom of faith is grounded through the actualization of baptism in obedience.[169]

Luther, on the other hand, finds that faith does not make baptism, but receives it.[170] In the Christian life human agency is therefore not primary, rather "in the encounter at the chosen meeting places it is God who takes the initiative," and "at these places, in these signs, through these means, he is present and active in the encounter with man."[171] This distances Luther from a progressive scheme of the Christian life. Therefore Karl Barth's baptismal theology is not in accord with Luther's baptismal theology, as Barth places baptism on the side of human response, while for Luther "faith does not attend to itself, but to Christ."[172] For Luther, Christian faith is literally faith in one's baptism, and the Christian therefore appear in Christ's story as object, not subject—"not the doer but the one on the receiving end of the good things Christ has done."[173]

For Luther Christian experience actually implies the recurrent experience of being terrified when turning to oneself and comforted when turning to Christ in his word. This is precisely how growth in faith and obedience takes place, learning from hard experience that there is nothing to hang onto in the face of sin, death and the Devil but Christ's promise. This is in line with how Luther, in the Catechisms, and in most depth

---

167. Volf, *Free of Charge*, 43: "Faith is the way we as receivers relate appropriately to God as the Giver."

168. Zizioulas, *Being as Communion*.

169. Hütter, *Suffering Divine Things*, 177–78. Cf. also ibid., 123, where Hütter agrees with Pannenberg that "participation in the relation of the Son to the Father by the Spirit changes the structure of self-identiy itself."

170. Trigg, *Baptism in the Theology of Martin Luther*, 82–83.

171. Ibid., 32.

172. Ibid., 225.

173. Cary, "Why Luther is not quite Protestant," 453.

in the Large Catechism, outlines and discusses how the baptized always remains a receiver, someone who passively suffers the work of God. But at the same time the "practice" of receiving baptism as God's gift of salvation—faith—is a matter of the heart. For Luther baptism becomes beneficial if it is accepted as God's command and ordinance. Therefore "neither the hand nor the body can do this, but rather the heart must believe it."[174] Luther even writes "without faith baptism is of no use."[175]

Altogether, when developing an understanding of human agency in Christian practices it is important to depart from understanding of the "practitioner" as fundamentally a receiver. Luther describes the "practice" of receiving as clinging to, grasping and holding firmly. This comes to the surface when Luther deals with infant baptism. In an expression that, at first glance, may seem contradictory to his assertion that "without faith baptism is of no use" Luther claims that "we do not put the main emphasis on whether the person baptized believes or not, for in the latter case baptism does not become invalid." The point is that faith does not make baptism, rather faith receives baptism.[176]

Therefore the presence of Christ, both in the "practice" and in the "practitioner" is rooted in how "the practitioner" always remains a receiver *coram Deo*, someone who suffers the work of the triune God, where the baptized in baptism becomes one with (the present) Christ. This is a crucial point in the continuous construction of the Christian self. At the same time Christ is still present in the "practice" due to "the Word and commandment of God," and therefore "baptism does not become invalid if it is not properly received or used, . . . for it is not bound to our faith but to the Word." The point for Luther is to underline the independence of God's saving work in Christ for human beings—there is nothing human beings can do to "undo" this work of God.[177]

At the same time the receiver of the sacrament—in this case the Lord's Supper—has an assigned role to play within the practice of the sacrament. Luther underlines that "all those who let these words be addressed to them and believe that they are true have what the words

---

174. BC, 451.

175. Ibid.

176. BC, 460-63. "Invalid" is "*unrecht*" in the German original; cf. BELK, 701.

177. But it is also important to pay attention to Luther's rhetorical front in this case, which is the radical wing of the Reformation, the sectarians. Luther even goes as far as to say that "baptism does have existence and value, precisely because it is wrongly received." BC, 463-64.

declare. But those who do not believe have nothing, for they let this gracious blessing be offered to them in vain and refuse to enjoy it." Luther even stresses that people who abstain and absent themselves from the sacrament for a long period of time are not to be considered Christians. This is because Christ did not institute the sacrament in order for us to treat it as a spectacle, but he commanded "Christians to eat and drink it and thereby remember him."[178]

This accords with how Luther underlines in *Confession concerning Christ's Supper,* as in the Large Catechism, the relationship between faith and the Sacrament. Luther writes "that our administration of the Supper consists of two parts, viz. the Word and the eating, and that the Word requires faith and spiritual eating along with the physical."[179] Ultimately faith for Luther is about the receiving heart.[180] For Luther it is even this receiving *faith, which asserts* the manifold existence of Christ.

Altogether, Luther firmly underlines that the sacrament belongs to the receiver, as does the Word. First-tablet Christian practices are recognized by how they shape the "practitioner" into a receiver by the very nature of these practices.[181] This is the fundamental structure of the *notae ecclesiae.* They are marks, which *mark* those to whom they are given into receivers. Luther sees God's merciful love as something that belongs to the receiver: "For all of it is given, not to him that has the office, but to him who is to receive it through this office."[182] Therefore the new self born in baptism is a *beggar* before God.[183] It is Christ who baptizes, preaches, absolves and offers the Sacrament to the receiver, the beggar. The baptized human being is *being shaped* by Christ. For Luther, man in this life is "pura material Dei ad future formae suae vitam."[184]

---

178. BC, 470–71.

179. LW 37:193.

180. BC, 272. Cf. also Hoffman, *Theology of the Heart,* 23, 241. "When Luther spoke about God as residing in the heart of the believer, he was not only speaking objectively. He spoke from experience. The rational terms for unity between God and man took on meaning for Luther through mystical knowledge," and "the soul's mystical rest in God—as Luther saw it—is the subjective side of the objective symbols."

181. LW 41:151.

182. LW 41:156.

183. Lathrop and Wengert, *Christian Assembly,* 154.

184. Asheim, *Glaube und Erziehung,* 223.

The New Finnish Interpretation of Luther

> Sic ut Christus obiectum fidei, imo non obiectum, sed ut ita dicam, in ipsa fide Christus adest.[185]

The Finnish Luther research, with its focus on salvation as divinization, has challenged a mere forensic interpretation of the doctrine of justification in Luther's theology. But how has human agency been understood in the Finnish Luther research, and particularly in relation to baptismal theology? The "new" interpretation of Luther has grown out of an Orthodox-Lutheran dialogue, where one of the focuses has been to let Lutheran soteriology enter into dialogue with the Eastern Orthodox notion of *theo(poie)sis*—salvation as deification. This Finnish research on Luther offers interesting perspectives on the presence of Christ. The Godfather of this new interpretation, Tuomo Mannermaa, underlines that Luther understands the presence of Christ in a very concrete way, as Christ and the Christian becomes one person. This is referred to as the 'happy exchange', where the human being becomes a partaker of God's attributes.

Mannermaa underlines that for Christian holiness this still means that Christians have to turn again and again to the objective reality that is outside them and makes them holy. What is particularly helpful with the Finnish Luther research in looking at human agency in Christian practices is how it opens up for rediscovering Christian existence as a continuum. Mannermaa claims that the idea of the presence of Christ as determinative for the continuity of the Christian existence, for Luther, rests on the "incessant sighs of the Spirit" (Rom 8:26). Therefore, Mannermaa maintains, that "this hidden spiritual life is truly 'happening' and effective in believers, even though they cannot always perceive it in themselves."[186]

Christian holiness in the light of this new interpretation of Luther therefore contains a certain element of transformation, but that transformation is defined through the concept *conformitas Christi*. Faith is a *union with Christ*, a "place" where the believer is conformed in and to

---

185. LW 26:129.

186. Mannermaa claims, based on an analysis of Luther's theology—chiefly the Lectures on Galatians (1531 and 1535)—that "when a human being believes in Christ, Christ is present, in the very fullness of his divine and human nature, in that faith itself." Mannermaa, *Christ Present in Faith*, 86–88.

Christ. At this "place" Christ, as the true subject of the "practice" faith, "draws us into himself, and transforms us":

> Luther's understanding of transformation contains two aspects. On the one hand our transformation in Christ involves a continuous change into the form of Christ (*conformitas Christi*). Its purpose is complete conformity with Christ, which occurs in the resurrection. On the other hand the transformation involves an ever deeper enclosure in Christ and his righteousness. Faith makes us like those chicks whom Christ the mother hen protects under his wing so that we can be healed and trained to full conformity with our Protector. When joined with Christ, a Christian trusts not himself, but in the complete righteousness of Christ.[187]

The Finnish Luther interpretation has not given much explicit attention to baptism. But it is underlined that the meaning of baptism is found in how the death of sin and the resurrection of the new person become effective in the baptized person as God unites himself with the sinner both through the sacramental act of baptism and through faith. Therefore the Christian should direct his confidence away from himself toward Christ. The role of the *practitioner* in Christian life is therefore fundamentally that of the receiver, of someone who is *being shaped*. For the new Finnish interpretation of Luther both imputed righteousness as well as effective, transforming righteousness, are based on the fact that through justification Christ is dwelling in the Christian, and the Christian is given to participate in Christ.

What is important here is the way Luther fundamentally finds that God gives his Spirit to us through the sacramental life of the church, through the *communio sanctorum*, where the word is preached and the sacraments are shared. In all of this the Holy Spirit produces faith in Christ and enables the receiving of Christ with all of his gifts. The gifts distributed by the triune God are given to be both received—and shared—in the sense that "what God gives man receives, that it may be given to be the neighbor."[188] Therefore the life of the baptized Christian is a construction site, where God is at work, and where God calls the Christian to follow Christ's example of unselfish love, and to live by the Golden Rule in every relation of life.

---

187. Peura, "Christ as Favor and Gift," 61–62.
188. Peura, "What God Gives Man Receives," 90–95.

Altogether, the new Finnish interpretation of Luther shows that guarding the doctrine of justification as radically divine agency does not necessarily mean that the Christian life cannot be described in more dynamic terms. The everyday baptismal life may be described as a union with Christ, as a dynamic *conformitas Christi*. From this perspective one may speak about transformation in Lutheran theology. The risk of solemnly stressing this approach to the Christian life, however, without at the same time underlining, as Mannermaa does, that Christians have to turn again and again to the objective reality that is outside them and makes them holy, is that human agency in Christian practices may be obscured. Therefore it has to be underlined, as I have already pointed out based on the work on practices by Reinhard Hütter, that theologically speaking, the Holy Spirit is the real subject of first-tablet Christian practices.

The Role of Human Agency in Christian Practices

How then should human agency in Christian practices be understood? Both Reinhard Hütter and David Yeago have been accused of misreading Luther on human agency. In developing a Lutheran understanding of *human agency*—of the "practicing human subject" in (Christian) practices—it is also important to pay attention to Luther's creation theology. So what is the role of creation theology in the construction of the Christian self? Luther gives a poignant and clear description of the fundamentals of this theology in the Large Catechism. Human beings are fundamentally God's creation. This means God that is the giver of life, and the one who constantly sustains body, soul, and life, members, great and small, all senses, reason and understanding. At the same time the triune God is the provider of food and drink, clothing, nourishment, spouse and children, servants, house and farm, etc. Furthermore this view on creation, and ultimately on the presence of the triune God, extends to all creation. God "makes all creation help provide the benefits and necessities of life—sun, moon, and stars in the heavens; day and night, air, fire, water, the earth and all that it yields and brings forth: birds, fish, animals, grain, and all sorts of produce."[189]

---

189. Luther joins his creation theology with his cosmology, where evil forces also play a role: "We confess also that God the Father has given us not only all that we have and what we see before our eyes, but also that he daily guards and defends us against every evil and misfortune, warding off all sorts of danger and disaster" (BC, 432–33).

Human agency in Christian practices, even in second-tablet Christian practices, is therefore fundamentally made possible by the triune God's sustaining agency in and through creation. In a theology of Christian practices one therefore has to distinguish clearly between the saving agency of the triune God through the church's core practices, and the enduring presence of the triune God, which makes human agency in other practices possible. This distinction is parallel to the distinction between the diffintive and repletive mode of presence. This important distinction is made clearer by engaging Lutheran anthropology, and the Lutheran doctrine of sin, in particular. Furthermore, one has to take into account that human agency in Christian practices is an ambivalent agency, due to the complex anthropology, and the doctrine of sin, as human agency may be corrupted.

From this perspective it seems the critique of Hütter and Yeago misses the point, but it is interesting and partly clarifying in the way it points to crucial elements in Lutheran anthropology and soteriology which are challenged by the Christian practices paradigm—the *simul* doctrine, teleology, human agency and the distinction between justification and sanctification.[190] Yeago and Hütter, labelled the Thomistic Turners by Radical Lutheranism, are accused of re-introducing a third use of the law, whereas Radical Lutheranism would focus on the fruits of the spirit as the approach to the good works coming from the life of the Christian. What *is* interesting for this study is the attempt to make baptismal theology the center of the critique of the Thomistic Turn, and more indirectly the Christian practices paradigm. Radical Lutheranism stresses the external and forensic element as constitutive for the Christian life and is therefore critical of any attempt to speak too ambitiously about union with Christ. Rather, it would emphasize that Christ, who is the form of faith, is also the freedom that works in the baptized to do good for a neighbor in need.

Here we are at a crucial point: Radical Lutheranism's insistence that only when a self is "displaced in faith and Christ is centered in one's life through the daily re-affirmation of baptism," God is glorified and the law fulfilled," is an important reminder in developing further the understanding of human agency in Christian practices. It is of fundamental importance that the Christian de-centered self is a self constituted by another, Christ. It is also a self constituted *for* others, the neighbor and the world.

190. Mattes, "The Thomistic Turn in Evangelical Catholic Ethics," 84.

Thus the Christian's (life) story takes on a "narrative identity" as it becomes one with Christ's story. Therefore "the only way to affirm the law is to allow the gospel to limit it to the affairs of this life. If we wish to overcome Gnosticism, then we must allow the autonomous 'sacred self' to die daily in remembrance of baptismal waters so that a new self formed in and by Christ can rise in joyful love of God and eager service to the neighbor."[191]

The baptized, the re-born Christian, is a new being. To what extent and in what ways this new being takes on concrete social forms—or "practices"—is one of the most controversial questions of this study. Although the Finnish Luther research and Radical Lutheranism disagree on how to understand the relationship between justification and human agency, they are both reluctant to outline in very concrete terms—or "practices"—the life of a Christian. This is where Hütter, and Yeago in particular, differ and conflict with both Radical Lutheranism and the new Finnish interpretation of Luther, although for different reasons.

What the new Finnish Luther research and Radical Lutheranism also have in common is that they hesitate to outline how the contemporary context may influence the shape of the Christian life socially in the light of Lutheran theology. Apparently, then, different concepts of how Christ is present in the *practitioner* in Christian practices, different soteriological conceptions, may still lead to a rather uniform "ecclesiology"— a rather parallel outlining of Christian life and community. This brings to the fore the ecclesiological implications of this theme, which I will discuss later in this chapter.

Altogether, a Lutheran understanding of human agency in Christian practices may be systematized in the following way: *First of all*, human beings are born receivers; in every aspect of life depending on the god who created them. Luther's explanation of the First Commandment in the *Large Catechism* is a clear example of this understanding. The role of human beings is therefore to receive God's gifts with joy and gratitude, and share these gifts with their neighbor, throughout life.

Secondly, this relationship is corrupted through sin and human beings therefore struggle to be at the producing and not the receiving end of the relationship—both aiming at self-righteousness and despising a mutual solidarity of gifts with their neighbor and all creation. In this sense human agency is ambivalent.

---

191. Ibid., 80, 89.

Thirdly, in baptism human beings are re-made, or re-born, receivers. In baptism the triune God is the one who acts, the one who saves. Therefore, faith has a causative, rather than a responsive character. With a primacy of the efficiaous Word, Luther wants to emphasize that God gives himself to those receiving his gifts in baptism, in preaching, and in the Lord's Supper whether or not the gift is greeted with faith.

Fourthly, without giving in to subjectivism, there is still a role for the *practitioner*—that is to receive. But when that happens, it is Christ who acts in the practitioner through the Holy Spirit.

Fifthly, this relationship—where the practitioner is always at the receiving end—remains throughout life. This is formative for a Lutheran understanding of human agency in Christian practices. Therefore the core practices, or the first-tablet Christian practices, are genuinely practices only if they are understood in a strictly pneumatological fashion. This shifts their logic considerably. Now the Holy Spirit is to be understood as the real subject of these practices and their teleological focus is soteriological and eschatological. Therefore the only "excellence" in question involves a person's growth in faith, or sanctification.

Sixthly, the first-tablet Christian practices are what the new self born in baptism "does." In these practices the human being is always present, and even always *actively present*, through listening, receiving, responding, praising, and rendering obedience. But still this human activity does *not* constitute these practices. Rather, the human being is always the *recipient*, always remaining in the mode of pathos. Therefore the human being receives a new form, modeled through the work of the Holy Spirit.

Justification Versus Sanctification?

The construction of the Christian self may also be interpreted in the light of the tension between justification and sanctification. The relationship between justification and sanctification is an often-debated theme in Lutheran theology. How may the here developed understanding of human agency in Christian practices help to discern between justification and sanctification? German Lutheran theologian Oswald Bayer tries to develop a distinct Lutheran approach to how the nature of Christian life is to be interpreted and how this pertains to the relationship between justification and sanctification. Bayer works out his scheme in opposition to two traditions which have influenced contemporary modern theology heavily; Pietism and the Enlightenment. Both these traditions are victims of subjectivism, according to Bayer, as they see sanctification as a matter of personal and individual development and orientation.[192]

For Bayer this is contrary to Luther's own approach. Bayer agrees that Luther stressed personal responsibility, but claims that Luther understood sanctification in an objective manner. It is first and foremost the work of God, the Holy Spirit, according to Bayer. Bayer makes references to Luther's explanation of the third article of the Creed in the Large Catechism and *On the Councils and the Church* to prove this. Bayer finds that Luther, in speaking about "sanctification," simply speaks about justification. Bayer argues this based on the nature of God's righteousness towards sinners, and a cosmological interpretation of the world as a great court room.

Bayer finds that justification is an all-encompassing concept for Lutheran theology, and he claims that in the context of the modern search for identity human beings are forced to justify themselves, and therefore there is a need deep within each human being to prove our right to exist.[193] According to Bayer, what constitutes the whole life of human beings is disclosed with particular clarity before the court of law.

For Bayer Luther's concept of justification is the (only) proper response to this problem, as this champions a passive righteousness of faith, "in the sense 'that we let God alone work in us and that in all our powers we do nothing of our own.'"[194] Bayer concludes by pointing out that faith is neither a theory nor a praxis of self-fulfillment. Rather, it is a passive righteousness. This is the work of God in us that is experienced with suffering, dying both to justifying thinking and justifying action. But the meaning here is not that faith is both unthinking and inactive. Rather, by faith, both thinking and action are renewed.[195]

The new life in faith, granted freely by the passive righteousness of Christ, is not an escape from this world, however. Rather, we are still in the world, and we enter into a new wordliness. Because of this the "new creation" is a return to—or even conversion to—the world, not a retreat

---

192. Bayer, *Living by Faith*, 58–59. In his original preface to the German edition of his book, Bayer sees this as a problem, which emerged in the later Melanchthon, and that Pietism and its sibling, or cousin, Methodism both laid such emphasis upon sanctification that "the Reformation understanding of justification was more or less obscured." Bayer, *Living by Faith*, xii.

193. Ibid., 1, 9, 21, 40.

194. Ibid., 19. Bayer quotes "von den guten Werken"; LW 44:72

195. Bayer, *Living by Faith*, 25.

from it.[196] By this righteousness "my life story, together with all others, is justified by God, by grace alone, *gratis*, for nothing."[197]

By discussing the inter-relationship of justification and sanctification, Bayer indirectly gives a distinct contribution to the development of a Lutheran understanding of the presence of Christ in Christian practices. Although Bayer never addresses the topic of practices explicitly himself, he indirectly deals with it, particularly in his discussion of the interrelationship between justification and sanctification. Fundamental to Bayer's theological view is his emphasis on the passive righteousness of faith. This takes place only by virtue of the Word (*solo verbo*), and Bayer underlines that it is therefore the "nature" of God to create out of nothing. God is the Creator by the Word alone. It also follows from this that God therefore justifies the ungodly by his Word, creating a new self for the old Adamic self. This Word which, creates is an external Word (*verbum externum*), and it is simultaneously a bodily Word. Therefore Article V of the CA is the decisive article, according to Bayer, because the institution of the Word is the most fundamental institution.[198] Bayer also points out that this preached, bodily Word is Jesus Christ himself. The preached Word which comes to us by word of mouth "is Jesus Christ himself now present with us."[199]

According to Bayer, a theology that takes the passive righteousness of faith as its focal point may prevent from the Pietist and Roman Catholic fallacy to monitor growth of faith and love, in the life of the Christian. This is important for Bayer, because "the moment we turn aside and look back at ourselves and our own doings instead of God and God's promise, at that moment we are again left alone with ourselves and with our judgment about ourselves."[200] But Bayer also tries to develop a theological language for the relationship between sanctification and progress. He writes that:

> Progress is, to be sure, made in the ethical sphere, in the area of works, in our actions, in our political involvement. But it is not absolute progress. It is ethical progress without since been prepared. The concept of progress is no longer a salvation concept. It loses the religious fascination that it has as a perverted salvation concept. It also loses its fanaticism in the area of politics. As

---

196. Ibid., 28.
197. Ibid., 35.
198. Ibid., 42–45.
199. Ibid., 49.
200. Ibid., 44.

ethical progress, progress divorced from the question of salvation is really secular progress.[201]

Like Oswald Bayer, Church historian David C. Steinmetz also pictures Luther's idea of the Christian life as a life shaped by radical freedom and spontaneity. Steinmetz claims that Luther was reluctant to specify the ideal shape of the Christian life in too much detail. Steinmetz refers to how Luther sometimes could oppose the *imitatio Christi* piety of the later Middle Ages. Luther sarcastically noted that successful imitation would actually require Christians to be born of a virgin, have brown eyes, and walk on water. Steinmetz finds that imitation piety of such a kind is the antithesis to what Luther finds to be a proper theology of vocation: He was always emphasizing that Christians are called to serve God in their own space and time, not in the space and time of the apostles.[202]

Steinmetz elaborates further on the tentative nature of Christian life by underlining that Luther was reluctant to specify the form of Christian life too narrowly, because of his conviction that the essential form of the Christian life is freedom. As true Christians trust Christ for their salvation, rather than their fidelity and good works, good works may come as the spontaneous overflow of the lively confidence in God.

Similarly, Gerhard O. Forde and Radical Lutheranism find that sanctification is *the art of getting used to justification*. But the problem is that Forde does not discuss in any depth how this art is performed or trained. The *Sitz im Leben* of this art—or practice, if you like—is hardly elaborated. It seems to be a matter of spontaneity.[203] Forde does admit that there is a certain growth in sanctification, but this is a growth in grace, being captivated more and more by the grace alone. Forde also relates this to Luther's idea of progress as returning to the beginning, as in returning to one's baptism.[204]

Altogether, the weakness in these approaches to sanctification that Bayer, Steinmetz and Forde propose is the lack of addressing in any width the concrete shape of the Christian life. A too narrow and episodic

---

201. Ibid., 65–66.

202. Steinmetz also refers to how Luther "drew far more comfort from the failings of the biblical characters than from their virtues." Steinmetz, *Luther in Context*, 139–40.

203. Forde, *A More Radical Gospel*, 226–27. Forde asks what sanctification looks like, and he says that "when I think about such sanctification, I think about several things: spontaneity, taking care, vocation, and attaining a certain elusive kind of truthfullness and lucidity about oneself." Ibid., 242.

204. Ibid., 240–41.

definition of sanctification makes it hard to address the experience of change or even transformation in the life of the Christian. Luther himself—as I have tried to prove previously in this subchapter—offers a bolder and fuller approach to experience, sanctification and the Christian life. Although Bayer is fundamentally right in pointing out that the Christian life is shaped by a radical focus on God's action in the present moment, Bayer hesitates to develop fully the Christian life as part of a larger *continuum* of God's saving and restoring work in the world.

Discussing and outlining more concretely the shape of the Christian life has also become more urgent in a context where the traditional role of the church and Christianity is rapidly changing. I agree with Bayer, Steinmetz and Forde that the nature of the Christian life and the role of Christian practices should be considered, in a certain way, as *tentative*. The Christian life is characterized by great freedom and spontaneity. But that does not mean that the nature of the Christian life is a-contextual or without shape. In other words, the fact that the Christian life, through the practices of the new self, may take on social forms does not necessarily hinder freedom and spontaneity.

The Christian life is always both progress (*coram hominibus*—biographically and (potentially) ethically) and regress (*coram Deo*—by the constant returning to baptism due to the remaining influence of the power of sin and evil). In the light of this distinction, human agency in Christian practices may be understood as fundamentally, and in a double way, God's agency: First and foremost God's saving agency through the first-tablet Christian practices (i.e. the diffinitive presence of Christ), and secondly, God's sustaining agency, making human action possible (i.e., the repletive presence of Christ).

AN ECCLESIOLOGY OF PRESENCE AND PROMISE

Engaging Lutheran Ecclesiology in a Post-Christendom Context

The Christian practices paradigm is in many ways an ecclesiological insider critique of the self-understanding of the church of Western Christendom, and its failure to rethink its own identity in a time when the *corpus Christianum* is no longer a viable notion to interpret the role of the church and Christianity within the society in the Northern and Western hemisphere. Evaluating the ecclesiological implications of the presence of Christ in Christian practices means first of all asking where the church is to be found.

Ecclesiological reflections always involve reflecting on the context in which these reflections take place, both with regard to the context of the church and society, and the historical context.[205] Towards the end of *Suffering Divine Things*, Reinhard Hütter very briefly reflects on what a contextual catechetical theology for a secularized Europe should look like. He argues that a catechetical theology at the end of the twentieth century obviously must look different from one in the sixteenth century at the same place. It must also differ from one in Muslim Syria in the eighth or ninth century or in Japan in the nineteenth century.

The aim of the learning of faith (in a secularized Europe) is to nurture and foster a "mobile faith."[206] This is a faith for the life journey as a whole. Hütter labels the ongoing learning of faith *peregrinational* learning. This learning takes place as "a continual actualization of baptismal recollection . . . amid the most varied contexts of life and with interpreting these life situations within the context of the praxis of faith itself."[207]

When Luther defends the validity of baptism, we sense Luther's sixteenth-century context strongly. Luther writes on the validity of baptism that "even though a Jew should come today deceitfully and with an evil purpose, and we baptized him in good faith, we ought to say that his baptism was nonetheless valid."[208] First of all, this reveals Luther's rhetorical approach to Jews and Jewish faith, which is highly problematic from the perspective of a twenty-first century reader.[209] Secondly, it also reveals how Luther inevitably operates within a Christendom paradigm, where the church is defined not in opposition to the state and civil society, as an alternative ("practice") community, as one may find in the pre-Constantinian period. The church and Christians are a part of the whole *Corpus Christianum* of the Western world. But Luther's state is not the liberal and plural a-religious post-Enlightenment national state

---

205. Ferel points out that Paul Althaus reflects on the different baptismal contexts of St. Paul and Luther, and claims that for St. Paul baptism is a baptism of repentance, whereas for Luther the focus is on baptism as an event that directs the whole life of the person as sinner; cf. Ferel, *Gepredigte Taufe*, 207.

206. Cf. here, for instance, Norheim, *Kan tru praktiserast*, 20.

207. Hütter, *Suffering Divine Things*, 190–91.

208. BC, 463.

209. For a broader reflection on this theme, cf. Lohse, *Martin Luther's Theology*, 336–45.

of contemporary Europe, but a state where the elector also serves as a political leader of the church—explicated in the famous principle from the peace of Augsburg in 1555, *cuius regio, eius religio*.

Although Luther also rushes to underline the particularity of church and Christians, which departs from baptism, he still sees Europe (and in particular Saxony) as a Christian hemisphere, where Turks and Jews are viewed as the minority outsiders—a possible threat to the *Corpus Christianum*.[210] This is one of the main differences between the US-based Christian practices paradigm and Luther's own approach. The Christian practices paradigm has emerged from a distinct understanding of how Christianity and the church is in a phase of transition, as the Western church and its theology is no longer operating in the climate of a Christendom society, and therefore it has to address the contemporary context differently.

The ecclesiological-contextual differences between Luther and our time are remarkable. Whereas Luther aimed at reforming an old church getting complacent about its core identity, the church in the Western world is mostly faced with a liberal state in a religiously plural context. In this context the challenge of re-creating communal and corporal Christian identity takes on a different momentum than for Luther. This calls for a more ambitious interest in the shape of Christian life, as the institutions which Luther trusted so greatly—in particular the family, but also schools—has been altered to an extent that in most cases have made most citizens illiterate when it comes to faith formation.

Christian Practices and the Notae Ecclesiae

> If one seeks to divorce the church as *congregatio sanctorum* from its distinguishing marks, the Word and the sacraments, it shows that one has a completely different concept of faith, and thus a completely different doctrine of justification from the reformers.[211]

It is sometimes claimed that Luther's search for a merciful God does not correspond with the search for meaning in life in a late modern

---

210. Cf. here how Luther argues that "outside this Christian community, however, where there is no gospel, there is also no forgiveness, and hence there can also be no holiness." BC, 438. Cf. also BC, 465: "Those who are outside of Christ can only grow worse day by day."

211. Grane, *The Augsburg Confession*, 93.

context. But Luther's opening question in the third part of *On the Councils and the Church*—"how will or how can a poor confused person tell where such Christian holy people are to be found in this world?"[212]—seems to address the longing of many late modern humans—the question of where to find an authentic community or fellowship.[213]

The "marks of the church" could be considered a part of Luther's Reformation breakthrough.[214] Looking at the *Confessio Augustana* (CA), it is evident for Melanchthon (and Luther) that whatever the church is, it transcends time, place and person. Therefore the "church" in CA VII–VIII, is *not* some separate, pure Lutheran denomination per se or any other social or political entity. Therefore the articles on the church belong together with the articles, which precede them. The faith and holiness of the assembly is defined in CA IV–VI. But Wengert also points out that, by defining the church in other terms person or place Melanchthon was forced to invoke the marks of the church.[215]

If we look at the inherent ecclesiology of Luther's catechisms, it is interesting to note how Luther argues for the daily use of the catechisms. The argument Luther uses for this daily use of the catechism is parallel to his way of arguing where the church may be found: "In such reading, and meditation the Holy Spirit is present and bestows ever new and greater light and devotion, so that it tastes better and better and is digested, as Christ also promises in Matthew 18(:20), 'Where two or three are gathered in my name, I am there among them.'" So by the work of the Holy Spirit, through this practice, Christ himself is present. The important point here is how Luther underlines the role of the Holy Spirit.

To use and meditate on the contents of the catechisms is for Luther grounded in God's command to his people in Deuteronomy 6: Therefore the believer should meditate on the precepts of the Lord while sitting, walking, standing, lying down, and rising, and should keep them as an

---

212. LW 41:148.

213. Cf. Lathrop and Wengert, *Christian Assembly*, 3. Asheim argues—against MacIntyre, who places Luther in line with Macchiavelli and Hobbes—that Luther's anthropology is individualistic in the modern sense. Rather, Asheim claims, the idea of community is fundamental to Luther and his anthropology—Luther's most central treatises from around 1520 all bear witness to this, according to Asheim. But Luther's interest in community is mainly an ecclesiological interest—a focus on the church as a community. Cf. Asheim, *Hva betyr holdninger*, 113.

214. Lathrop and Wengert, *Christian Assembly*, 19.

215. Ibid., 62–63.

ever-present emblem and sign before the eyes and on the hands.[216] In a striking metaphor, in the explanation to the third article of the Creed in the Large Catechism, Luther defines the church as a unique community: "the mother that begets and bears every Christian through the Word of God."[217]

Luther further elaborates on the particular term used in the Creed, the *communio sanctorum*. He sees it as an equivalent to the Holy Christian church, but he also relates it to the term *ecclesia*, assembly.[218] Luther finds that the word "church" actually means nothing else than a common assembly.[219] In this sense, Luther advocates a participatory approach to church. He claims that being a member of the church is to be "a participant and co-partner in all the blessings it possesses." Ultimately this community is recognized as a place where sins are forgiven through the holy sacraments and absolution "as well as through the comforting words of the entire gospel."[220] Luther even talks about the Christian church and the forgiveness of sins as "means" through which the Holy Spirit works to increase holiness on earth. Luther also interprets the articles of the Creed in an eschatological and historic-linear perspective as he claims that creation is behind us, and even redemption has taken place. But "the Holy Spirit continues his work without ceasing until the Last Day, and for this purpose he has appointed a community on earth, through which he speaks and does all his work."[221]

Ultimately, the *notae ecclesiae* are closely related to Luther's baptismal theology. In his Sermon on the Baptism of Jesus of January 13, 1544, Luther builds much of his ecclesiology on one point in this story—that the heavens were opened. For Luther, the church as an event happens every time the preacher tells that the heavens are still opened and points to places where that opening occurs.[222] Therefore Luther finds that baptism, as one

---

216. BC, 382.

217. BC, 436.

218. Cf. here also Grane's argument on how the term *congregatio sanctorum* in CA VII in many ways defines the content of *communio sanctorum*: "The use of *congregatio* (assembly) is no doubt meant to avoid the ambiguity that *communio* could have occasioned" (Grane, *The Augsburg Confession*, 90).

219. BC, 437.

220. Luther states negatively, that the opposite is also true: "Outside this Christian community, however, where there is no gospel, there is also no forgiveness, and hence there can also be no holiness" (BC, 438).

221. BC, 439.

222. Lathrop and Wengert, *Christian Assembly*, 107. When Luther preaches about the baptism of Jesus, he stresses that in this baptism we see how we benefit through our

of the marks of the church, in fact as the first of them, is the very center of the Church's life, and that it therefore constitute the character of the church as a whole. This constitutive role of baptism is important in outlining the ecclesiological implications of the Christian practices paradigm in the light of Lutheran baptismal theology. This also makes "the present tense of baptism" an important ecclesiological theme. It means that baptism cannot be confined to the past—it acts as a call in the present.[223]

One of the outstanding features of Luther's ecclesiology in *Against Hanswurst* is that Luther finds that the marks of the true church are not hidden but open for all to see. Although this treatise is very polemical, Luther also discusses ecclesiological matters, trying to distinguish what makes a true church. Luther claims that he can prove that the Reformers have "remained faithful to the true ancient church."[224] Luther then goes on to prove that the church of the Augsburg Confession is a true church, also in the sense that it has remained faithful to tradition, because it has kept the chief marks of the church as constitutive for being church. Luther claims that by remaining true to the marks of the church, we act in accordance with the practice of the ancient church.

But although the *notae ecclesiae* are there for all to see, this does not mean that the church can be identified in a final or triumphalist way. Luther's attitude to the mixed church is fundamentally different to that of Calvin.[225] This means that the very real presence of Christ in (Christian) practices—is revealed to us under the sign of the cross, which is, according to Luther, the way God actually goes about revealing himself.[226] In Lutheran theology the hiddenness of Christ and the hiddenness of the church belong together in a certain way. This does not mean that the church as such is an abstract entity. The church is *real*, but in this world, living under the cross, the church in its fullness is hidden.[227]

What is worth noticing is Luther's lack of focus upon the boundary of the Church as he talks about the *notae*. Rather, Luther tends to focus on the Christological center of the church rather than defining

---

baptism; cf. Ferel, *Gepredigte Taufe*, 170.

223. Trigg, *Baptism in the Theology of Martin Luther*, 196, 199.

224. LW 41:194.

225. Trigg, *Baptism in the Theology of Martin Luther*, 192.

226. Lahtrop and Wengert, *Christian Assembly*, 106.

227. Cf. Trigg, *Baptism in the Theology of Martin Luther*, 180–81, but see also the insightful critique of ecclesiologies that tend to dichotomize the church we experience and the church in which we believe in Hegstad, *The Real Church*.

its outer boundaries. On the basis of this, the boundary of the church in Lutheran ecclesiology is baptism.[228] But at the same time the church has to be understood as an assembly. Luther's concept of the marks of the church addresses the catholicity of the church by focusing on the assembly constituted by those marks. The marks are the *catholic*, universal things that are found throughout God's world, constituting local assemblies of people all over the world, which are in communion with other such assemblies in other places, as they all exist by the power of the Spirit. Therefore both the locality and the particularity of the church belong to the essence of such catholicity.[229]

Altogether, Luther's development of a theology of the marks of the church is situated within the historical development of Luther's theology: Justification by faith alone led Luther to see the church not as an institution but as the gathering of believers in Christ. But then, when this notion came under attack, Luther developed the idea of *notae ecclesiae*. At the same time, the theology of the marks of the church is complemented with Luther's idea of the hidden church all through Luther's theology. This is probably because Luther realized that defining the church as an assembly of believers also meant that it is, in some sense, hidden. It is hidden in the sense that the church is hidden in persecution, in weakness and under sin.[230]

Developing the ecclesiological implications of a Lutheran understanding of the presence of Christ in Christian practices leads to the conclusion that the church is not constituted through outer boundaries but rather through its Christological and soteriological center, the first-tablet Christian practices, the marks of the church, which creates the church, as the public of the Holy Spirit in "space" and time."[231]

Penance As a Christian Practice

In the light of Lutheran ecclesiology, the church is the place where sins are forgiven in Christ. Those engaging Christian practices in contemporary theology do not write much on penance. This may be read as another example of what I characterized as a soft soteriology and idealistic

---

228. Trigg, *Baptism in the Theology of Martin Luther*, 176, 193, 197.
229. Lathrop and Wengert, *Christian Assembly*, 8.
230. Ibid., 90–93.
231. Hütter, *Suffering Divine Things*, 165.

ecclesiology. Penance, the fourth mark of the church in Luther's list in *On the Councils and the Church*, is situated between the first three, traditionally held as sacraments, and the last three, applications of the first three. This is a witness to the special position of this mark. Penance as a practice also actualizes some of the more urgent matters in the debate on Christian practices, namely the matter of human agency in (Christian) practices.

David S. Yeago claims that the way Luther understands penance, or the office of the keys, as a sort of public discipline represents a major challenge to contemporary ecclesiological reflection and the tendency to foster an individual approach to church life in the late modern Western church. Yeago stresses the public aspect of Luther's treatment of the keys, which, in his opinion, has largely disappeared. Yeago therefore maintains that the public exercise of the keys is not only an instrument of the Spirit's work of sanctification directed towards the individual sinner; it also has a public dimension.

To practice penance in contemporary church life is to rediscover the practice and exercise of the adult catechumenate. Yeago also relates the exercise of the office of the keys through the catechumenate to baptism, as the catechumenate represents baptism as reception into a community of *disciples*, which is called to a distinctive life and witness. Yeago finds that this has a positive dramatic effect, even on soteriology, as salvation means coming under the rule of Jesus. It is not mere contentless divine acceptance. Rather it is sharing in the life and mission of the people of Jesus.[232]

For Luther penance and baptism are closely related.[233] This implies that the daily repentance through contrition under the law and through faith in the Gospel is simultaneously a daily return to baptism and a daily approach to the Lord's Supper. Altogether, the whole life of the Christian is a daily repentance. Fundamentally, this implies the mortification of the old Adam followed by the resurrection of the new man, which both take place in Christians as long as they live. Luther therefore criticizes the idea that penance is a second plank to swim upon, following the first plank, baptism. According to Luther in the Large Catechism, this view of baptism takes away the value of baptism, "making it of no further use for us." Luther presents his view using the metaphor of baptism as a ship. Baptism is a ship that does not break up because it is founded in God's

---

232. Yeago, "The Office of the Keys," 95–117.

233. For further elaboration of this, cf. Peters, *Kommentar zu Luthers Katechismen*, 4:79; Stolle, "Taufe und Busse"; and Steinmetz, *Luther in Context*, 137, among others.

ordinance. But it may happen that the baptized slip and fall out of the ship. But here Luther admonishes those who fall out of the ship to swim back to the ship and hold fast to it, "until they can climb up again and sail on in it as before."[234]

Thus Luther relates medieval soteriology, which focuses on conversion, and the idea of progress in the life of a Christian. Although Luther exhorts his audience to pray for the fruits of progress, Luther sees conversion in baptism as something that is unique and unrepeatable. On the other hand, conversion in penance or penitence must be repeated again and again. Therefore the Christian is *semper penitens*. The Christian is always in need of conversion, always in need to begin over again.[235]

Basically, for Luther penance as daily conversion is therefore drowning the Old Adam or "mortification of the flesh." The "walk of life" in penance is formatted by baptism. Luther finds that to live in repentance is to walk in baptism.[236] This way of life not only announces new life but also produces, begins, and exercises it.[237] From this quotation it seems that Luther even understands penance—or *practicing baptism*—in more cyclic-repetitive terms. For Luther, to return to baptism is to "resume and practice what has earlier been begun but abandoned."[238]

Altogether, Luther's approach to penance is directed by his understanding of baptism. Luther may on occasion refer to penance as a sacrament, but then he sees penance as a part of baptism. The part of penance on which Luther puts the most weight is therefore the declaration of forgiveness, the absolution. This is also closely related to the fact that for Luther the Word of God is a Word always calling us to repentance.[239] I therefore find, partially in line with Yeago, that rediscovering the importance of penance is one of the main challenges in developing the whole concept *practicing baptism* ecclesiologically. But developing penance as a Christian practice, as a way the Christian self is continuously shaped and constructed, needs to be done with great contextual sensitivity, if

---

234. BC, 466. This is another example of how baptism for Luther is something the Christian should "make use of."

235. Trigg, *Baptism in the Theology of Martin Luther*, 165–66.

236. "so gehest du in der Taufe." BELK, 706. Cf. the subjunctive form of the verb.

237. BC, 466. Cf. the verbs used in the German original: "wirkt, anhebt und treibt." BELK, 706.

238. BC, 466. The German verbs used, "wiederholet und treibt," further underline the repetitive character of baptism as a practice. BELK, 706.

239. Cf. BC, 465; and Asheim, *Glaube und Erziehung*, 161.

we wish to follow Luther. Luther offers an interesting pastoral-contextual argument for a twofold use of the keys, both public and private. Because the consciences of people are different, the keys need to be exercised differently.[240] Even in the *Visitation Articles* it is stated that teaching lay people about the practice of penance and contrition must be done pedagogically, in particular, children need to be taught gradually.[241]

Ethical Progress and Christian Practices

How does an ecclesiology emerging from an evaluation of the marks of the church relate to what may be called ethical progress? In other words, to what extent is the *notae ecclesiae* also an ethical concept? Oswald Bayer claims that the significance of baptism is forgotten if the distinction between ethical and metaphysical progress is forgotten. For Bayer, to "practice baptism" has an ethical emphasis. He even claims that ethical progress is only possible by returning to baptism. For Bayer baptism marks the intersection of the old world and the new. Baptism leads into a new perception of the world.

Bayer therefore depicts *practicing baptism* as the (only) way to make ethical progress. The new life of the baptismally founded self is fundamentally tentative and spontaneous, but it is also constructed socially. Bayer stresses the tentative aspect, as he is concerned about protecting sanctification from becoming enthusiastic and fanatical. Talking about the Christian life as a continuous return to baptism also helps Bayer to add a linear perspective on Christian life. In addition to living in God's promise, Bayer also emphasizes the importance of living in the institutions that God's Word has sanctified.[242]

Similar to Bayer, Swedish Lutheran theologian Gustaf Wingren, in his study on vocation in Luther's theology, finds that Luther's teaching on vocation opposes any claim to imitation, as every situation is unique. Therefore Wingren argues that right ethics does not correspond to a certain fixed outward behavior, but rather in the ability to meet, in calmness and faith, what may come in life. Wingren places the concept of vocation within an eschatological framework—rooted in baptismal theology. Wingren further

240. LW 41:153.

241. LW 40:295.

242. Bayer, *Living by Faith*, 66–70. Bayer puts great weight on Luther's doctrine of the three estates—the Church, the economy, and the political sphere—as "Luther talks of sanctification not merely *in* institutions but also *through* institutions" (ibid., 60).

argues, based on an evaluation of Luther's idea of the hiddenness of Gud and the not-yet character of human life, that that in everyone's vocation there is a cross, and on this cross the old nature is to be crucified. Therefore vocation is ordained by God to benefit the neighbor.[243]

Wingren maintains that vocation for Luther is about divine love coming to earth, the same love as was in Christ. Radically, Wingren finds that, for Luther, excluding the neighbor also means excluding Christ.[244] Wingren also reflects on this third part of the *Confession concerning the Lord's Supper*, where Luther speaks about the "common order of God's love." Similar to what I have already argued, Wingren emphasizes the constitutive importance of "love" for what I have labeled the second-tablet Christian practices. Wingren underlines that such love is the inner willingness to do and bear all that is required by vocation, and do it gladly and without resistance. But at the same time, Wingren hastens to underline that there is nothing in the exercise of one's vocation or love, which could save man.[245]

Therefore Wingren argues that, vocation always involves one's relation with others, and that love for others is the fulfillment of vocation. Therefore "it is the vocabulary of vocation itself, the terms 'station' and 'office,' which Luther uses when he speaks of spontaneous love toward others."[246] Wingren poignantly concludes that "it is one's neighbour, not one's sanctification, which stands at the heart of the ethics of vocation."[247]

Both Bayer and Wingren take as their (implicit) point of departure a break with Pietism. It is worth asking if this may be the reason for what appears to be a blind spot for both Bayer and Wingren, namely to see the church as a particular community and as the primary context—the starting point—of the Christian life. This is where Reinhard Hütter offers an ecclesiological alternative, maintaining that the communal, Christian life is the ground from which Christian ethics arises.[248] Based on this premise, Hütter tries to re-order the role of the "law-gospel" system in Lutheran ethics. Hütter finds that God's commandments both presup-

---

243. Wingren, *Luther on Vocation*, 1, 3, 29, 171, 181, 243. Wingren finds that *vocatio* for Luther can mean different things, but most frequently it is used—along with *Beruf*—as outer status or occupation.

244. Ibid., 30–31.

245. Ibid., 63–64.

246. Ibid., 120.

247. Ibid., 182.

248. Hütter, "The Christian Life," 286.

pose the ecclesial context of particular practices within God's economy of salvation and, while rooted in this context, they are not limited to this context. They are also "co-extensive with our scope as human agents. They are therefore primarily directed to "the concrete creaturely contexts in which we find ourselves." Hütter therefore concludes that Christian ethics in the tradition of the Reformation is the remembrance of God's commandments, and at the same time the interpretation of the innumerable challenges, complexities, and perplexities that human beings encounter in the world in the critical and wholesome light of God's commandments.[249]

Lutheran ethics are ethics of formation shaped by certain practices, where the focus is on the neighbor. Martha Ellen Stortz focuses particularly on the role of prayer. She finds that a practicing Christian is someone who is trained in the practice of prayer. Based on this fundamental practice the Christian acts in the world and on behalf of their neighbor. Stortz therefore underlines that prayer, along with the other practices of Christian discipleship, may inform moral vision, as an invitation to a life attentive to and oriented towards God in a way that may enable us to see the world with God's eyes.[250]

There is a great complexity in Luther's approach to ethics—a wavering between the internal and the external, between the renewal of the inner person and a life in service of the neighbor.[251] Stortz and Hütter's interest in developing a Lutheran understanding of what it means to be a practicing Christian in today's contemporary context challenges Wingren and Bayer's take on Lutheran ethics. The problem with both Wingren and Bayer, who both (at least implicitly) presuppose a Christendom society, is that their eagerness to criticize a pietistic approach to sanctification runs the danger of diminishing important aspects of Luther's own understanding of sanctification and the life of the "practicing Christian" as a communal life. Failing adequately to emphasize the church as the primary context of the Christian life is a potential shortcoming, particularly in a post-Christendom context, where the need to interpret and embody the Christian life as a whole is voiced. Ignoring the church as a community with a social form and with practices shaping its particularity is therefore particularly problematical for ministry in a post-Christendom context,

---

249. Hütter, "The Twofold Center of Lutheran Ethics," 52–53.
250. Stortz, "Practicing Christian," 55, 72–73.
251. Cf. Peter, *Kommentar zu Luthers Katechismen*, 1:93.

where fewer and fewer young people have any experience of such a practicing community before coming into ministry.

In a post-Christendom context the more dynamic and continuous understanding of the relationship between sanctification and ethics outlined by Hütter and Stortz challenges the more static approach of Wingren and Bayer. This short analysis of the ethical implications of Luther's baptismal ecclesiology in the light of how Christ is present in Christian practices underlines once again the need to reflect hermeneutically and contextually on what it means to develop an understanding of this theme today.

Altogether, there is a double structure in the way an ecclesiology emerging from an evaluation of the marks of the church relates to ethics and ethical progress: Practicing the first-tablet Christian practices has an indirect but clear ethical side as it leads to the practicing of the second-tablet Christian practices—the church's *diakonia* for the sake of the neighbor and the world. This in turn helps with discovering the *vocatio* of all Christians. In this dynamic continuum, the communal practice of penance is of particular importance, as it continuously turns the baptized to the triune God and his forgiveness. Resting in the mercy of Christ, the baptized is called to the second-tablet practices and the neighbor.

The diaconal paradox of an ecclesiology emerging from the marks of the church is therefore that the marks of the church form the center of the church as assembly. This in turn point to another center in the life of a Christian, that is, meeting the other, the neighbor, outside the city gate. This meeting is where the marks of the church lead—or send (*missio!*)—the practitioner: As Christ suffered outside the city gate, those marked by the liberating freedom and forgiveness of the marks of the church are sent to suffer with Christ outside the city gate (the assembly)—for the neighbor, and for the life of the world.[252] Even this meeting is a way of *practicing baptism*—a continuous return to the gifts of God, which turns everyone into a receiver, a beggar, before Christ.

Christian ethics departing from baptismal theology is therefore fundamentally a liturgical enterprise. Bernd Wannenwetsch underlines, based on an analysis on the way *anakainosis* is used in both Titus 3:5 and 2 Cor. 4:16, that baptism and the remembrance of baptism in a special way may be seen as the context for a renewal of judgment. Wannenwetsch, based on this and pointing to Romans 12:1f, argues that "ethical worship"—understood as "worship in the everyday life of the world"—cannot

---

252. Lathrop and Wengert, *Christian Assembly*, 144.

be dichotomized over against liturgical worship, since the *logike latreia* is characterized by the link with *anakainosis* in a clear reference to baptism. I agree with Wannenwetsch who concludes that a renewal of ethical discernment is rooted in baptism and the remembrance of baptism. This sets off the change, which constitutes the Christian life and which also keeps it going. This is a "transformation from the abstractions of the powers of the world to life in the form of worship—life in the Spirit, life in the 'logic' of the Spirit."[253]

Christian Practices Between Soteriology and Ecclesiology

The two fundamental questions for Luther in the third part of *On the Councils and the Church* are: What makes a person or a people holy? And: Where is the true and authentic church to be found? Immediately, looking at Luther's two questions, it seems ecclesiology and soteriology are closely knit together, particularly if sanctification equals justification, as Oswald Bayer and Radical Lutheranism seem to think. But in *On the Councils and the Church* Luther also explicitly points out that the Holy Spirit leads us in our daily vivification and sanctification of faith. Here Luther discerns justification from sanctification.[254]

Anne Marie Aagard advocates what I have described as a "thick ecclesiology." She aims to rethink what it means to be church in such a manner that the church is not utterly ghetto-ized, but at the same time does not reject the church's identity as a Christian church.[255] Aagard argues that Luther situates the first seven marks of the church in a *continuum* with the following seven "marks"—the seven commandments of the second tablet of Moses. For Aagard this way to outline Lutheran ecclesiology makes room for a thicker ecclesiology—understanding the church as a "broader" network of Christian practices in the political or public sphere. This is much in line with what Yeago advocates. The crucial point is the interpretation of the seventh mark of the church, the cross, Aagard claims. She distances herself from interpreting this as a "private" mark.

253. Wannenwetsch, *Political Worship*, 37–38.

254. LW 41:144: That there is always a holy Christian people on earth, in whom Christ lives, works, and rules, *per redemptionem*, "through grace and the remission of sin," and the Holy Spirit, *per vivificiationem et sanctificationem*, "through daily purging on sin." Cf. here how the work of the Holy Spirit is described in terms that shape the theological content of the concept *practicing baptism*.

255. Aagard, *Identifikation af kirken*, 11.

Rather, she claims that it relates to the church's "corporative lifestyle."[256] Aagaard's ecclesiology is therefore more ambitious when it comes to the church's *diakonia*. For instance, Aagaard advocates an asceticism which she labels the "practice of mercy." This practice is always directed towards the neighbor. Aagaard argues that mercy is the only faithful motif for re-creating the world.[257]

This "thick ecclesiology" does not imply that Aagard is uninterested in distinguishing between soteriology and ecclesiology. Quite the opposite, for Aagaard, Luther knows clearly how to distinguish between soteriology and ecclesiology. Aagaard even uses the first mark of the true church as a criterion for disclosing idolatry. She relates it to the church of Nazi Germany, where institutionalized idolatry replaced the right preaching of the Word and public confession. Aagaard also relates her study to *Against Hanswurst*. Aagaard once again elaborates on the distinction between ecclesiology and soteriology and underlines that although Luther maintains that every baptized person is *simul iustus et peccator*, congregations are not liberated from their obligation to reflect critically and make an effort to let the true church grow forth through the marks of the church.[258]

Aagaard therefore outlines the more counter-cultural aspect of a *notae* ecclesiology. She sees an ecclesiology based on the marks of the church as a protection against a privatized church, where the church may enter into conflict with powers and government, as the church is born by the Holy Spirit of Christ, and not the spirit of the world. Aagaard poignantly points out that the kingdom of God is not built through politics, but it can be lost through politics. In stressing this, Aagard also indirectly points to the relationship between the practice of penance and the second–tablet Christian practices: Ecclesiological malpractice of the second- tablet practices (for instance, stealing), may in turn lead to mal-practice of the practice of penance, by failing to confess stealing as something which is against the will of God.[259]

Focusing on the constitutive role of the seven first marks of the church, or the church's core practices, "high ecclesiology" seems like a fitting heading for Hütter's ecclesiology. Hütter's main focus is advocating

---

256. Ibid., 21.

257. "The practice of mercy," in Danish: "barmhjertighedens praksis"; cf. ibid., 262–63.

258. Ibid., 21, 31, 33.

259. Ibid., 263.

theology as a church practice related to the core practices of the church, and thereby to the salvific-economic *telos* of the church. Hütter points out that the church is known fundamentally through its center, through the core practices.[260] What Hütter does not elaborate on in a sufficient way is the radical ecclesiological complexity, expressed in Luther's radical cosmology, or succinctly put, that by bringing a child to baptism the church confesses before God that it is actually "possessed by the devil."[261]

Oswald Bayer, on the other hand, underlines that church is (also) an order of creation. Bayer finds that the church is a universal entity, and not a particular entity. It is a church without walls, although Bayer also admits it was instituted by God prior to household and government. This church exists in the word and in faith, by the fact that God calls Adam (and so all humankind) into life, and in this way "preaches" to man and puts his word before him. Later Bayer outlines the consequences of this view, stressing that the only particularity of the church is its divine service, the *Gottesdienst*, which discloses the world as creation. Bayer stresses this also in order to safeguard what he finds to be central to Luther's thought, creation as God's gift.[262] The problem for Bayer is that this kind of ecclesiology runs the risk of ending up with a church which is "all ears," as the church, in the strict sense, according to Bayer, takes place—only and rather episodically—where the gospel is heard.

Such an "episodic" ecclesiology may become irrelevant, particularly for young people. For most young people the meaning of faith is experienced and fostered in a community, where for many the non-episodic but continuous quality of the community may be the inherent good news of becoming and remaining a member of this community. Communal sanctification then has to be something other than avoiding thinking about sanctification in self-monitoring terms. Rather, the church has to offer a *Sitz im Leben* for discovering the contours of living a life shaped by baptism. I would therefore suggest that Bayer's way of understanding church—compared with the "high ecclesiology" of Hütter and the "thick ecclesiology" of Aagard—may be labeled "thin ecclesiology," in the sense that Bayer is eager to make sure that not everything is church.

The response from Radical Lutheranism, to Hütter's evangelical catholic attempt to merge the MacIntyre-ian practice concept into

---

260. Hütter, *Suffering Divine Things*, 193, 165.
261. Schlink, *Theology of the Lutheran Confessions*, 194.
262. Bayer, *Theology the Lutheran Way*, 86, 91.

Lutheran theology, which is partly inspired by Bayer, does not solve this problem in Bayer's ecclesiology, rather it maximizes it. The problem with the critique of Radical Lutheranism is that it appears almost a-contextual in its form, and it does not catch nor address a common feature of the practice(s) movement—its engagement with late modern culture. This reveals an inherent problem within Radical Lutheranism—its rather episodic ecclesiology and rather abstract take on the Christian life.[263]

In relation to this problem, it is noteworthy that Luther always insists on the corporal nature of the church, both historically and contextually.[264] Of great importance for this discussion is the comment Luther makes towards the very end of *On the Councils and the Church* about the corporal shape of church practice(s) and church life. It is a life that needs an order, shaped by solidarity, where the needs of the individual do not stand over the mission of the church. Luther makes a reference to a wedding or another social event, commenting that no one should offend the bride or the company by doing something special or something that interferes. Rather one should join the rest, and sit, walk, stand, dance, eat, and drink with them. In other words, "it is impossible to order a special table for each individual, and also a special kitchen, cellar, and servant."[265] Ironically, this comment serves as a warning to much of the individualistic "*pro me*" church life coming out of the Reformation—and it is also a potential warning against a too "thin" ecclesiology.[266]

But how does this critique of the potential ecclesiological deficit in the ecclesiology of Bayer, Wingren, and Radical Lutheranism in a post-Christendom context relate to Luther's insistence on the Word of God as primary? This seems to support the rather episodic "preaching first/only" ecclesiology of Bayer, and in particular Radical Lutheranism. Timothy J. Wengert's study on the marks of the church also seems largely to support Bayer's approach, but Wengert, more than Bayer and Wingren, emphasizes the church as a sent community. This speaks for a further

263. Cf., for instance, how troublesome it is for Mattes to define the countercultural element in Radical Lutheranism; Mattes, "The Thomistic Turn in Evangelical Catholic Ethics," 83.

264. Luther maintains that there has always been, even since the days of Cain and Abel, and will be, until the Second Coming of Christ, a church: "The Children's Creed teaches us (as was said) that a Christian holy people is to be and to remain on earth until the end of the world" (LW 41:148).

265. LW 41:174.

266. Cf. Wannenwetsch, "Lob der Äusserlichkeit," 389.

engagement of the corporal elements in Lutheran ecclesiology in order to develop a missional Lutheran ecclesiology.[267] My argument against Bayer and Wingren is not that they misinterpret Luther, but that they fail to engage the corporal and missional potential of Luther's ecclesiology in dialogue with a culture where the primary knowledge of Christianity—both in practice and theory—is vanishing.

Here the way Bernd Wannenwetsch engages the marks of the church may represent a way forward. He also applies Luther's ecclesiological elaborations in *On the Councils and the Church*. Wannenwetsch points out that here Luther speaks about the "lovely forms," which we need to practice and exercise, in which the Holy Spirit sanctifies and vivifies us. Wannenwetsch uses this to argue that these external forms of the *missa*—or the seven "core practices" or "marks" of the church—are exactly the means which God uses to address the inner human being *coram Deo*. The pious human being is therefore not faced with an abstract justification process, but rather this human being undergoes—with heart, mind and all faith—these external "means of grace." On this basis Wannenwetsch maintains that Christian piety in a Reformation perspective is not about making inner experiences into external things or forms, rather this piety is nothing other than exercising the lovely forms, the means of grace of the Mass, the concrete practices, which Luther calls the marks of the church. Wannenwetsch also makes the epistemological—and ontological—claim that there is godly reality behind these forms, a certain shape of God, which it would be possible to experience and which justifies making these forms into an object to shape or form.[268]

To further uncover the missional-corporal drive in Lutheran ecclesiology we need to look at how Luther relates baptismal theology and ecclesiology. The relationship between the two is not as simple as one would think—that baptism marks the boundaries of the church. Actually, the relationship between baptism and the boundary of the *communio sanctorum* is highly problematic in Luther's theology, both because of Luther's emphasis on the mixed church and the need for a continuous reformation of the church, but also because of the *simul*-structured anthropology and the cyclic element in the life of the Christian. As the

---

267. Lathrop and Wengert, *Christian* Assembly, 146: "God *marks* the assembly with Word and Sacrament, with prayer and proclamation (under the cross), and *sends* us into the world marked with those very gifts for all."

268. Wannenwetsch, "Lob der Äusserlichkeit. Evangelische *praxis pietatis* als gottesdienstliche Frömmigkeit," 401.

Christian, the church is continuous need of reformation—*ecclesia reformata semper reformanda*.[269]

Another source for further elaborating on the corporal, missional element of Lutheran ecclesiology is found in the second part of the treatise *Confession concerning Christ's Supper*. Here Luther discusses the concept of participation in the body of Christ, based on 1 Corinthians 10:16. Based on this text, Luther also argues why the celebration of communion in principle is an "open" event, in the sense that it happens before God, and it is not for human beings to distinguish who is eating/participating worthily. Luther writes that it is "evident that *koinōnia*, 'participation in the body of Christ,' is nothing else than the body of Christ as a common possession, distributed among many for them to partake."[270] But Luther goes on to claim that those taking part in the broken bread, are not only the worthy, but even Judas and the unworthy. Ultimately therefore, it is the missional drive, the sending of the triune God, which may make Lutheran ecclesiology "thick." All claims to a thick ecclesiology are always rooted in the centrifugal power of the Christological center of the church—the core practices.

Crucial to Luther's ecclesiology is therefore the idea that the church is found where sins are forgiven. Luther underlines that wherever the Christian Church exists, the forgiveness of sins is to be found. From this perspective Luther joins the Cyprian motto *extra ecclesiam nulla salus*: "Outside this Christian Church there is no salvation or forgiveness of sins."[271] Based on this, the church is defined in the strict, constitutive sense through the first-tablet Christian practices. But second-tablet Christian practices also have a role to play, in the sense that they indirectly offer a possible "negative" definition of church: As the church is the place where sins are forgiven, failure to confess and confront a mal-practice of second-tablet practices, like stealing or lying, may offer an example of what is *not* church. In that sense, the failure to serve the neighbor and world in need is a betrayal of both the missional and the centrifugal power of the first-tablet Christian practices, and subsequently, if this is not confronted and confessed, a failure to practice church as the place where sins are confessed and forgiven. Fundamentally, what is at stake for Luther in most of his disputes with ecclesiological implications is soteriology,

---

269. Trigg, *Baptism in the Theology of Martin Luther*, 57, 201.
270. LW 37:353–57.
271. LW 37:368.

and deeply imbedded in this, anthropology. All in all, there is therefore an intimate connection between soteriology and ecclesiology in Luther's theology. The present Christ, who saves humans here and now, is given to the world through the marks of the church; through the core practices.

In all this, the pursuit to re-discover the shape and theological bias of the new Christian self, as *practicing baptism*, cannot rest assured with just referring to piety as a matter of freedom and spontaneity.[272] Defining Christian life merely through spontaneity and freedom at best leaves the church with an individualistic and at worst an elitist approach to faith formation. The problem with the rather meta-idealistic attempt to frame Lutheran spirituality as a "spontaneous spirituality" of ultimate freedom is that it fails to reckon on the concreteness of Luther's own approach to things abundantly found in his letters and sermons and in the Catechisms. For Luther it was important that living as a Christian, by *practicing baptism*, was something very concrete and practical. It was not something extraordinary; rather it was about remaining faithful to Christ and your neighbor in every aspect of everyday life.

Living by faith, *practicing baptism*, the church has to let itself be re-created and shaped by the church's core practices, which "in practice" also re-constitutes a communal church and faith as a way of life. This communal way of life is a sending to the neighbor and to God's world. Hence the paradox of a Lutheran ecclesiology finds its crux in the development of a missional ecclesiology: The church has to reclaim its identity as a *community of beggars before God* where everything is given to be received and shared with the neighbor and all of creation. Living thus, it becomes more than an *episodic community*. In the context of ministry, this is also important in order to proclaim the good news in manifold ways.

Therefore *practicing baptism* is a fitting concept to understand the nature of the Christian life. It is also a helpful concept to help discern between ecclesiology and soteriology. *Practicing baptism* is about constantly receiving the forgiveness of sins, and where sins are forgiven in the name of Jesus Christ, there is the church. In *Against Hanswurst* (1541) Luther ranks baptism as the prime mark of the church and, underlines that without baptism, the sacraments and the keys are of no use.

---

272. Probably Luther could have had much more to say about the use of baptism in the everyday life of the Christian, but due to the rhetorical scheme he used when he wrote about baptism and to the fact that he became ill on several occasions, we have "lost" some of Luther's more practical elaborations of what it might mean to practice baptism; cf. Ferel, *Gepredigte Taufe*, 248.

This is because baptism is the first and most important sacrament. It is also because Luther finds that baptism is the source and entrance to all grace and forgiveness of sins. Hence baptism becomes the entrance to, or anchor for, all other practices. If practicing faith is not anchored in baptism, it becomes works and merit, a holiness based on works.[273] But based on baptism, as a redemptive act of the triune God, the church as the public of the Holy Spirit is freed to be enrolled in a new fellowship, a new order, practicing *the common order of Christian love*.

THE CHRISTIAN LIFE AS PRACTICING BAPTISM

To Live by Your Baptism

> In baptism, therefore, every Christian has enough to study and practice all his or her life.[274]

Apart from sketching a catechetical theology for a secularized Europe in the epilogue of *Suffering Divine Things* (2000), Reinhard Hütter pays little explicit attention to the shaping role of baptism for a Lutheran approach to Christian practices. But Hütter speaks about the "continual actualization of baptismal recollection," which takes place in all the different contexts in which the Christian lives and acts.[275] This actualization is for Hütter situated within the larger narrative of the Christian *peregrinatio*. Based on Galatians 3:27–29 Hütter argues that baptism constitutes the church as a unique public. This public is "governed by God's *oikonomia*, God's household rule."[276] This is similar to how Luther, in both *On the Councils and the Church* (1539) and in *Against Hanswurst* (1541), underlines the ecclesiologically constitutive role of baptism. It is at the very center of the church's life. Next to the Word, it is the primary mark of the church. It stamps its mark on the whole of the life of the church and the Christian. Baptism is therefore something the Christian, the baptized, should make use of—or "put into use"—throughout her or his life journey.[277]

---

273. LW 41:195–99.
274. BC, 461. In German: "lernen und üben." Cf. BELK, 699.
275. Hütter, *Suffering Divine Things*, 191.
276. Hütter, "The Church," 43.
277. BC, 462, cf. the German original "uns nutze machen." BELK, 699. Further Luther claims that "we must regard baptism and put it into use in such a way that we may draw strength and comfort from it when our sins or conscience oppress us, and

To look at the wider implications of the concept *practicing baptism*, we have to look at how this is explicated at greater length within the Catechisms, and particularly in the Large Catechism. Here Luther always pictures baptism *in the present tense*. So when God is appearing, working or speaking in baptism, Luther's focus is *not* confined to the time of the actual baptism, rather Luther exhorts "to attend to God's presence and word in baptism, now."[278] Luther fundamentally pictures *practicing baptism* as a way to live a life shaped by the first commandment. It is to "fear, love, and trust God above all things," as Luther writes when explaining the First Commandment in the Small Catechism, which forms the introduction to all the other commandments—"we are to fear and love God, so that we . . ."[279]

Living by the First Commandment as a life in Christ is "special" because it also implies to "trust God above things." This understanding of God, as the one in whom we put our trust, is even more broadly explicated in the Large Catechism, where Luther writes: "A 'god' is a term for that to which we are to look for all good and in which we are to find refuge in all need. Therefore, to have a god is nothing else than to trust and believe in that one with your whole heart."[280]

According to Luther, therefore, baptism opens the doors to a life where the baptized sees everything (good) in life as a gift from God, as Luther does in his explanation of the first article of the creed:

> I believe that God has created me together with all that exists. God has given me and still preserves my body and soul: eyes, ears, and all limbs and senses; reason and all mental facilities. In addition, God daily and abundantly provides shoes and clothing, food and drink, house and farm, spouse and children, fields, livestock, and all property—along with all the necessities and nourishment for this body and life. God protects me against all danger and shields and preserves me from evil.[281]

To practice one's baptism is to receive life as a gift, daily, a gift, in which God again and again brings me life through his liberating gifts.

---

say: 'But I am baptized!' And if I have been baptized, I have the promise that I shall be saved and have eternal life, both in soul and body."

278. Trigg, *Baptism in the Theology of Martin Luther*, 33.
279. BC, 351.
280. BC, 386.
281. BC, 354.

Even Luther's explanations of the second and the third articles of the creed, each in their own way, explain further the contents of the concept *practicing baptism*. This life is a life in Christ, where Jesus Christ is the Lord of the believer. It is a life pictured through "organic" verbs, such as "belong to," "live under" and "serve him." Luther's outlining of the Creed does not focus on the past, on who Jesus was, rather he focuses on what Jesus has done for us and who Jesus is in the life of the believer. Luther pictures a Christ who is present as someone I can "belong to," "live under," and "serve" here and now.

In Luther's brief outline of the significance of baptism in the Small Catechism, the contents of his concept of what it means to practice one's baptism daily is clear: The old creature with sins and evil desires in us is to be drowned and die daily through contrition and repentance, and a new person is to rise up to live before God in purity and righteousness.[282] Luther's most poignant and profiled definition of what it means to "practice baptism," however, is found in his concluding paragraphs on baptism in the Large Catechism:

> Therefore let all Christians regard their baptism as the daily garment that they are to wear all the time. Every day they should be found in faith and with its fruits, suppressing the old creature and growing up in the new. If we want to be Christians, we must practice the work that makes us Christians.[283]

In the final and fourth article on baptism in the Large Catechism Luther changes the form of the verbs from the past tense to the subjunctive tense.[284] By this change Luther may want to underline the "tentative" nature of Christian life. It is not so that the daily repentance follows as a causal law upon the event of baptism, but baptism opens the doors to a new life for the Old Adam. This new life *coram Deo*, as the Latin text says, is in line with St Paul's "walk in a new life." The new life is parallel to the outline of repentance in CA XII. *Practicing baptism* is in this sense a daily repentance. But by using the subjunctive form of the verb, Luther also effectively underlines that this is not the work of the believer himself, but the work of Christ in the believer.

282. BC, 360.

283. BC, 466. The verb "practice" is a translation of the German "treiben." Cf. BELK, 707.

284. Cf. also the German original "*soll* ersäuft werden und sterben (etc.)," and "ein neuer Mensch, der in Gerechtigkeit und Reiningkeit für Gott ewiglich *lebe*." BELK, 516. Thanks to Hans Wiersma for pointing this out to me.

Altogether, the first-tablet Christian practices have a soteriological *telos*. The practitioner actually receives Christ through them.[285] Therefore, baptism—being born again in Christ—is both constitutive and exemplary. But baptism is not confined to the past, it has a "present tense": As the Christian wanders before God it is always the *promise* of baptism that the Christian *practices*. Or rather, it is in and through the promise of baptism that the triune God through the Holy Spirit practices his work in the Christian. This is why *practicing baptism* is a fitting concept to grasp the nature of the Christian life.

Discerning the Presence of Christ in Christian Practices

We need to distinguish between God's economy of creation and God's economy of salvation in looking at both more universal practices and distinctly Christian practices. Universal practices support the sustenance and enhancement of human life. They therefore belong to God's economy of creation. But what makes them possible, and which at the same time represents their final fulfillment, is revealed through their particular Christian equivalent, as this equivalent communicates and reflects God's own practice. Hütter finds the practice of "forgiveness" to be a good example of this. Therefore the enactment of more universal practices is rooted in the church's core practices, Hütter finally claims.[286]

How then should the understanding of the presence of Christ in Christian practices be interpreted in the light of Lutheran theology? Should the list of "practices" that Luther's lists in *On the Councils and the Church* be understood as a 7+7 list, where the last seven marks are practices equivalent with the seven commandments of the second tablet of Moses, as Anne Marie Aagard claims? Most interpreters of Luther would, however, agree that Luther gives a certain primacy to the three first marks—the Word, baptism and the Lord's Supper—and partially

---

285. Hütter on many occasions relates this to the relationship between the *fides quae creditur* and the *fides qua creditur*, cf. Hütter, *Bound to Be Free*, 143: "Traditionally put, in Christ as the 'form of faith' both the content of faith (*fides quae creditur*) and the act of faith (*fides qua creditur*) are inseparably one." Cf. similar elaborations on this theme in Hütter, "Hospitality and Truth," 225; Hütter, "The Church," 36–37; and Hütter, *Suffering Divine Things*, 42–44.

286. Hütter, "Hospitality and Truth," 206–7. In *Bound to Be Free* Hütter sorts practices in two circles, where the inner circle consists of the church core practices, whereas "the outer circle is an open, extensive list, being mainly and expansion of the first and last practices of the inner circle." Cf. Hütter, *Bound to Be Free*, 36.

also the fourth mark, the office of the keys. The fifth, sixth and seventh marks are really explications of the first three or four marks.

An analysis and discussion of Luther's elaborations on the sixth and seventh marks will show why it is not fully appropriate to picture Luther's list as a 7+7 list, as a *continuum* as Aagard does, although the practices belonging to the first and second tablet of the Decalogue must not be interpreted as two separate entities either. Luther claims that the Christian life is a life where we practice "the work that made us Christians," namely baptism. The wording or rhetoric Luther uses to argue this is basically the same rhetoric he uses when he advocates the importance of prayer as a "practice" in the life of Christians. On both occasions Luther starts his argument with a premise: "if we want to be Christians."[287] Following this premise comes an outlining of a certain "practice"—here prayer—and prayer is outlined as living by one's baptism throughout life.

In his elaboration of the First Petition of the Lord's Prayer, Luther relates prayer to baptism. Baptism is the starting point of a new relationship to God, because God's name is given to us, and we enter into a life where the triune God through the sacraments "incorporates us into himself." The outcome of this is a new life "where everything that is God's must serve for our use."[288] In both *On the Councils and the Church* and in the Catechisms Luther gives the Lord's Prayer a prominent role, as he unfolds the meaning of the sixth mark—prayer.[289] Luther links prayer to the Second Commandment as he finds that praying is what the Second Commandment teaches, to call upon God in every need. According to Luther, the Christian should do this incessantly and even "drum into" God's ears the prayer that God may "give, preserve, and increase in us faith and the fulfilment of the Ten Commandments and remove all that stands in our way and hinders us in this regard."[290]

In line with John 12:24, Luther materializes the meaning of sanctification through his elaborations on the sixth and the seventh marks of the church. The sixth mark is altogether a very "flexible" mark, as Luther includes not only praise and thanksgiving, but also the creed, the Ten Commandments and the catechism used in public.[291] The practice of

287. BC, 441.
288. BC, 445.
289. LW 41:164.
290. BC, 440–41.
291. LW 41:164.

prayer is also to "constantly pray that God will bring forth his gifts in us. This we call Christian goodness."[292] Under the article "True Christian Prayer" in the *Visitation Articles* it is also pointed out that Christians owe the government both payment of taxes, respect and honor. Therefore Christians should also pray for the government.[293]

The flexibility and broad understanding of the sixth mark as a "practice" underlines that Luther in many ways sees this mark as the practical explication of the first three (or four) marks. But when Luther elaborates on the seventh mark, he adds a different rhetoric to the scheme. Luther's definition of this mark may be broad, but it is not as "flexible": Those who adhere to the Word of God, Christ himself, must expect persecution and resistance. Luther relates this mark of the church to the introduction to the Sermon on the Mount, Matthew 5:11: "Blessed are you when men persecute you on my account." The outlining of this "practice" also adds depth to the concept of *practicing baptism* as Luther underlines that when baptized is condemned or plagued because of Christ, he or she is also sanctified, as this "mortifies the old Adam and teaches him patience, humility, gentleness, praise and thanks, and good cheer in suffering."[294]

In talking about the seventh mark of the church, Luther uses the same kind of metaphorical language as he uses when he describes what it means to "practice the work that makes us Christians."[295] By putting this as the seventh and final mark, Luther marks a border towards the coming seven commandments, which Luther claims we need "not only to apprise us of our lawful obligations, but we also need it to discern how far the Holy Spirit has advanced us in his work of sanctification."[296] This quotation underlines the "double character" of the seven "practices" of the second tablet: On one hand, they are not instituted by Christ, which is the main criterion for Luther when he makes his list of the seven marks of the church. On the other hand, they are needed to discern how far the Holy Spirit has advanced us in his work of sanctification.

It is the Word and ordinance of God, which validate the presence of Christ in a "practice," according to Luther. In other words, the presence of Christ is not validated through the belief of the "practitioner." This

292. LW 40:302.
293. LW 40:283.
294. LW 41:165.
295. BC, 466.
296. LW 41:166.

also implies that it would be more difficult for Luther to speak about the Holy Spirit as the true subject of the seven first-tablet Christian practices, than of the seven following second-tablet practices. We see this point clearly explicated as Luther underlines firmly how the sacrament—both baptism and the sacrament of the altar—belongs to the one who receives it. Luther writes, that "it does not rest on man's belief or unbelief but on the Word and ordinance of God."[297] This implies that although Christ is and has always been present in this world, through some specific "practices," which are instituted, commanded or ordained by Christ himself in Scripture and promised for our salvation through the Word, we may find true, salvific fellowship with God through Christ who is present in these "practices" according to his promise. These are the practices, which makes church happen—through worship, through a distinct liturgy.[298]

Based on this, Luther emphasizes the fundamental difference in quality between practices which offer us God's saving presence—forgiveness of sins—and "practices" which may be Christian in the sense that through them we may exercise the "common order of Christian love." This does not imply that such practices are less important, but they serve another purpose. Altogether, *love* is made the focal point of all Christian practices: First-tablet practices offer God's saving love in Christ. Second-tablet practices are ways to practice the common order of Christian love.

For the shape of the Christian life this implies that the Incarnation and baptism are not mere models for the practitioner to imitate, but events that model the shape of the Christian life. This implies that the baptismal ethics of the Christian life has to do with faith, active in love. It has to do with being discipled by Christ in the lasting effect of the promise given through the word of God in baptism. The freedom to love emerging from this is the gift of serving the neighbor. From this perspective second-tablet Christian practices are "Christian" in so far as they serve as ways to practice baptism. Based on this I will suggest the following theological definition of Christian practices:

Christian practices are ways to practice baptism. By putting faith in the gift of Christ's promised presence through the first-tablet practices, God's baptized people are freed to participate in the common order of Christian love through a variety of practices serving the neighbor and the continuous enhancement of God's created world.

---

297. LW 37:367.
298. Cf. for instance Wannenwetsch, "Lob der Äusserlichkeit," 411.

The Work of the Triune God and Human Agency in Christian Practices

In baptism, the baptized is baptized in the name of the triune God—Father, Son and Holy Spirit. In the Large Catechism we see how intimately connected Luther's theology of the Holy Spirit is with his theology of the presence of Christ in Christian practices: "For where Christ is not preached, there is no Holy Spirit to create, call, and gather the Christian church, apart from which no one can come to the Lord Christ."[299] Reinhard Hütter therefore claims that, theologically speaking, the Holy Spirit is the real subject in the church's core practices. But how should the work of the triune God and human agency in Christian practices be discerned?

A further look at *On the Councils and the Church* may help to deepen the insights here. In *On the Councils and the Church* Luther points out what the triune God wants to do through the church's core practices—also called the "holy possessions": "God himself wishes to be effective and wants them to be his water, word, hand, bread, and wine, by means of which he wishes to sanctify and save you in Christ, who acquired this for us and who gave us the Holy Spirit from the Father of this work."[300] At the beginning of the third part of this treatise, Luther distinguishes between the work of Christ, and that of the Holy Spirit. Christ's work is described as redemption, or "*per redemptionem*," whereas the work of the Holy Spirit is described as giving life and sanctifying—"*vivificationem et sanctificationem*."[301]

Luther explicates further on the interdependency between the work of Christ and the work of the Holy Spirit through the marks as he underlines that it is impossible for human beings to know anything about Christ, or believe in him, unless it is "offered to us and bestowed on our hearts through the preaching of the gospel by the Holy Spirit."[302] Talking about the presence of Christ in Lutheran theology is therefore always an exercise in Trinitarian theology: God the Father is the one who upholds the world by his power, and He is the one who sent his Son for the life of world. From this perspective, the Holy Spirit is the active agent and true subject in Christian "practices."

---

299. BC, 436.
300. LW 41:172.
301. LW 41:144.
302. BC, 436.

The new life in Christ is not a life we beget on our own. Faith in Christ is given to us through the Gospel by the Holy Spirit. It is also the Holy Spirit who enlightens and makes holy. The Holy Spirit does so by "abundantly" forgiving all sins. In his explanation to the third article Luther writes that:

> I believe that by my own understanding or strength I cannot believe in Jesus Christ my Lord or come to him, but instead the Holy Spirit has called me through the gospel, enlightened me with his gifts, made me holy and kept me in the true faith, just as he calls, gathers, enlightens, and makes holy the whole Christian church on earth and keeps it with Jesus Christ in the one common, true faith. Daily in this church the Holy Spirit abundantly forgives all sins—mine and those of all believers. On the Last Day the Holy Spirit will raise me and all the dead and will give to me and all believers in Christ eternal life.[303]

From this perspective, Reinhard Hütter is right in claiming that the Holy Spirit should be considered the true subject in the church's core practices. Likewise, the "practices" of the Catechisms are only "practices" if we consider the Holy Spirit as the true subject in these practices. Hütter also underlines that, although the Holy Spirit is to be considered the real subject in the church core practices, human beings are always actively present in the practices—listening, receiving, responding, praising and rendering obedience. Hütter's point is that this activity does not constitute the church's core practices.[304]

I find this distinction by Hütter to be sufficient to avoid introducing human agency into the concept of salvation. In a way, even *human* agency is really God's "agency," as God is the one who upholds all creation. This "agency" is of course not God's salvific agency. An example of this is how Luther deals with prayer: With an implicit reference to Romans 8:26, Luther underlines that God takes the initiative to prayer. He puts the words we are to use into our mouths and help us to approach him in prayer. But although the Holy Spirit is the true subject of a "practice" like prayer, human beings are also active in the practice. Luther puts forth earnestness in prayer as a virtue, and he writes that "we must feel our

---

303. BC, 355–56.
304. Hütter, *Suffering Divine Things*, 132.

need, the distress that drives and impels us to cry out. Then prayer will come out spontaneously, as it should."[305]

As I have already pointed out, human beings are born as receivers in their relationship to God, but sin has corrupted this relationship. Baptism restores this relationship, as the baptized is united with Christ and given the Holy Spirit. Looking at Christian practices, this implies that every kind of agency in Christian practices is in a certain way God's agency. For the first-tablet Christian practices, this implies that the practitioner is receiving the work of the Holy Spirit—new life in Christ. When it comes to the second-tablet Christian practices, it is the sustaining presence of the triune God which makes such practices possible. But in all this, the created human being (the *imago Dei*), is of course active—by speaking, listening, singing, feeling, caring, remembering etc. In this sense, rooted in the *inhabitatio Christi* of baptism and the *cooperatio*-motif of the new life in the Holy Spirit, the baptized human being is a partaker in the work of the triune God through both the first-tablet Christian practices, and the second-tablet Christian practices. This motif is not fully developed in Reinhard Hütter's elaborations on practices.

What remains less clear in Hütter's project is how to understand human agency in those practices which are not strictly core practices, but which may still be considered Christian practices. Here Kathryn Tanner offers a helpful contribution to the discussion. She discusses the practice of "welcome"—a typical example of a practice, which Hütter would label as a practice belonging to the outer circle of practices that extend and support the inner circle of church core practices. This outer circle, according to Hütter, is an open and extensive list. It is "mainly an expansion of the first and the last practices of the inner circle."[306] Tanner claims that in order to establish meaning in Christian practices one needs to look "away from the Christian practice itself to its relations with similar practices in the wider society."[307]

Tanner's approach challenges and completes Hütter's approach to practices in a constructive way: Hütter's distinction between universal practices belonging to God's economy of creation, where human agency is the constitutive, and the practices belonging to God's economy of salvation (the church's core practices), where the Holy Spirit is to be

---

305. BC, 443–44.
306. Hütter, *Bound to Be Free*, 36.
307. Tanner, "Theological Reflection and Christian Practices," 242.

considered the real subject, is helpful in determining the more doctrinal aspects of Christian practices. Tanner's approach, on the other hand, helps theological reflection to relate human agency, or more precisely human experience, in Christian practices to the wider context of human life in history and society. This elaboration on the distinctions between the work of the triune God and human agency in Christian practices will serve as a foundation for the forthcoming discussion.

Christian Practices—introducing a Third Use of the Law?

Closely related to the question of human agency in Christian practices is the question of how to understand growth in faith, and to what extent Christian practices really introduce a third use of the law. Even though Reinhard Hütter clearly states that the Holy Spirit is to be considered the real subject in the church's core practices, Hütter and his theological ally David S. Yeago have been accused of introducing growth in faith and a third use of the law in a way that is alien to Lutheran theology.[308]

Does talking about Christian practices and growth or maturing in faith necessarily introduce a third use of the law in a way that is foreign to Lutheran theology? In his article in "The Promise of Lutheran Ethics" Hütter claims that the critical core fallacy of modern Protestant Ethics is its assumption that everything, even ethics, can be derived from one article, namely justification by grace through faith alone.[309] Hütter argues that this has led to an exclusive focus on the 'theological use' of the law, where the main point is to (merely) prepare human beings for the word of forgiveness. Hütter's ambition is to rediscover Luther's theology of Christian freedom. He finds that much of Lutheran theology has tended

---

308. Cf. Hütter, "The Twofold Center of Lutheran Ethics," 182: In footnote 12 on this page Hütter joins Yeago in his critique of Radical Lutheranism and the Luther renaissance in the 1920s, which Hütter claims is deeply indebted to Kantian ontology: "Since the law/gospel distinction is placed in no wider context, but is itself the context into which everything else in theology must be integrated, the grounds for the oppressiveness of the law must be sought in the law itself."

309. Hütter here explicitly critiques Forde and Radical Lutheranism: "Gerhard Forde's chapter 'Christian Life' in *Christian Dogmatics*, 2, eds. Carl Braaten and Robert Jenson (Philadelphia: Fortress, 1984); 395–469, is one case where this problematic concentration on and thereby overstretching of the doctrine of justification become quite evident. While I profoundly agree with most of what Forde lays out under the doctrine of justification, it nevertheless swallows up everything else pertinent to the Christian life" (Hütter, "The Twofold Center of Lutheran Ethics, 181).

to dichotomize the opening dialectic of Luther's *The Freedom of a Christian* (1520): "A Christian is a perfectly free lord of all, subject to none. A Christian is a perfectly dutiful servant of all, subject to all."[310] Hütter claims that this dialectic has not been maintained; rather the second half has been neglected or forgotten.

To regain this dialectic Hütter does not want to dissolve the dialectic of law and gospel, but he wants to relate it to Christian freedom. According to Hütter, this freedom is given a particular *gestalt*. The shape of such a Christian freedom is a way of life according the commandments, the Sermon on the Mount and the double love commandment.[311] Hütter does in a certain way advocate a third use of the law, but this is not his main point. His main point, it seems, is similar to what Yeago stresses when he elaborates on the fourth mark of the church, the office of the keys. Yeago points out that by being baptized to a life in Christ, Christians are received into a community of disciples. This community is called to a distinctive life and witness. Yeago finds that this has a positive dramatic effect as salvation now becomes coming under the rule of Jesus, sharing in the life and mission of his people.[312] The ambition to re-introduce this "rule of Jesus" is why both Hütter and Yeago engage Christian practices in contemporary Lutheran theology.

The critic of Hütter and Yeago by theologians affiliated to Radical Lutheranism is important as it points to crucial theological problems, which are not fully answered by Yeago and Hütter (ala the *simul* doctrine, teleology, agency and service[313]). The problem is that the critique fails

---

310. LW 31:344

311. Hütter writes: "While I agree with the insight that the 'third use of the law' intends to maintain, it is crucial to distinguish between 'law' on the one hand and 'commandment,' 'mandate,' 'torah' on the other hand. Due to the condition of sin, 'law' in both its first and second use has an enforcing, restraining, and convicting character. This is not inherent in God's law but is the result of the radical human enstrangement from God. As the *gestalt* of the way of life with God—the embodiment of genuine human freedom—the enforcing, restraining, and convicting elements are lost . . . Let me be clear: In this life the struggle between 'spirit' and 'flesh' is not yet over. The enstrangement from God is broken 'in faith' but not yet fully overcome. Therefore the substantive dialectic between 'law' and 'gospel' still applies to Christians. In our still ongoing estrangement from God, God's law us as restraining and convincing. Yet by grasping Christ in faith, Christian freedom receives its distinct *gestalt* through a way of life according to the commandments: the Decalogue, the Sermon on the Mount, and the double-love commandment" (Hütter, "The Twofold Center of Lutheran Ethics," 182–83).

312. Yeago, "The Office of the Keys," 122.

313. Mattes, "The Thomistic Turn in Evangelical Catholic Ethics," 84.

to offer an account of how the Christian life may be become more than series of rather episodic events of being justified, as Radical Lutheranism seems eager *not* to identify Christian freedom with any particular way of life. Obviously, it is important to safeguard the theological principle that neither Christian practices nor anything else may improve your position *coram Deo*. But this rather obvious statement about the nature of justification should not silence all attempts to outline the shape of Christian freedom and address how Christian life relates to the changes, which every human life goes through. More importantly, it should not neglect to discover and develop the freedom of the common order of Christian love as a social practice.

Luther's explanation of the third article of the Creed seems to support the point Hütter tries to make in *The Promise of Lutheran Ethics*, where he advocates the shaping role of the Ten Commandments in Lutheran ethics—and in the life of the Christian. Luther writes:

> We need the Decalogue not only to apprise us of our lawful obligations, but we also need it to discern how far the Holy Spirit has advanced us in his work of sanctification and by how much we still fall short of the goal, lest we become secure and imagine we have now done all that is required. Thus we must constantly grow in sanctification and always become new creatures in Christ.[314]

Life in faith, life in Christ, always takes place in both the personal and social context of a person's maturing and growth. We have to distinguish between speaking about maturing in faith or growth in faith *coram Deo* and *coram hominibus*. The concept *practicing baptism*, rooted in the so-called present tense of baptism, and the understanding of how Christ is present in Christian practices, should help to address how Christ acts for, in, and through the Christian in the present tense. This is of particular importance in relation to ministry.

How are we then to speak about growth in faith or maturing in faith in a Lutheran manner? Is it possible at all? First of all, growth in the Lutheran scheme is open-ended, in the sense that it is radically immeasurable and hidden. It is directed towards the *Eschaton*. Luther expresses this point very lucidly as he criticizes the spiritualists of the Reformation, like Münzer, and claims that they have misunderstood the point about the sacraments working spiritually, invisibly and for the future.[315] Secondly, to "practice

---

314. LW 41:166.
315. LW 41:170.

baptism" is also to relate to the on-going shifts in human life. It may take on different shapes in different life stages and situations. Furthermore, in confronting the call to anti-nomism, Luther uses what he understands to be the correct understanding of the term "spiritual" to distinguish the role of good works in the life of a Christian. He underlines that his doctrine of good works is "spiritual and based on a distinction between good works for righteousness and good works for the glory of God." Therefore it is wrong to interpret good works as necessary for righteousness. Good works should be interpreted as necessary for the glory of God.[316]

Theologically to speak of growth in faith is to speak of growth in God's holy Word. It is about being discipled in the promise of the presence of Christ in God's holy Word. In his explanation to the Second Petition, Luther pictures growth in Christian living as growth in God's holy Word.[317] Even in the exposition on the Commandments in the Large Catechism, Luther sums up the content and meaning of the Commandments, and ultimately of life itself in a way that allows for at least speaking about doing good in relation to faith, but not about quantitatively or qualitatively growing in faith *coram Deo*: "You should do good to all people, help them and promote their interests, however and wherever you can, purely out of love to God and in order to please him, in confidence that he will repay you richly in everything."[318] Therefore it is not very helpful to argue whether a third use of the law is alien to Lutheran theology or not. It is probably more helpful to discuss whether Christian life may be interpreted as a social practice, a more or less concrete embodiment of Christian freedom in a particular way of life, or whether it has a largely episodic nature—defined by ultimate spontaneity.

Altogether, sanctification as getting used to justification (that is, growing into trusting the grace of the triune God) does not exclude speaking about Christian life as a way of life formatted by certain practices. However, distinguishing the importance of different practices for this growth is crucial: The first-tablet Christian practices root the baptized in the grace freely given, resting in the mercy of Christ. Christian practices of the second tablet are ways to exercise the common order of Christian love for the benefit of the neighbor and all creation. Maybe it is therefore

---

316. LW 37:249–50.
317. BC, 447.
318. BC, 430.

more helpful to speak about a second use of the gospel than a third use of the law when it comes to speaking about the first-tablet practices.

The Telos of the Christian Life

What does a Lutheran vision of the shape of Christian life look like? Does it have a linear or a cyclic shape? This may be a problem for the interpreter of Luther. The linear model, with its definite beginning in baptism, and a clear end in death and resurrection, and its progress in dying to sin in between, is strongly suggested by the *significatio* of baptism. On the other hand, this cannot be uncritically accepted in the light of Lutheran theology, as progress in the Christian life is a repeated return to baptism, not a progress away from the beginning of baptism.[319] Luther seems to have an eschatological rather than a teleological approach to Christian life, in the sense that Christian existence starts where all human efforts have come to an end.[320] Hütter and Yeago have (also) been criticized by Radical Lutheranism for introducing an Aristotelian, linear *telos* scheme for sanctification that is foreign to Lutheranism.

From one perspective a linear approach to the Christian life has some validity in Luther's theology, as the Christian moves from pride and self-justification to the beginning of a new life, through the ministry of law and gospel. The "linear" progress here is found in how the Christian progresses in the dying to sin and renewal which begins at baptism, and which is continued throughout life, and finally completed through death and resurrection.[321]

Oswald Bayer states this in an even more radical way, claiming that Luther's view of time stands opposed to any concept of time as linear development, in particular a Pietist one. Bayer argues that the crucial point for Luther is the distinctive combination and interweaving of the last judgment, the consummation of the world, and creation simultaneously. According to Bayer, Luther sees the future of the world as emerging from God's presence. This future of the world derives from the present-day newness of the presence of God. In the same way, the new creation now disclosed in baptism and the Lord's Supper turns the old, perverted world into the past and restores the original world as creation.

319. Trigg, *Baptism in the Theology of Martin Luther*, 95–96.
320. Asheim, *Glaube und Erziehung bei Luther*, 118.
321. Trigg, *Baptism in the Theology of Martin Luther*, 167–68.

But Bayer admits that this "non-simultaneous time is hard to conceive of, and also more especially, to live in."[322] The problem with this approach, as I have already pointed out, is that it easily—apart from the structuring role of the Sunday Mass, *Gottesdienst*—leads to a rather thin or abstract ecclesial life. The problem is also that Bayer's account of Luther here is too one-sided: towards the end of *On the Councils and the Church* Luther gives an argument for the linear approach to Christian holiness. Living by faith is pictured as a journey towards a goal, towards the Eschaton. On this journey the marks of the church are the principal parts which contribute to the sanctification of the Christian: "But we constantly strive to attain the goal, under his redemption or remission of sin, until we too shall one day become perfectly holy and no longer stand in the need of forgiveness. Everything is directed toward that goal."[323] But this is *not* really a scheme for growth. The focus is on the cosmological implications of faith and the church. Faith is lived within a linear narrative, where the main movement is cyclic, returning to one's baptism—which is what I understand by the concept *practicing baptism*.

The combination of the linear and the cyclic is also shaped by another continuous element in the life of the Christian, which is rooted in Luther's dramatic cosmology. Luther describes the devil as a furious enemy. Therefore Luther maintains that when "the Devil sees that we resist him and attack the old creature, and when he cannot rout us by force, he sneaks and skulks about at every turn, trying all kinds of tricks, and does not stop until he has finally worn us out so that we either renounce our faith or lose heart, and become indifferent or impatient."[324]

This is how Luther places the Lord's Supper within the larger narrative of the life of a Christian, which starts in baptism, but which is also full of tribulations. Luther finds that the Sacrament of the Altar is food for the soul, as it strengthens and nourishes the new creature, which comes out of baptism: "There are so many hindrances and attacks of the devil and the world that we often grow weary and faint and at times even stumble." Therefore the Lord's Supper is given as a daily food and sustenance so that

---

322. Bayer, *Living by Faith*, 64–65. For Bayer Luther's "time-scheme," or his take on metaphysics, is central to understand his theology. This scheme is also decisive for his take on sanctification. Cf. for instance Bayer's comment: "The gap between Luther on the side and Bengel and Hegel and their theological successors on the other can never be bridged."

323. LW 41:166.

324. BC, 469.

faith may be refreshed and strengthened and that it may become stronger and stronger. Therefore Luther claims that "the new life should be one that continually develops and progresses."[325] This is another proof that it is reductionism to picture Luther's idea of *practicing baptism* as simply a version of "snakes and ladders" where you always fall back on your baptism, and no progress is made. But *coram Deo* and in relation to God's justification by faith alone, no progress is made. So although the baptized Christian always remains *simul iustus et peccator*, *coram hominibus* and in the frames of the Christian's life narrative, one may speak about maturing in faith and development in the Christian's love towards his or her neighbor: The Christian may become more gentle, more patient, more meek, more likely to break away from greed, hatred, envy, and pride.[326]

The shape of the Christian life is both tentative and formative. On the one hand you find distinct Christian practices, on the other hand great freedom and spontaneity. The concept *practicing baptism* grasps this duality, as it contains both a cyclic and linear perspective on life in Christ. *Practicing baptism* means both daily and constantly returning to one's baptism (*cyclic*), but it also involves a *linear* and more peregrinational perspective on life in Christ: Through "practicing" the practices of the catechisms the believer is kept steadfast to the promise of Christ and the new life in Christ given in baptism. Luther describes this as a journey where the believer is to be "led into the Scriptures and make progress every day"—or more succinctly put in German—"in die Schrift bringen und täglich *weiter fahren*."[327]

This speaks for developing further a *narrative* approach to the Christian life, also in relation to Christian practices. In the light of Lutheran theology, there are what one may call two "colliding" or "conflicting" narratives—the linear and the cyclic narrative. The life of the believer is narratively structured as a baptism—as a continuous moving "through death to life and resurrection"—receiving, suffering, undergoing, participating in the work of the triune God. I therefore suggest that the narrative structure of the baptismal, Christian life, understood through the concept *practicing baptism*, holds the narrative shape of a comedy. It corresponds

---

325. Cf. the German original: "Denn das neue Leben soll also getan sein, dass es stets zunehme und fortfahre." BELK, 712. Once again the conjunctive form of the verbs underlines the tentative, and not determinative, nature of Christian life (BC, 469).

326. BC, 465.

327. BELK, 559; and BC, 386.

with how Northrop Frye has pointed out in *The Great Code* that the comedy is a narrative structure, which is roughly U-shaped.

According to Frye, apostasy in the biblical narrative is usually followed by a descent into disaster and bondage. This is then followed by repentance, where after comes a rise through deliverance, which brings the story back to a point more or less on the level from which the descent began. Frye finds that this is a literary pattern typical for the biblical narrative:

> This U-shaped pattern, approximate as it is, recurs in literature as the standard shape of comedy, where a series of misfortunes and misunderstandings brings the action to a threateningly low point, after which some fortunate twist in the plot sends the conclusion up to a happy ending. The entire Bible, viewed as a "divine comedy," is contained with a U-shaped story of this sort, one in which man, as explained, loses the tree and water of life at the beginning of Genesis and gets them back at the end of Revelation.[328]

The difference between a Lutheran and an Aristotelian approach to *passio*, suffering, is that in the Aristotelian scheme suffering humbles to lift up. It is the move from *potentialis* to *actualis*. In the Lutheran scheme—according to the theology of the cross—suffering continues to happen while we are still sinful. It takes as its point of departure justification as perfect passivity. Baptism is therefore the first and final example of what it means to practice suffering, understood as being totally bound to receiving and undergoing the liberating gifts of God. The main problem with Reinhard Hütter's proposal in relationship to this is his inherent teleological approach, instead of an eschatological approach.

In a teleological approach to practices, the tendency is towards practices as a tool to educate desires and to move them in the proper direction. Departing from the concept *practicing baptism* on the other hand, growth in faith is always related to how the triune God sanctifies due to His faithfulness through the present tense of His promise (in baptism). *Practicing baptism* is therefore a daily dying and rising with Christ. In this sense, baptism shapes the life of the believer into a U-shaped eshatological comedy. By this way of understanding living by faith through the concept *practicing baptism* the cyclic and the linear in the narrative

---

328. Frye, *The Great Code*, 169. Cf. also ibid., 79, where Frye notes, that "in I Peter 3:21 Christian baptism is called the *antitypos* of the saving of mankind from the flood of Noah."

structure of the Christian life is combined in a constructive narrative paradox—the U-shaped comedy.

The *telos* of the Christian life rooted in baptism is really *eschatological*, and not teleological in the Aristotelian meaning of the word, as it is directed to the final realization of the baptismal promise of eternal life in Christ through death. Practicing the first-tablet practices is a continuous return to the promise of baptism, life in Christ. For wordly matters, the *telos* of the Christian life rooted in baptism is fundamentally *diaconal*, as it is always directed to the other—the neighbor and all of creation—practicing second-tablet Christian practices, the common order of Christian love.

Practicing Baptism

Luther champions what he refers to as "the ordinary Christian life."[329] But Luther also uses a distinct metaphor to describe the rules of the communal life of a Christian. He compares being Christian to living in a particular city. When you live in a city, you ought to know and abide the laws of the city whose protection you enjoy.[330] This underlines a fundamental aspect of Luther's baptismal ecclesiology: *Practicing baptism* is a public thing, much like Reinhard Hütter's point that the church is the public of the Holy Spirit. And this "public thing" is not just a flow of episodic, forensic declarations of justification by grace.

The bearing concept in Luther's baptismal theology in relation to the life of the Christian is his focus on the "present tense" of baptism. To "practice" one's baptism all through life is to return by faith to repentance for sins, so that they may be forgiven. For Luther good works in the life of the Christian plays the role of killing the flesh—*mortificatio carnis*. Luther gives life in Christ a cruciform shape: Living under the cross is the shape of the Christian life, and this life is eschatological in its profile and direction. It is a *conformitas Christi*, which is also about being enrapt in the sufferings and tribulations of Christ—not only through physical suffering, but all the more being tried in conscience and in soul by the judgement of God. This "baptismal pedagogy" underlines that the baptized since baptism is marked by the sign of the cross; the daily dying and rising with Christ.[331]

---

329. BC, 413.
330. BC, 349.
331. Asheim, *Glaube und Erziehung bei Luther*, 219–22.

A Lutheran theology of Christian practices is about reclaiming the love of the triune God and how it shapes us. *Practicing baptism* is to practice the promises of Christ by undergoing the work of the triune God through the church's core practices. It is the invitation to rest in Christ's love for human beings, in perfect passivity. Resting in Christ's mercy, the receiver is incorporated in a *baptismal*, cruciform pattern of God's self-giving love. In this sense, all of life, living in the transition between the old and the new man, is a continuous preparation for the receiving of grace, seeking God through his Word.[332] Rooted in this grace, the baptized is freed to live a life where faith is active in love (Gal 5:6), practicing the common order of Christian love—*diakonia*—which benefit the neighbor and all of creation, and to the glory of God.[333] As we are drawn to Christ through the Holy Spirit, we are freed to be drawn to our neighbor, becoming Christ to our neighbor. In this sense *practicing baptism* is even a charismatic concept, celebrating the fullness of life in God through Christ, made available through the Holy Spirit—continuously empowering the new life in Christ.

Practicing baptism is being remade again and again by the triune God in the "image" of baptism. But unlike the MacIntyre-ian and Aristotelian anthropological perspective on the excellence inherent in practices,[334] a Lutheran focus on excellence is both fundamentally Christological and Trinitarian. Human and divine agency in Christian practices is discerned. We therefore need a combined linear-cyclic baptismal narrative to capture the nature and shape of this Christian life in the light of Lutheran theology: Baptism is the compass for the everyday (*linear*) life and maturing in faith and it is something a Christian always returns to (*cyclic*). *Practicing baptism* daily is to be brought into the presence of the kingdom of Christ again and again.

---

332. Jetter, *Die Taufe beim jungen Luther*, 342.

333. In a sermon on 1 Tim 1:5–7 on the Sum of the Christian Life, Luther underlines that "true love flows from a pure heart," and that "God has commanded me to let my love go out to my neighbor and kindly disposed to all, whether they be my friends or enemies, just as our heavenly Father himself does." LW 51:267. Luther firmly underlines that it is the Word of God that makes a heart pure; LW 51:269.

334. Cf. here MacIntyre's definition of social practices, which involves certain "standards of excellence" and extends the capacities of the ones involved in a practice; MacIntyre, *After Virtue*, 187.

4

Practicing Baptism

CONSEQUENTIAL CHRISTOLOGY IN CONTEXT

Theological Practice Revolutions

THOSE ADVOCATING CHRISTIAN PRACTICES try to engage a Christology that is passionate and consequential.[1] The Lutheran anxiety about practices reflects a radical skepticism on what of real theological substance is going on in the practices conversation, and also to which extent the focus on practices is a new way of introducing a righteousness of works. This chapter is set up as a critical dialogue between the theology of the Christian practices-paradigm and the Lutheran understanding of

---

1. Bonhoeffer's focus on the relationship between belief and practices plays an important role for many of the theologians within the Christian practices paradigm. Bass quotes *Life Together* in *For Life Abundant*, but perhaps most poignant to capture the impetus of the engagement in Christian practices is the role D. B. Bass ascribes to Bonhoeffer's famous term "cheap grace": "Cheap grace is the preaching of forgiveness without requiring repentance, baptism without church discipline, Communion without confession, absolution without personal confession. Cheap grace is grace without discipleship, grace without the cross, grace without Jesus Christ, living and incarnate" (Bonhoeffer, *The Cost of Discipleship*, 57; quoted in D. B. Bass, *The Practicing Congregation*, 57). Based on this, D. B. Bass outlines the hope of a new kind of mainline congregation, which is being "rebirthed around Christian practices." D. B. Bass, *The Practicing Congregation*, 59.

Christian practices developed in chapter 3 in order to answer three crucial questions:

- What makes a *practice* Christian?
- What makes a *Christian* practice?
- Where is the church?

Different contexts give rise to different questions—even theologically. At the beginning of the twenty-first century the lives of young people are fundamentally shaped by the ongoing media revolution, where the use of Internet, mobile phones, and diverse forms of social media are shaping everyday lives in new ways. At the same time there is a rising biblical illiteracy in the Western hemisphere.

The lack of biblical knowledge was an important impetus even for Luther's writing of the Catechisms. With the help of the newly invented printing tools, writing, printing, publishing and spreading the Catechisms was a media-borne "practice-revolution" in the way of the sixteenth century. Like Luther and Melanchthon, church leaders of today try to initiate "practice" revolutions or reforms like the Catechisms. The whole engagement in Christian practices in the US is an excellent, contemporary example of this.

The current engagements to rethink the churches' catechetical ministry also reflect the importance of different historical and theological contexts. Europe has a long history of close state-church relations and majority churches with bonds to both ruler and nation. The ecclesiological map in the US is largely determined by a free-church approach to state-church relations. Traditionally therefore congregational life in Europe has been more uniform than in the US, both when it comes to the range of different denominations and even ethnicity, although immigration is making the ecclesiological map in Europe more multi-faceted.

Historically, the differences between the sixteenth-century "practice revolution" and the late twentieth-century Christian practices paradigm are also notable. Compared with Luther and the other Reformers, those engaging Christian practices obviously have different questions as their fundamental point of departure. Luther asked, "How can I find a merciful God?" whereas Bass and Dykstra ask, "What does it mean to live the Christian life faithfully and well, and how do we help others to do so?" whereas Dean seems to ask, "How can the encounter with the passion of Christ through Christian practices change the lives of (American) teenagers?" For the whole approach to Christian practices it is quite determining what kind of questions form the point of departure. Among those interested in Christian practices one may also trace differences. Reinhard Hütter seems to be more concerned with re-shaping ecclesiology after Constantinism. Bass and Dykstra, and partly Dean, focus more on the shape of the everyday Christian life after Christendom through a rediscovery of Christian practices.

The Role of Baptism in the Christian Life

The main contribution from the "Christian practices paradigm" to contemporary theology is the way it re-conceptualizes the Christian life as a *way of life*—as a continuum—in multiple contexts. In a way it may be interpreted as a way to re-introduce the ancient slogan ascribed to Prosper of Aquitaine; *Lex orandi—lex credendi*: The rule of prayer is the rule of faith, and the other way around, which resembles Miroslav Volf's notion of "belief-shaping practices and practice-shaping beliefs."[2]

Bass, Dykstra and Dean do not elaborate broadly on the role of baptism in relation to Christian practices, this still needs to be discussed: they focus little on what baptism accomplishes, rather the focus is on what baptism presents—the Christian life is in baptism "fully and finally presented, visibly, tangibly, and in words." One of the more problematic claims is the claim that detached from a way of life abundant "the pouring of water accomplishes nothing."[3]

Without actually fully developing it, Dykstra and Bass, and in particular Bass, on several occasions, hint in the direction of the concept *practicing baptism*, which I developed in the previous chapter of this book. Bass points out that through baptism Christians have been given to "walk in newness of life" according to Romans 6:4, and Bass claims that the most important thing for the Christian community of today is to consider what this walk of life looks like. Bass also strongly suggests that this walk—this

---

2. Cf. how Dean uses this, Dean, *Practicing Passion*, 25. Lathrop also suggests a turn to the ancient *lex orandi est lex credendi*: "We might more confidently hold with the more modest proposal of fifth-century Augustinian Prosper of Aquitaine: the rule of beseeching—the urging of the apostle (in Tim 2:1) that prayers should be made for everyone and widespread response of the churches in actually doing that—establishes the rule of believing." Lathrop and Wengert, *Christian Assembly*, 9.

3. Dykstra and Bass, "A Theological Understanding of Christian Practices," 30–31.

"way of life shaped by Christian practices"—may be countercultural because "it is impossible to ignore the harm caused by our own patterns of consumption." Therefore Bass wants the Christian community to ask how our life together may "honor all creation as belonging to God and teach us to dwell rightly and faithfully within this creation."[4]

Compared with a Lutheran approach to baptism, the differences are noteworthy. For Luther, baptism as a "treaty" ("covenant") stems from the fact that God in his word encounters us through his promise. For Luther baptism is the concrete realization of a God-given, spiritual fact in our life.[5] Baptism, according to Evangelical-Lutheran confession, holds a double structure in the sense that the aim of the sacraments, which are signs and testimonies of God's will to mankind, is to arouse and strengthen faith in those who use them. But although the aim of the use of the sacraments is that faith may increase, the sacraments do not justify by the work done (*ex opere operato*). At the same time faith, which believes the forgiveness of sins is not a requisite in the use of the sacraments.[6] This double structure implies that baptism is necessary for salvation as an *opus operatum Dei* while at the same time its aim is to stir up and confirm faith in the promise(s) of the triune God.[7]

In CA IX it is stated that baptism is "necessary for salvation."[8] This statement is ordered within the rhetorical logic of the whole confession (CA), where the motivation for baptism—the *necessitas* of baptism—is both rooted in the radically complex anthropology of the Lutheran confession (CA II), the radically *theo*-logical drive of the soteriology (CA III–VII), and the radical gift character of the sacrament, instituted to "arouse and strengthen faith" (CA XIII).[9] But in our contemporary and plural context both the *why* and the *what* of salvation is not always obvious. In other words, if the necessity of baptism is not rooted in a larger logical structure, than just pointing to CA IX, arguing why baptism as a mutual sacrament of transition from the old to the new becomes much harder. The *why* of baptism therefore has to be founded in a *simul-juxtaposition* of *Trinitarian theology*, which emphasizes that God is love, and he has

4. Bass, "Ways of Life Abundant," 25, 22.
5. Jetter, *Die Taufe beim jungen Luther*, 213, 316.
6. BC, 46–47. CA XIII.
7. BC, 42–43 (CA IX); and Jetter, *Die Taufe beim jungen Luther*, 339.
8. "sit necessarius ad salutem." Cf. BELK, 63
9. Lathrop and Wengert, *Christian Assembly*, 56–58.

created us out of love, saved us in Jesus Christ and is calling us through his Holy Spirit, and *a radically complex anthropology*, which emphasizes that human beings are radically *imago Dei* and fallen sinners at the same time and therefore in need of being saved from sin and death.

Both the Small Catechism and CAXII outlines the same view on daily contrition and repentance on the basis of baptism. It is stated that repentance consists of two parts, both the recognizing of sin and faith, brought alive by the gospel or absolution. Upon the faith in the consoling work of Christ follows good works, which is a fruit of repentance.[10] Here we see how a radically complex anthropology is combined with a radical soteriology—and view on sanctification. Baptismal theology and the *necessitas* of baptism are rooted in this logic.

Someone who relates the engagement in Christian practices to baptismal theology and gets closer to this Lutheran approach is American Presbyterian theologian John P. Burgess in the book *After Baptism* (2005). But even though Burgess draws on Bonhoeffer and Luther, Burgess still focuses on how practices of faith may help to *fulfill* the vows made in baptism and maintain Christian identity as the baptized believer matures and grows up, which at least confuses the nature of baptism as a treaty. But Burgess also underlines that through Christian practices the practitioner receive God's word of promise, and that Christian practices shape the practitioner in the image of Christ, so that he/she may offer Christ to the world." Here the commandments are understood as identity markers and the Sabbath as a free zone to maintain the Christian identity given in baptism. Interestingly enough, Burgess, like Dean, refers to September 11 as a transformative event for the church and its approach to practices and disciplines. Burgess also joins in the critique of consumer society. For Burgess the problem with consumer society is that it offers us every good thing here and now.[11]

Fundamentally, the difference between a more Reformed view and a Lutheran view when it comes to baptismal theology is found in the weight the Reformed tradition puts on baptism as a mutual covenant. In the Reformed tradition this covenant is constituted (also) by the promises human beings give in the act of baptism—either by the baptized or the sponsors. Dykstra finds that the Christian faith is imbued with a promissory structure. Further, Dykstra claims that "this promissory structure is

---

10. BC, 45
11. Burgess, *After Baptism*, 16–17, 19, 134.

made especially clear and is enacted anew for each new Christian in the Sacrament of Holy Baptism."[12]

In the light of Lutheran baptismal theology the real presence of Christ makes baptism more than a covenant. The focus in baptism is on *what the triune God does in baptism*—and the lasting effects of this act. "The present tense of baptism" as a concept in Lutheran theology relates to the lasting presence of Christ in the promise of baptism. The new man born in Christ in baptism, lives in Christ throughout life, as Christ himself is present in faith. Therefore it is not the promises of the baptized or the sponsors, which secures the validity of baptism.

WHAT MAKES A PRACTICE CHRISTIAN?

The Incarnation As a Model or the Ontological Event that Models

The engagement in Christian practices so far lacks a clear and developed criteriology on how to discern and understand what constitutes the presence of Christ in Christian practices. The question whether Christ comes to the world through Christian practices also needs further elaboration. Here I will discuss how the Lutheran criteriology I have developed may contribute in developing such a criteriology. My particular focus will be on how this relates to the context of ministry.

Kenda Creasy Dean describes Christian practices, metaphorically, as a tool to "smuggle Jesus into the world through our own lives."[13] But if God uses the practices as a point of entry into the world, where is Christ before He gets "smuggled into the world" through the lives of the faithful and through Christian practices? Dean does not promote the idea that Christian practices "smuggle" Jesus into the word in *Practicing Passion*, but she gets fairly close to the same theological approach—that the real presence of Christ is really outside our world, and in need of being imported.[14] Dean and Dykstra are both reluctant to talk explicitly about the (full) presence of Christ in the world. Rather, it seems, Christ comes to us through Christian practices.

Those engaging Christian practices seldom reflect in depth theologically on how the Incarnation as an event affects the (continuous) presence

---

12. Dykstra, *Growing in the Life of Faith*, 105.
13. Dean and Foster, *The Godbearing Life*, 48.
14. Dean, *Practicing Passion*, 195.

of Christ in the world, and how to understand the presence of the second person in the Trinity prior to Incarnation. They tend to view the Incarnation as a model for ecclesiological action and Christian identity formation to a point where it runs the risk of undermining the historical character and ontological consequences of the Incarnation. Does the Incarnation just represent or model a potential divine presence, which once in a while may be present again and again through Christian practices?

Jürgen Moltmann, whom Dean refers to frequently, ultimately places the real presence of Christ in the messianic and eschatological future. For Moltmann the full real presence of Christ is bound to the eschatological future of the triune God. This future may in dynamic ways break into our reality in the here and now, but not fully. The problem with Moltmann's understanding of the presence of Christ is that it lacks a sufficient focus on Christ's presence here and now. Moltmann, in his theology of hope, places the real presence of Christ in the eschatology, and this presence *can be made present* in the world by the church as the kingdom of God, directed by the self-giving love of the Holy Spirit.[15] But even this happens sort of episodically, as an act of the reigning Christ seated to the right of the Father breaking through from heaven to earth. Dean seems to be writing with this theological background in mind when she underlines that "the church reconstitutes the suffering love of Jesus Christ in human acts of self-giving love that imperfectly draw us into Christ's passion through grace, making it present again and again."[16] One problem with Dean's focus on the passion of Christ is that it may run the danger of threating the Passion of Christ as a separate quality outside or distinct from the present Jesus Christ.

But there are also obvious strengths to this more dynamic understanding of the presence of Christ, particularly in how it addresses human experiences of growth, passion, and the longing for a more holistic lifestyle. However, a theology of the different modes of Christ's presence allows speaking about a full real presence here and now in a nuanced way. The main problem is that the Incarnation first and foremost becomes a model for the Christian life, and not the event, which makes life in Christ possible in the first place. This also brings to the fore crucial anthropological, soteriological and ecclesiological implications. First of all, human

---

15. Cf. Kjølsvik, *Kreuz und Auferstehung als Geschichte—und Gegenwart*, 310.
16. Dean, *Practicing Passion*, 157.

agency is obscured. Secondly, when the Incarnation is a model, and not the event that models, it is far easier to develop an idealized ecclesiology.

Reinhard Hütter speaks about how faith uncovers the inherent interconnectedness of practices of the economy of creation and the economy of salvation. This is a hermeneutical key to discern the presence of Christ in Christian practices: First look for Christ (in the practices) where he promised to be, then the disciples of Jesus will learn to recognize him elsewhere.[17] In other words, the first tablet Christian practices may serve as a prism in discerning what may make other practices Christian.

In the context of ministry this is crucial. If the Incarnation and baptism are mere models, rather than events that model, the focus tends to be more on what humans can do to imitate or produce Christian behavior. If the incarnation and baptism are events that model and shape our identity and common (play-)ground of ministry, the focus is (or at least should) be on exploring what Christ, through the Holy Spirit is doing in our midst, and how we may be engaged in the work of the triune God in the world—in our particular context.

Baptism As a Model Or the Soteriological Event That Models

Bass, Dykstra, and Dean all tend to understand baptism the same way they understand the Incarnation. Baptism may serve as a model for the Christian life and for all Christian practices, but it is not the event that models—and shapes—Christian life here and now by stamping its mark upon the whole. Here the Lutheran understanding of the "present tense of baptism" challenges the baptismal theology of the Christian practices paradigm. In both Lutheran theology and for those engaging Christian practices in practical theology, Incarnation theology and baptismal theology are closely connected, and the way they relate directly influences the conceptualization of the Christian life. Incarnation theology and baptismal theology are altogether very influential for the way the Christian life is pictured.

Schematically this may be sketched in the following way:

---

17. Cf. Stortz, *A World according to God*, 163. The role Stortz here gives "the resurrection practices" is similar to the way Hütter enfolds the role of the church's core practices: These practices characterize and constitute the church, and by doing so they point to where Christ is to be found in the world.

The Christian practices paradigm	A Lutheran approach to Christian practices
The Incarnation as a model	The Incarnation as the event that models
Baptism as a model	Baptism as the event that models
Imitatio Christi	*Conformitas Christi*

Two different approaches to Incarnation theology and baptismal theology result in two different approaches to the Christian life. Whereas many of those engaging Christian practices focus the Christian life through the concept *imitatio Christi*, in Lutheran theology the leading metaphor for the Christian life is *conformitas Christi*. This stresses passivity—receiving—as the point to which the Christian always returns. Hence, *imitatio Christi* as a concept is not neglected, but is always reinterpreted in the light of what the triune God has done and is doing as a process of *conformtias Christi*, cf. Romans 8:29. Christian life is, therefore, theologically speaking, not mimicry, but first and foremost about undergoing—suffering—the work of the Holy Spirit through the gifts of the triune God. As I will discuss further later in this chapter the biggest problem with interpreting baptism and the Incarnation mainly as models and not events which model is that it runs the risk of obscuring human agency in Christian practices.

Altogether, Lutheran baptismal theology differs from the dominant focus on baptism in the Christian practices paradigm in that it focuses on the present tense of baptism: Christ is present for the baptized here and now. The baptismal event is not just a model for Christian life. This ontic reality of the promise of Christ's presence in the baptized is a constant invitation to live a life shaped by the church's core practices.

At the same time Lutheran theology celebrates both the particular and the universal presence of Christ. But by distinguishing the two, a certain dual relationship is established. This duality is found in the distinction between first- and second-tablet Christian practices: For Luther first-tablet practices—the church's core practices—are practices which celebrate and mediate the particular, real-salvific presence of Christ. Practices stemming from the second tablet are Christian practices insofar as through these practices we may exercise the common order of Christian love. That is to become Christ to our neighbor, and take part in how God through his love constantly sustains and renews the world. Participating in these practices is a way of *practicing baptism* as baptism liberates the baptized, being loved freely, to the freedom of loving and serving freely. The Christian self therefore exists both in Christ and in the neighbor.

In the context of ministry this dual relationship allows for a more positive approach to contemporary culture, and a more focused approach when discerning what makes the centre of congregational life and ministry. *Practicing baptism* is the movement of the triune God—who shapes us in this duality; to on the one hand, celebrate the joys of Christ's universal presence in the midst of all relations and all creations, and at the same time celebrate and beseech the particular presence of Christ rooted in the present tense of baptism and through the church's core practices that baptism points to.

Ordering Christian Practices

Reinhard Hütter finds that his work in *Suffering Divine Things* is fundamentally different from the works of Bass and Dykstra, which according to Hütter focus on practices from the perspective of the economy of creation, whereas his work on practices insists on giving primacy to the Holy Spirit in the church's agency in general and in the Christian life in particular. Hütter finds that theologians with a fundamentally non-sacramental, Congregationalist ecclesiology, often tend to favor either practices of witness, if they along the Barthian lines prioritize the economy of salvation, or favor what may be called everyday practices, if they along liberal Protestant lines, prioritize the economy of creation with practices that sustain human flourishing.[18]

Altogether, the most weighty premise given by the Christian practices paradigm when it comes to arguing what constitutes the presence of Christ in a practice is that "in Christian practices, the 'goods' are the presence of Christ, guaranteed by the shared nature of practice ("Where two or three are gathered together, I am in their midst." Matthew 18:20)."[19] It is hard to disagree with this argument. Even for Luther it is the Word and ordinance of God, which validate the presence of Christ in a "practice." What is stated with more clarity in the light of Lutheran theology than within the Christian practices paradigm is that the presence of Christ in (Christian) practices is not validated through the belief of the "practitioner," as the sacrament, belongs to the one who receives it. I have argued

18. Hütter, "The Christian Life," 297–98.
19. Dean, *Practicing Passion*, 173–74.

that when participating in those practices, which are not necessarily Christian, but which belong to the second tablet of Moses, it is important to state we are always surrounded by the repletive presence of Christ; The Christ, the Son of God, who created the world and upholds it along with the Father and the Spirit.

Within the Christian practices paradigm, there is little reflection on how Jesus' promise of presence to the gathered assembly relates to the duality between his universal presence (the *repletive* mode) and the particular-salvific presence (the *diffinitive* mode). This *simul*-structure in Luther's Christology, that Christ is radically present in all creation for the enhancement of life, but distinctively and radically present in a special way in the church's core practices for the forgiveness of sins, is important for a criteriology on how to discern how Christ may be present in (Christian) practices: From this perspective, second-tablet practices may be "Christian" in so far as they serve as ways to practice baptism, as faith active in love.

When it comes to a criteriology on how to discern the presence of Christ in Christian practices, Dean, Dykstra and Bass do not differentiate between different modes of presence. But you may find traces in their writings with a certain affinity towards Luther's idea of the diffinitive category of presence.[20] But in general, by Dean in particular, it is emphasized that Jesus Christ comes to the world through us.[21] That Jesus Christ "comes to the world through us," and that imitation of Christ is a way to "wobble towards God" remains problematic—not only from a Lutheran perspective, but also philosophically. The problem is also partly linked to terminology. The terminology used is not always very precise when it comes to discerning the presence of Christ in Christian practices. Dean, Bass and Dykstra all use both traditional terms such as "means of grace"[22] and more "open" or vague terms like "a sense of presence." Christian practices knit together in a way of life, according to Dykstra, have the "power to place us where we can receive a sense of the presence of God."[23]

---

20. "Christian practices do more than re-enact historic events to shape young people into members of religious communities. In every practice, Jesus enters the room though the doors be closed. The church reconstitutes the suffering love of Jesus Christ in human acts of self-giving love that imperfectly draw us into Christ's passion through grace, making it present again and again" (ibid., 157).

21. Cf. ibid., 150–51.

22. Dykstra, *Growing in the Life of Faith*, 45.

23. Ibid., 63.

Dykstra argues that certain practices are in fact conditions making it possible for us to recognize the risen Lord. He even claims that "the engagement in the practice of service is a *condition* for the knowledge of a reality absolutely central to faith—the reality of the resurrection presence."[24] But what are the epistemological implications of this? It is important to ask where this reality outside our knowledge really exists, or if this is actually a kerygmatic epistemology à la Bultmann.

According to Bass, different ways of life, which respond to the freedom of God, are "made manifest and available in Christ." What Bass means by this is not quite clear, but the present Christ seems to be a prerequisite for Christian practices. What kind of presence this is remains unclear, but it seems that Bass identifies this way of life with "Jesus' reconciling work."[25]

In the context of ministry the dual approach to practices offered by Lutheran theology, adds clarity to the engagement in Christian practices: The church's core practices, or the first-tablet Christian practices, are special in the sense that they constitute and characterize the center of the church's ministry. But at the same time, due to the continuous universal presence, the repletive presence of Christ, a large range of practices may be Christian practices. These are the practices that are ways to exercise the common order of Christian love, serving the neighbor, trusting in the promise of Christ's lasting presence.

What *make* practices Christian are therefore not (practicing) Christian people. The opposite is true, however, that first-tablet Christian practices may *make* people Christian. In the context of ministry this radical openness paves the way for organizing Christian ministry with radical open outer borders. This is particularly important in developing youth ministry in a post-Christendom context.

WHAT MAKES A CHRISTIAN PRACTICE?

The Doctrine of Sin, Radical Evil and Christian Practices

By relating the interest in Christian practices to paradigmatic events such as the Columbine shootings and 9/11, Dean implicitly, and maybe unintentionally, relates it to the problem of radical evil. Although the contours

---

24. Dykstra, "Reconceiving Practice," 46.
25. Bass, "Ways of Life Abundant," 23–24.

of a cosmological drama are drawn out, the role of God's opponent, Satan, and the doctrine of sin is not discussed in any breadth. Rather, the problem for the Christian is maintaining identity in a pluralist consumer society, with the result that the concept of sin becomes rather unclear in Dean's theology. Sin is pictured as identity confusion, as a denying of your true self.[26]

Radical evil and the doctrine of sin and its relationship to Christian practices need to be discussed. When discussing Christian practices, sin and radical evil has to be related to something more than just the dynamics of consumer culture. I have suggested that the Christian practices paradigm is characterized by a "soft soteriology" and an "optimistic anthropology" as opposed to a more "radical soteriology" and more "complex anthropology" in the Lutheran tradition.

In developing the anthropological and soteriological consequences of a Lutheran approach to the presence of Christ in Christian practices, focusing on human agency, I found that human beings are fundamentally receivers in their relationship to God. But sin has corrupted the human beings' trustful, receiving relationship to their Creator. In baptism, however, this relationship is restored, in the sense that baptism makes human beings into receivers again.

Therefore, when it comes to practices, human agency in practices is fundamentally about receiving. From a certain perspective, the Holy Spirit should be considered the real subject of the church's core practices, which models what God may give also through second tablet practices. But although the practitioner is always at the receiving end, he or she acts with all her senses, abilities and assets the baptized suffers—*passio*—the work of the triune God in these practices. This is, from a certain perspective, also the case with second-tablet Christian practices. In these practices human beings are receivers, as the sustaining, repletive presence of the triune God is the precondition for all human agency in the first place.

Bass and Dykstra seem to deliberately avoid more classic Christian metaphors when it comes to describing the Christian life. This is particularly evident when it comes to classic baptismal metaphors like "dying to sin" and other metaphors, which relate to baptism and the Christian life as a way to practice baptism. Obviously classic metaphors need to be challenged, but the problem with Bass and Dykstra's metaphorical

---

26. Cf. Dean, *Practicing Passion*, 173–74.

language is that instead of challenging old metaphors they just replace them with rather idealistic new metaphors with less clarity.

Dean's soteriological terminology is synthetic in the sense that it aims at synthesizing and incorporating adolescent passion into divine passion. Dean uses the scaffolding of medieval theology to give grounds for her chief arguments, but this medieval approach also brings about some theological challenges. What does Dean mean by the distinction between *extrinsic* imitation of Christ, *intrinsic* identification with Christ—and finally *union* with Christ?[27] In her eagerness to see identity formation as transformation, Dean may run the risk of over-emphasizing development and growth as the key terms in a theology of Christian practices.

With great relevance to this matter, the Polish philosopher Kolakowski claims that the best way to guard the vulnerability of humanity is to keep the idea of original sin and the Devil. Kolakowski finds that guilt is all mankind has, apart from sheer physical compulsion, in order to impose rules of conduct on its members, and all it has to give those rules the form of moral commandments. Therefore Kolakowski finds that Christianity is opposed to humanism, if by "humanism" one means a "doctrine implying either that there are no limits whatever to human self-perfectibility or that people are entirely free in stating the criteria of good and evil."[28]

In the context of ministry this difference may be important in relation to how the experience of suffering and (radical) evil is approached both in preaching and in pastoral care. Whereas Luther would point at Christian practices as tools to fight the Devil, the Christian practices paradigm underlines that Christian practices are tools for growth and transformation. This marks a radical difference. Although Luther is in many ways a stranger to a post modern reader, at the same time his willingness to address evil strikes a chord: *Practicing baptism is a matter of life and death.* A complex and nuanced baptismal anthropology offers a more realistic and direct approach to this theme. For a generation who have grown up with terror attacks as a part of everyday reality a more complex anthropology may serve as an important and critical resource.

While Luther understands and explains things happening as confrontations between God and Satan, Dean et al. are very hesitant to speak about evil in a cosmological sense. Although the shaping role of events

---

27. Ibid., 163.
28. Kolakowksi, *Religion, If There Is No God*, 196, 201.

such as 9/11 and the Columbine shooting is focused, the main focus is on how these events may reinforce martyrdom and passion as virtues in ministry, not on how the (radical) evil element of such events challenges theology. The question is whether the Christian practices paradigm really has a language to interpret radical evil.

Fundamentally, this has also to do with why God became human in Christ, and therefore Christian anthropology and its relationship to human brokenness and failure—to sin.[29] The ability to address anthropological complexity is a strength with the concept *practicing baptism*. Ministry, and youth ministry in particular, has to foster the fine balance of celebrating the giftedness of (young) people and being a place where the truth about humans—even in their brokenness, shame, guilt, sin and failure—may be spoken and dealt with in truthful and caring ways.

Baptismal Anthropology and Christian Practices

Dykstra and Bass make an idealistic claim, which may ultimately compromise the saving action of God in baptism. Their ambition to focus on Christian practices as a tool for transformation force them to too easily diminish the saving powers of baptism. These ambitions come to the fore in expressions like "the possibility of a way of life shaped by a positive response to God."[30] There is little space given to Christian practices as a daily way of "dying to sin."

There is also very little focus on what the act of baptism accomplishes, rather the focus is on what baptism presents—in baptism the Christian life is presented fully and finally, visibly, tangibly, and in words. This approach is problematic, for many reasons. It runs the risk of devaluating the work of the triune God in baptism, and it also runs the risk of de-valuating the eschatological character of the Christian community.

Bass and Dykstra also make the radical claim, drawing on Romans 6:3–4, that when baptism is detached from a way of life abundant, as it the case in the Corleone baptism, "the pouring of water accomplishes nothing." Although Bass and Dykstra add that they cannot be sure what becomes of the little godson in *The Godfather*, they seem quite skeptical about his prospects, as "it is clear that the godfather himself has only a life-style of

---

29. In the light of Lutheran theology "sin is what is opposed to God's law." M. Root, "Continuing the Conversation," 57.

30. Dykstra and Bass, "A Theological Understanding of Christian Practices," 16.

abundance, not a way of life abundant, however impressive the riches and might he secures for himself."[31] This rather unsupported claim also makes it harder to safeguard against the notion that Christian practices are just another way of being saved by works. But this approach to the Corleone baptism raises a whole range of questions: Why is the Corleone baptism necessarily an abuse of baptism, and if it is an abuse, what does the abuse consist of? And finally: how can we be sure that "the pouring of water accomplishes nothing" if it is detached from a way of life abundant?

Kenda Creasy Dean does not make any clear link between faith and baptism. Likewise she does not focus on faith in more classical terms as *fiducia*—(God-given) trust. Dean seems to think of faith as an inherent slumbering quality or potential within every human being. The role ascribed to baptism in relation to Christian practices is in many ways parallel to the role of the Eucharistic. The sacraments are "feeding stations" for the Christian in his or her sanctification. They are part of the identity formation task—to let sanctifying grace make possible the *imitation* of Christ. In other words, they are means of "divine self-communication, in which God bestows sanctifying grace that makes imitating Christ possible."[32]

In her eagerness to see identity formation as transformation, Dean emphasizes development and growth in the Christian life. The problem here is the tendency to see Christian practices merely as tools of Christian identity formation. But at the same time Dean's approach to Christian practices may serve as a fruitful "counter-critique" to the Lutheran tradition. Dean's approach resonates in part with Swedish theologian Anna Karin Hammar's attempt to develop an authentic baptismal theology in the tension between interpreting the tradition and the situation.[33] Hammar suggests that by making the baptism of Jesus formative for Christian baptism, the baptismal paradigm of dying and rising with Christ is challenged by the paradigm of baptism as new birth. The latter paradigm is, according to Hammar, a more authentic paradigm in a late modern context, as it corresponds better to contemporary challenges related to justice, peace, and the integrity of creation. Hammar even finds that by focusing on baptism as new birth it also has the advantage of making for ecologically sound "foot-prints" in Sweden. It also grasps the particular

---

31. Ibid., 30–31.
32. Dean, *Practicing Passion*, 136.
33. Hammar, *Skapelsens Mysterium*, 27–39.

sociological traits of Sweden as marked both by individualism and social welfare and social care in a better way.[34]

Bryan Spinks, whose work Hammar uses, writes about the relationship between the two chief baptismal metaphors, baptism as *tomb* and baptism as *womb*:

> In many of the rites the theme of rebirth/regeneration and font as womb predominate, and although the death/resurrection theme of Romans 6 is frequently present, it usually takes second place; womb, not tomb is the major focus. The theme of repentance took on a deeper meaning in the West through the theological influence of St Augustine, though the dramatic renunciation found in the classical rites shows that rejection of sin and evil was always an important theme. In the Eastern rites, though, the emphasis was on restoration of the old Adam in Christ rather than concern with Original Sin.[35]

The problem with Hammar's attempt is that although she quite rightly re-introduces the *womb* (baptism as new birth) as an *additional* paradigm and "shift of emphasis" as opposed to the *tomb* (baptism as dying and rising with Christ), she uses the new birth paradigm to formulate an *alternative* baptismal anthropology. Instead of speaking about original sin or "inherited sin" (cf. the German "Erbsünde" and the Swedish "arvsynd") Hammar introduces a counter concept—"inherited responsibility." Here Hammar seems to neglect that Spinks underlines how the dramatic renunciation found in the classical baptismal rites shows that rejection of sin and evil has always been an important theme. One possible outcome of this anthropology—and its inherent cosmology—is that baptism as a soteriological practice is confused or even jeopardized. The lack of soteriology in this conception of baptismal theology is evident, as "the baptized person is seen not as having been liberated from the guilt of original sin but rather as having been equipped for encountering destruction in life and society."[36] In Hammar's scheme *practicing baptism*, or Christian practices in general, is something which takes place only on the economy of creation, not on the economy of salvation.

This approach, although claiming in its preface to be Lutheran, runs into serious conflict with important features in Lutheran baptismal

---

34. Ibid., 220–21.
35. Spinks, *Early and Medieval Rituals and Theologies of Baptism*, 158.
36. Hammar, *Skapelsens Mysterium*, 222.

theology—chiefly how Luther equates practicing baptism with penance. Both the baptismal event as soteriological drama and baptism as the act through which the Holy Spirit is given, are downplayed to such an extent that it becomes problematic in the light of Lutheran baptismal theology. If this is an attempt to propose an additional baptismal paradigm, the main problem occurs in the way a realistic Lutheran anthropology is neglected here, and as a result of this, there is no real need for a soteriology. Inherent in this anthropological fallacy is the way this theology fails to address radical evil, although it claims to take an incarnational approach, rather than a monistic or a dualistic approach.

As a complementary approach, however, Hammar's proposal may be an important contribution in the context of ministry. *Practicing baptism* is about fighting for justice, peace, reconciliation and a sustainable ecological development, as baptism restores our relationship to God and the created world, as Hammar quite rightly outlines. But human beings' inherited responsibility does not come (first) through baptism, it is in a certain way liberated through baptism, as the baptized self through baptism is freed to live a new life in Christ and in the neighbor.

Lutheran theology may run the risk of developing a too narrow language for baptismal theology. The strength of Hammar's proposal is that it highlights some of the neglected aspects of the concept *practicing baptism*. But by letting a certain interpretation of baptism as new birth define anthropology as a whole, *practicing baptism* becomes a first use of the law—defined in the light of eco theology. The problem arises however when the additional baptismal paradigm of the "womb" is used to formulate an alternative anthropology.

The baptismal theology Hammar develops creates an unnecessary dichotomy. The dying-and-rising paradigm does not have to exclude interpreting baptism as new birth, quite the opposite. It is by developing the *interconnectedness* between baptism as a "womb" and as a "tomb" that the full breadth of the concept *practicing baptism* may be developed. As Bryan Spinks points out, Luther links the death/resurrection theme with the regeneration theme in his 1519 treatise *The Holy and Blessed Sacrament of Baptism*.[37] In the biblical narratives the metaphors of the womb and the tomb are closely united, as in Romans 6. The reason Hammar comes to this conclusion is probably her ambition to perform

---

37. Spinks, *Reformation and Modern Rituals and Theologies of Baptism*, 4–5. LW 35:30: "The significance of baptism is a blessed dying unto sin and a resurrection in the grace of God, so that the old man, conceived and born in sin, is there drowned, and a new man, born in grace, comes forth and rises."

a "non-exclusive theological approach" to baptism and baptismal theology. Therefore baptism for Hammar is chiefly baptism into "communion with all of life and with all humanity." Because of this Hammar labels this concept "particular universalism," but it is hard to see the particularity of the inherent ecclesiology.[38]

In the context of post-Christendom ministry, and youth ministry in particular, a retrieval of baptismal theology must address the question of radical evil and make use of baptismal theology in its fullness in order to argue why the new birth in baptism is needed in the first place. Fundamentally communion with all human beings is something that takes place with our first birth—on the economy of creation—although the new birth in baptism strengthens this tie of solidarity with all humanity. Hereby the particularity of baptismal anthropology and soteriology (and hence also ecclesiology) may not be neglected.

Human Agency in Christian Practices

The role of human agency in Christian practices is something, which requires further discussion. Craig Dykstra claims that to come to faith implies recognizing that "the context of all our growing and living is the world in which, over which, and through which the Spirit of God known in Jesus Christ reigns."[39] Maybe there is a parallel here between Hütter and Dykstra, as Hütter speaks about how the Holy Spirit is the true subject of the church's core practices, whereas Dykstra speaks about how Christian practices may be "habitations of the Spirit"?[40]

In much of Protestant theology, the eschatological reality of the "new creation" is fully present in the word as promise, but in the present world still hidden as its own future. Therefore Hütter in an article in 2007 argues that one way to describe the central issue at stake between Catholic and Orthodox theologies on the hand and most of Protestantism on the other hand is what kind of reality the Spirit's agency effects in the Christian life. Hütter notes that for both Catholics and Wesleyans, the essence of perfection is love. This leads him to critically examine some of the Lutheran approaches to the Spirit's agency in the Christian life. In relation to the discussion of the theology of the *Joint Declaration* (1998),

38. Hammar, *Skapelsens Mysterium*, 221–22.
39. Dykstra, *Growing in the Life of Faith*, 37.
40. Ibid., 78.

Hütter argues for a connection between Methodist/Reformed theology and Catholic theology, as opposed to a "stricter" Lutheran approach. This becomes evident, particularly in the anthropology. Hütter here points to the still ongoing theological controversy whether original sin in the baptized constitutes a mere potency (JDDJ 2000: §30) or an active reality to be ended an overcome only with the person's death.[41]

Hütter places himself, at least in his 2004 *Bound to be Free*, in the Calvinist tradition, or more precisely Lutheran theologians who draw primarily upon Luther's treatise *On Good Works* (1520). Such a theological approach tends to promote a (more) spiritual interpretation of the Decalogue as "the blueprint for good works engendered by faith active in love." Hütter finds, pointing to the contributions of Joest (1967) and Jüngel (1988) that most genuine Lutheran accounts of the Christian life, there is no conceptual integration of *passio* and *cooperation*; no relationship between "the believer suffering the Spirit's ongoing salvific agency at the very centre of the Christian life on the one hand and the human mandated to cooperate with God's sustaining agency as creator on the other."[42]

Hütter argues that although these Lutheran accounts rightly focus on the *primacy* and *casual agency* in justifying faith and salvation, because human beings cannot be free agents in their relationship to God in matters of faith because of the condition of sin. For Hütter, these accounts, betray what he sees as a univocal, competitive account of divine and human agential causality. They therefore also fail to appreciate the genuine transcendence of divine causality in the matter of salvation. Therefore Hütter opts for a non-competitive account of divine and human causality, where "the Christian person, and hence the Christian life, is constituted in the externality of the promissory address of the gospel, which undercuts any notion of a received set of habits intrinsic to the believer's person."[43]

Despite of Hütter's emphasis on the externality of the promissory address of the gospel and its constitutive role for the first-tablet practices, one has to ask critically if the term "practice" in and for itself is so rooted in an Aristotelian understanding of human agency that Christian practices inevitably become righteousness of works. Ivar Asheim points out that Aristotle's virtue ethics is fundamentally

---

41. Hütter, "The Christian Life," 288–89.
42. Ibid., 290–91.
43. Ibid., 293–95.

social or communitarian in its nature, as excellence is realized through community, and as anthropologically speaking man is fundamentally a community being. Asheim interprets the Nichomachian Ethics of Aristotle and finds that justice is a typical virtue, which combines the individual and social aspect of virtue ethics, as justice as a virtue is both something you might inhabit or embody personally, but it is also something, which is realized through community.[44]

Focusing the Christian life through "practices" does not necessarily lead to a righteousness of works. The problem with Hütter's proposal is his failure to distinguish clearly enough between a teleological and an eschatological approach to practices, and the importance of such a distinction to further distinguish between human and divine agency in Christian practices. If I read the 2007-Hütter right, we also disagree on the impact of sin on the life of the Christian. Here I would emphasize, that sin is an ongoing reality.

As noted earlier, there is a paradoxical duality when it comes to the direction of the Christian life: On one hand, the Christian life biographically and (potentially) ethically is *progress (coram hominibus)*. On the other hand, the Christian life is soteriologically and eschatologically *regress (coram Deo)*, by the constant returning to baptism due to the remaining influence of the power of sin and evil. I have therefore argued for understanding human agency in Christian practices as fundamentally God's agency in a double manner: First and foremost it is God's saving agency through the church's core practices (i.e., the diffinitive presence of Christ), and secondly it is God's sustaining agency, making human action possible (i.e., the repletive presence of Christ).

This distinction between human and divine agency in Christian practices may take as its point of departure the fact that the presence of Christ in the heart of the believer is, not a unity in divine essence, but a unity based on the justification of Christ.[45] It is not a mystical union in essence in the Platonic sense. It is based on God's justifying work for us in Christ. Quite simply: Christ in our hearts is Christian justification. This is the focal point of Lutheran mystical theology, and also the focal point for change and ethical renewal in the life of a person, not the contemplation on God's ungraspable essence.[46]

---

44. Asheim, *Hva betyr holdninger*, 35.
45. Braw, *Mystikens arv hos Martin Luther*, 148.
46. Ibid., 235. Cf. also Peters, *Kommentar zu Luthers Katechismen*, 2:208.

In the context of ministry it is important to preach and celebrate the fact that baptism is *the* fundamental, formative act for a communal Christian life.[47] This is a challenge in a culture where authenticity is construed individually. Therefore within the context of ministry there have to be communal ways both of remembering one's baptism, like making the sign of the cross by the baptismal font as a part of the common liturgical life, and of teaching and reflecting on the importance of baptism for the everyday Christian life. This may help to focus on the Christian life as a gift, proclaiming the liberating freedom of God's agency in the baptized.

Furthermore, in ministry, and in youth ministry in particular, distinguishing between human and divine agency is important also in order to link baptism to a theology of hope. *Practicing baptism* is an eschatological concept in the sense that by *practicing baptism* through a daily dying of the old person and the resurrection of the new, we get a foretaste of the hope into which we are baptized, that faith and baptism are historically and eschatologically fundamentally bound together in the present tense of baptism.[48]

Conversion and Christian Practices

I will now turn to another theme, which actualizes the problem of how to understand human agency in Christian practices, namely conversion. In more evangelical and pentacostal approaches, conversion is often more emphasized than in contributions emerging from the more established churches. The question is how to speak of conversion on the basis of baptism and in the light of baptismal theology. Kenda Creasy Dean elaborates on the relationship between conversion and practices, and she claims that the practices themselves may be a sort of conversion.[49]

In Lutheran theology the first conversion is hearing God's Word and calling to repent in baptism, after which follows a daily conversion, a continuous turning to the promises of the triune God in Christ—effectively shaping the life of the Christian through the present tense of baptism. The difference between Dean's concept and a Lutheran approach to conversion is that in Lutheran theology daily conversion is always rooted in

---

47. Ibid., 2:95.
48. Ibid., 2:103, 120.
49. Dean here quotes Hauerwas and Willimon, saying: "Acquiring practices is another way to say conversion" (Dean, *Practicing Passion*, 159–60).

and shaped by baptism and how the triune God moves the Christian in baptismal ways.

One way to relate conversion as transformation to Lutheran theology, in the way the charismatic renewal speaks about it, is through the *Christus Praesens* motif in Luther's theology, that Christ himself is present in faith, and in the way Luther speaks about the use of baptism in the Large Catechism. Luther underlines the daily effects of baptism and maintains that the gifts of baptism will aid the baptized in his or her daily struggle. The concept of rebirth belongs here, as Luther quotes Titus 3:5. But there are also notable differences, for instance in the charismatic renewal's rather ambiguous relationship to the role of baptism as the believer strive to develop a conscious experience about Christ's presence by faith.[50]

Altogether, the different approaches to conversion in relation to Christian practices may be best understood through the difference between the two concepts of *imitatio Christi* and *conformatis Christi*. Dean et al. tend to focus on Christian formation through the concept *imitatio Christi*, whereas I have argued that *conformitas Christi* should be the preferred notion, departing from the concept *practicing baptism* as the *leitmotiv* for the Christian life. Lutheran soteriology always asserts the importance of Christ given for me, for us, the *pro me* and *pro nobis*. Finnish Luther research has shown that this also includes a dynamic approach where Christ is active in the Christian. But this always happens within the notion of *conformitas Christi*.

What then is the defining difference between the two concepts of *imitatio Christi* and *conformitas Christi*? From one perspective the Christian life is a sort of mimicry, in the sense that by performing Christian practices the things Christ commanded are practiced. But again, this happens in the passive form. The practitioner suffers the work of God.[51] The concept *conformitas Christi* underlines that the practitioner is suffering—undergoing—the work of the Holy Spirit. Therefore Christian practices are the fruits of the spirit, not the fruits of human mimicry. The difference is also found in this: *conformitas Christi* is not an ethical practice. It is about the flesh being mortified and resurrected by the Word.

---

50. Antola, *The Experience of Christ's Real Presence in Faith*, 79, 95, 100, 164.

51. This is parallel to how Jenson, based on *The Freedom of a Christian* (1520), finds that, "According to Luther, the soul *becomes* what it *hearkens to*. If the soul attends to the world's solicitations it becomes itself worldly. If it attends to Satan's councils of despair it is rapt into itself. If it attends to the story of God's righteousness it becomes righteous." (Cf. Jenson, *Systematic Theology*, 2:295)

For Luther, therefore, the Holy Spirit lives in the believer according to its essence (*quod substantiam suam*).⁵² Internally the Christian is not wholly transformed, but is, as Luther says, using a standard Augustinian simile, like the injured man in Jesus' parable of the Good Samaritan, who has been lifted up, but is still in need of healing. For Luther this gradual healing is related to baptism.⁵³

Some Luther scholars would claim—based on Luther's *On Good Works* (1520)—that the *unio mystica* of God's presence in the heart may also lead to ethical renewal.⁵⁴ In the *Treatise on Good Works* (1520) Luther starts by proclaiming that "there are no good works except those works God has commanded, just as there is no sin except that which God has forbidden."⁵⁵ Therefore the commandments should be the focus of the Christian. In this treatise Luther also maintains that all good works exist in the work that God does, faith in Christ. And "from faith these works receive a borrowed goodness."⁵⁶

In the context of ministry, Lutheran baptismal theology may address transformation and conversion through the concept of *conformitas Christi*, underlining that for a Christian to "walk as Jesus did" (1 John 2, 5b) is about letting the triune God do his work with the person through Christ. In a success- and performance-oriented culture, to focus the Christian life as a gift in this way is a crucial way to proclaim the gospel of the Christian everyday life. This life is about placing oneself at the "places" where Christ transforms—within the context of those practices through which human beings are conformed to Christ: By letting the old self die and the new self rise in Christ the believer may, through Christ, be set free to practice the Golden Rule—the common order of Christian love, serving their neighbor and stewarding God's created world. In this way *conformitas Christi* may become the starting point for discovering the Christian life as a life for the other, a life under the cross.

---

52. Braw, *Mystikens arv hos Martin Luther*, 143.

53. Root, "Continuing the Conversation," 57.

54. Braw, *Mystikens arv hos Martin Luther*, 91. Cf. here also WA 6:248.14–15: "eitel götliche lust, freud und frid ist da mit allen andern wercken und tugenden."

55. LW 44:23.

56. LW 44:24.

The Seventh Notae Ecclesiae As the Crux of the Concept Practicing Baptism

The seventh mark of the church—the cross, or discipleship in suffering—materially sums up the anthropological and soteriological implications of a Lutheran theology on Christian practices. The seventh mark serves as a material criterion to put the anthropological and soteriological implications in the right place. The problem with the Christian practices paradigm is that the radical aspect of soteriology may be lost. The crucial question in relation to this paradigm, is: Do we really need Christ to be delivered from evil, or is Christ needed first and foremost as a tool to put our identity in the right place?

Dykstra and Bass speak of life abundant in very positive, optimistic terms. But what if life in God may also involve suffering and pain? What if life abundant is not purely good, in the way we picture "good"? Here rooting Christian practices in the concept *practicing baptism*, which finds its final material criterion in the seventh mark, offers an alternative approach to these questions. One of the chief differences between the Christian practices paradigm and a Lutheran approach to practices is that whereas Dean in particular pictures Christian practices as a tool to "produce" steadfast Christian identity, in the Lutheran scheme that identity is from one perspective always radically "new" and "made new" in the present moment. There are even distinct soteriological reasons for why a clear criteriology on how Christ is present, is important.[57]

The seventh mark also shows the difference between the two concepts of *imitatio Christi* and *conformitas Christi*. Christian life is about how believers are modeled – shaped by the triune God – through the Incarnation and baptism. These are events which still shape the present and the future. The Incarnation and baptism are indeed also models, but they are models showing how Christ is working in and on human beings, not models for mimicry.

---

57. Peters, *Kommentar zu Luthers Katechismen*, 4:124.

The Christian practices paradigm	A Lutheran approach to Christian practices
The Incarnation as a model	The Incarnation as the event that models
Baptism as a model	Baptism as the event that models
Imitatio Christi	*Conformitas Christi*
Soft soteriology	Radical Soteriology
Optimistic anthropology	Complex anthropology
Focus on teleology	Focus on eschatology

In the context of ministry this means that baptism becomes the radical source of Christian freedom. This freedom is soteriologically founded, not a mere identity quest. Basically therefore, the difference between a Lutheran approach to the relationship between baptism and Christian practices and the baptismal theology of the Christian practices paradigm is a disagreement on the *what* of baptism. But the freedom emerging from baptismal waters has to be celebrated, for instance, by developing different contextual versions of the fourth core practice, the practice of forgiveness. In the light of Lutheran theology, baptismal freedom may be practiced and preached. The power of baptism is something to *use* throughout life. Baptism as the radical source of the new obedience is also celebrated: All in life becomes a gift—all creation and the neighbor, whom the baptized is freed to serve—as the baptized is sent on a mission of freedom, the freedom to serve. As a result of this, even the enemies may be suffering the common order of Christian love.

WHERE IS THE CHURCH?

The Real Church in a Shifting Context

Is the concept *practicing baptism* really a Christendom concept? The ongoing dissolution of the Christendom paradigm in the Western world is altering the conditions for catechetical training and youth ministry, and it is crucial to ask in which way the more holistic "way of life"-ecclesiology of the Christian practices paradigm challenges the intimate connection between soteriology and ecclesiology in Lutheran theology, where the church is not constituted through her outer boundaries but through her center, the core practices. This chapter sets up a critical dialogue with the ecclesiology of the Christian practices paradigm and Lutheran ecclesiology in an attempt to formulate an ecclesiology superseding the gospel community as a mere episodic community constituted by forensic declarations of justification.

Reformed ecclesiology has traditionally been an ecclesiology focusing on the visible church—the church as the city upon the hill. For such a church the proclamation of what the church is often comes from the holy deeds of God's people, not from God's word. This visible church demonstrates and proclaims the reign of God. The church is supposed to be a lighthouse for the world. Implicit in such an ecclesiology is a rather ambiguous relationship to contemporary culture. Implicit in such an ecclesiology is also the threat that God may withdraw God's presence from his people if they do not obey his commandment.[58]

Bass and Dykstra are eager to underline the universal potential in focusing on (Christian) practices. They explicitly state that they do not focus just on the church. What remains unclear in their approach is whether their account of how practices may be "a coherent and meaningful whole that gets embodied in a shared way of life" is just another way of saying what the church is or what the church could or should have been.[59] The ecclesiology of Bass and Dykstra could lead to the ecclesiological notion that there are really hidden traces of the church in every culture—at least where coherent and meaningful whole gets embodied in a shared way of life.

Focusing on the church as hidden or revealed has recently been challenged by an alternative proposal by Norwegian Lutheran theologian, Harald Hegstad, who proposes that the (visible) church should be understood genuinely as the "real church." Hegstad argues that there is only one church, the real church, and this church is the church which is present in the world and which we may experience. For Hegstad this church is identical with the church to which we confess our faith in the Creeds. Hegstad emphasizes, similar to Bass, Dykstra, and Dean, that the "real" church is fundamentally constituted through Jesus's promise in Matthew 18:20.[60]

---

58. Cf. here John Winthrop's speech "City upon a Hill" from 1630 as a classic example of this. Here Winthrop says that "wee must Consider that wee shall be as a Citty upon a Hill, the eies of all people are uppon us; soe that if wee shall deale falsely with our god in this worke wee have undertaken and soe cause him to withdrawe his present help from us." (Cf. for instance http://www.mtholyoke.edu/acad/intrel/winthrop.htm.) It has to be underlined, though, that although this is an important trace in parts of contemporary reformed ecclesiology, it is not fitting for all of reformed ecclesiology today.

59. Bass, "Ways of Life Abundant," 32.

60. Hegstad, *The Real Church*, 2, 17–20.

Idealized Ecclesiology?

Within the Christian practices paradigm there is a tendency to define the church and the body of Christ as identical terms. I have therefore argued that the ecclesiology of the Christian practices paradigm tends towards an idealized ecclesiology. This ecclesiology seems to be closely connected with the inherent anthropology and soteriology of the paradigm enfolded in the *imitatio Christi* motif. Simply by looking at the questions that guide Dykstra and Dean we can see that there is an idealistic element to it—even hinting at how the church should imitate the inner life of the triune God.[61]

The problem with this tendency—even in ministry—is that this runs the danger of becoming an art of *theologia gloriae*. First of all, the terminology used when describing the contours of this way of life tends to be somewhat idealistic, for instance in the *leitmotiv* the "life-giving way of life." Even more problematic is how a high and optimistic view of the church or the Christian community, at least in its ideal form as a transforming community nurturing and offering a life-giving way of life, is coupled with an equally pessimistic view on culture, in particular consumer culture. What is problematic at times is also that the "way of life" ecclesiology identifies the Christian community as Christ's body in the world to such an extent that there is little room for ecclesiological complexity. The church as the body of Christ, the way it is outlined within the Christian practices paradigm, tends to picture this body in ideal terms without any notable failure—or even sin.

All in all, the optimistic anthropology, the soft soteriology and the idealized ecclesiology of the Christian practices paradigm reveals a tendency towards a realized eschatology. The authors are generally eager to see the transformation towards a life-giving way of life here and now. Whether this is due to a sort of cultural blindness, or if it is because there are few publications within the Christian practices paradigm that include studies of actual Christian communities, unfolding how messy and complicated congregational life may be, is hard to tell.

---

61. Cf. for instance Dykstra, "Pastoral and Ecclesial Imagination," 60: "How can, and how do our lives and our life together participate in a way of life that reflects the Life of God, both when we are gathered as church and when we are dispersed into countless disparate circumstances? What is the shape of the contemporary life that truly is life-giving in and for the sake of the world? And how can the church foster such a way of life, for the good of all creation?"

Two quotes from Dorothy C. Bass challenge my criticism here, however. She underlines that "because communities engage in given practices in a wide range of circumstances, the variety and creativity in precisely how they are performed in specific settings is enormous," and even, more importantly, she maintains that "because communities engage in these practices forever imperfectly—faltering, forgetting, even falling into gross distortions—theological discernment, repentance, and renewal are necessary dimensions of each practice and of the Christian life as a whole."[62] Particularly the last quote points in the direction of themes that could correct the tendency towards an idealized ecclesiology within the Christian practices paradigm.

Even within the Lutheran camp of the practices conversation there are approaches, which may bring about challenges. Martha Ellen Stortz sums up the role of the so-called resurrection practices. According to Stortz, they define where the church is to be found.

> Wherever you find people baptizing, there you find the body of Christ in the world. Wherever you find people breaking bread together in the name of Jesus, there you find the body of Christ. Wherever you find people forgiving and being forgiven, there you find the body. Wherever you find people honoring their dead in memory of the one who was raised from the dead, there you find the body. Wherever you find people making and keeping promises in imitation of an ever-faithful God, there you find the body.[63]

The problem with this proposal is the focus on the church as mere imitation, instead of *conformitas Christi* as the starting point for imitation. Here actually Radical Lutheranism may contribute to developing an ecclesiology for engaging Christian practices in the context of ministry. The positive side of Radical Lutheranism is its focus on how to use the promise of baptism in combination with the seventh mark, the cross. Therefore, *practicing baptism* is about getting involved in suffering—in the everyday troubles and joys of both young and old. The promise of the triune God in baptism gives us a mandate, a commission, to enter into suffering, because in baptism the triune God has given the baptized the gift to nag God for the rest of his life. In this sense, *practicing baptism* is a bit like Jacob's fight with God's angel in Genesis 32:21–32.

62. Bass, "Ways of Life Abundant," 29.
63. Stortz, *A World According to God*, 163.

In ministry, and youth ministry in particular, it is important to pay attention to these tensions. In the abyss of suffering that some people experience, coining the concept *practicing baptism* through the seventh mark of the church, the cross, seems like a viable way forward.[64] Furthermore, making suffering, anthropological complexity and brokenness a test criterion also when it comes to ecclesiology, offers an important critique to ecclesiologies, which tend to over-emphasize the immanent, like Pete Ward's *Liquid Church* (2002).[65] It is also not quite clear how Hegstad's ecclesiological concept, *The Real Church*, relates to these tensions.

The Church As Both Communio Sanctorum and Congregatio Sanctorum

In the Lutheran tradition, as in many others, the church can be defined both as *communio sanctorum* and *congregatio sanctorum*, both as a fellowship transcending time and place and as a participatory event.[66] The ecclesiology of the Christian practices paradigm strives to be local and contextual at the same time. But how does it relate to the church as both local and universal, as both *communio sanctorum* and *congregatio sanctorum*? And how should this tension be dealt with in the context ministry?

The engagement in Christian practices appears to be a genuinely ecumenical enterprise. The scholars involved in this discussion come from a wide range of different denominations. However, there is little reflection on the tension between the church as both universal and local. The tendency goes in the direction of a *communio*-ecclesiology. Miroslav Volf makes three points when it comes to how the presence of Christ is linked to local and universal ecclesiologies:

---

64. For an example of how this may be done through preaching in the context of youth ministry, cf. my article Norheim, "Have You Come Here to Play Jesus?"

65. Cf., for instance, Ward's use of immanent, rather than salvific-economic trinitarian theology (and the concept *perichoresis*) as a role model for how the church should flow or move in a liquid, contemporary culture. This may also potentially lead towards an idealized ecclesiology, with a diaconal-ecclesiological deficit. Ward, *Liquid Church*.

66. For an extensive, historical overview of the different ways to translate and interpret *sanctorum communionem/communio sanctorum*, see Paul, "Sanctorem communionem." For a discussion of this tension in the context of Nordic youth ministry and in the light of Lutheran baptismal theology, cf. Norheim "Practicing Baptism: The Church as Communio and Congregatio Sanctorum."

1. The whole of Christ is present through Christ's Spirit in every congregation assembling in Christ's name to profess faith in him—and so every church is "independent" or "self-complete"—the independence of a local church does not mean that other churches are denied in every instance the right to intervene in its life.

2. The very presence of Christ through the Spirit, which makes each local church "independent" of other churches, simultaneously connects churches with one another.

3. Professing faith in Jesus Christ as universal Savior and Lord implies, as well as openness on the part of the church to all human beings.[67]

Based on this, Volf defines the nature of the church by focusing on the open and welcoming assembly in the name of Jesus, where baptism and the Lord's Supper is celebrated. Further Volf claims that it is the presence of Christ, which constitutes the church, and this presence is mediated through the whole congregation. Volf therefore finds that when focusing on the particular presence of Christ and the Spirit, it is fair to say that wherever the Spirit of Christ is present in its *ecclesially constitutive* activity, there is also the church.[68]

But how does the concept *practicing baptism* relate to Volf's ideas here? Volf claims that "on the basis of a common baptism, all Christians have become priests and all realize their priesthood in their own way on the basis of their respective charismata."[69] This is in line with how Robert W. Jenson underlines that the gifts bestowed by baptism are not mysterious endowments inserted into the interiority of the individual. Rather, the gifts of baptism belong to the baptized individual only as a member of the church, as these gifts are the several aspects of the Spirit who gives himself to the church.[70]

For Volf, baptism makes the human being into an ecclesial being.[71] Volf, more than many of the other theologians in the practice(s) discussion, elaborates on the ecclesiological consequences of this: Baptism gives the baptized a new identity, because the baptized becomes a mem-

---

67. Volf, "Community Formation as an Image of the Triune God," 218.
68. Cf. ibid., 219, 213, 231, 215.
69. Ibid., 235.
70. Jenson, *Systematic Theology*, 2:196.
71. Volf, *After Our Likeness*. Volf, along with Hütter, joins in Zizioulas's understanding of this.

ber of a new community. It is not possible to be initiated into Christian faith without being socialized into the life of a Christian church.[72] Volf underlines this programmatically by saying that in baptism you become a Christian, in the Eucharist you live as a Christian.[73] Baptism is formative for the new life in Christ, which is a pilgrimage.[74] But Volf concludes, based on Trinitarian theology that :

> A participative model of the church, therefore, requires more than just values and practices that correspond to participative institutions. The church is not first of all a realm of moral purposes. Rather, it is the anticipation, constituted by the Spirit of God, of the eschatological gathering of the entire people of God in communion of the triune God.[75]

But what does this participative model of church look like in ministry? In all this it is important to keep in mind that the confession stating the belief that we believe in the "*sanctorum communionem*"/"*communio sanctorum*" has always been complex, and never uniform. But in these individualistic times, there might be a psychological need for the church to be united with those who have advanced further, who have reached fullness, in order, departing from where we are, to enter the same path with them.[76] In that sense, a participative model of church is radically an eschatological model of church.

Such an eschatologically founded ecclesiology leads to a radical openness in ministry. In a sermon on 1 Timothy 1:5–7 on the Sum of the

---

72. Ibid., 173. Cf. also: "The invisible church—*communio sanctorum*—exists concretely only in the plurality of visible churches, which is why membership in the invisible church is bound to membership in a visible church. A person cannot be fully initiated into the Christian faith without being socialized into a Christian church." Volf elaborates further on this: "The church cannot simply be a social organism, since a person is not simply born into it, but rather is *reborn*. Christian faith presupposes personal faith with its cognitive and volitional dimensions, which is why associative elements are essential for the social structure 'church.' Hence as I understand it, the church is a mixture of the social type that Max Weber called 'church' into which a person is born, and the social type he called 'sect', 'which a person freely joins'" (ibid., 180).

73. Ibid., 42, 152–53.

74. Ibid., 199–200.

75. Volf also points out that classical free church ecclesiology takes as its point of departure Jesus' words in Matthew 18:20. Volf, "Community Formation as an Image of the Triune God," 235, 216.

76. Paul, "Sanctorem communionem," 59.

Christian Life (1532), Luther writes about the Sunday Mass that "all who are assembled together are assembled in real and high service of God."[77] The celebration of the real presence of Christ in the mass constitutes the sending of the Messianic community—a mission—to the world, where the movement of baptism is more than just a model.[78] This radical, eschatological openness of ministry is formative for an ecclesiology of Christian practices in the context of ministry.

Moreover, in ministry the celebration of Christ's victory over death and the powers of evil in the mass may be a helpful point of departure. Ultimately, a Christian ethical identity is a liturgical identity. Bernd Wannenwetsch, based on Charles Taylor and Alasdair MacIntyre's narrative approach to identity, claims that ethical identity springs from worship, and it is "performative" and "homologous."[79] It is the constant rehearsal of this performance that needs to be nurtured in ministry in order to develop such a narrative identity, much in line with the U-shaped, narrative identity that I outlined earlier in this book.

Ultimately, Luther understood the church as a fellowship of people recognized by mutual participation and sharing in the gifts of the triune God. In the light of Lutheran theology, therefore, the *communio* and the *congregatio sanctorum* are intimately interrelated: This implies that the church as *communio* is defined through its *congregatio*, and the church as *congregatio* is rooted in its *communio*. This double ecclesiological reality is defined through baptism in an exemplary way. As the birthplace of faith, baptism frees the baptized from the grip of sin and death and opens creation anew, and makes the baptized one with God and his people. Founded in God's grace and the power of the death and resurrection of Christ through baptism, the baptized are free to receive life as gift and as a *vocatio*, a calling to serve Christ in every aspect of life.

Ministry in this shifting world has to realize that it is often perceived as one out of many activities in the evolving market of spare-time activities. The hope for such a ministry is how it re-imagines community by

---

77. LW 51:261

78. Cf. here how A. Root advocates, with Bonhoeffer: "If the church is to be the concrete place of Christ in the world, the church must refuse sectarian exclusion from the world. Rather, just as the community is upheld by the distinct relationships of people within the church, in the same way the church community, to remain community, needs the world to serve as its counterpart, the place where the church discovers its own distinction in care, service and love for the world" (A. Root, *Revisiting Relational Youth Ministry*, 110).

79. Wannenetsch, *Political Worship*, 221.

engaging the tradition—i.e. the marks of the church—in dialogue with the particular context. Here the meal of Jesus Christ could function for some people as a first encounter with the gospel.[80]

Christian Practices—Mission or Maintenance?

What kind of (young) people are usually targeted with the focus on Christian practices? Very many of the Christian practices projects in the US, like *Way to Live*, *On Our Way* and *Practicing Passion*, involve parents (theologians) who engage in the faith and way of life of their children. But one question remains largely unanswered within this conversation: How should it influence a theology of Christian practices if the practicing community consists of mainly non-baptized participants?

Dean claims to write from a missional perspective, but she hardly discusses what practices are needed in a situation where most of the young people are not baptized or are unfamiliar with faith. Dean addresses a context where most young people are related to church in one way or another. She does not explicitly discuss whether her proposal should be outlined differently in a setting where the vast majority of adolescents are either unbaptized or are absolutely unfamiliar with Christian faith and life.

It seems that so far the focus on Christian practices in ministry does not put sufficient emphasis on those who do not come to church, or youth group or grow up in a so-called Christian family. Critically one may therefore ask: Is the focus on Christian practices really a maintenance strategy or a mission strategy? Do the practices have a more distinct missional side? Is the formation of a Christian practices program just another "come to us" thing? Ecclesial maintenance strategies are very often fear-driven and anxiety-driven strategies as organizations focusing on maintenance tend to spend most of their time, energy, and other resources on self-preservation.[81] So what is really "the missional impetus" in the Christian practices paradigm?

There is an obvious link here to the tension between the church as *communio* and *congregatio sanctorum*. This may be a particular challenge in a Europe, where there has been a long history of state-church relations. The whole engagement in Christian practices challenges the idea of what it means to be church, and especially to what extent the church should be

---

80. Lathrop and Wengert, *Christian Assembly*, 131.
81. Hamm, *Leadership for a Postmodern Age*, 63. 63.

understood as something particular, something different from the (nation) state, as there is an inherent claim on the particularity of the church in the Christian practices paradigm. John Howard Yoder maintains that in Paul's proclamation of the universality of the Gospel on Areopagos in Acts 17, "there is no backing away from the particularity of the Jesus story, no soft-pedaling of the missionary imperative."[82]

Is *practicing baptism* then a Christendom model? It can be, if baptismal theology is used to avoid elaborating the distinctiveness or particularity of a life rooted in baptism, as is the case in Hammar's proposal. Here the attempt to develop a non-exclusive baptismal theology, maybe unintentionally, is used to advocate a secular Christendom model, where it is difficult to claim that baptism may be the foundation of the church modeled as a community of disciples, a community which may also be potentially counter-cultural.[83]

But *practicing baptism* does not have to be a Christendom concept or model. Quite the contrary, rooting the concept *practicing baptism* in a distinct Lutheran understanding of the (diverse) presence of Christ paves the way for an ambitious Lutheran, missional ecclesiology. Combining the *simul* structure of the presence of Christ, that Christ is both radically present in all of creation in the repletive mode and radically present in the core church practices according to his diffintive-salvific mode, could be a starting point for a missional ecclesiology. Such a theology would both acknowledge the importance of the local culture and context, and the importance of the particular practices of the Christian community.

What then are the contours of the concept *practicing baptism* as a missional imperative? Here I will sketch out very briefly three focal points in the developing of missional ministry in an emerging post-Christendom context, where *practicing baptism* serves as a guiding principle or concept.

Forgiveness and reconciliation: Human diversity is both a result of creation design (created as men and women), but also the result of living in a fallen world. From this perspective, *practicing baptism* also means

---

82. Yoder, *Body Politics*, 39.

83. Dulles argues that discipleship after Easter, due to the (repletive) presence of Christ, is "a broader one, since Christ can now be found in every place and situation." There is an obvious link from this to the so-called discipleship model of church: "The discipleship model motivates the members of the church to imitate Jesus in their personal lives. It also makes them feel at home in a Church that must always find its way in a rapidly changing and fluid situation, a pilgrim Church still distant from its goal" (Cf. Dulles, *Models of the Church*, 216, 214).

discovering new ways of being church, where a new type of mutuality evolves. Based on Galatians 3:27–28 baptism formats the church as a fellowship based on a "Christological mutuality" between men and women, between older and younger, between slaves and masters, between Jews and Gentiles.[84] *Practicing baptism* is therefore practicing the change inherent in being a fellowship in Christ. By *practicing baptism* we therefore practice the power of the resurrection. This also brings us on a journey of reconciliation. The most obvious starting point for this is Pauline baptismal theology: In Galatians 3:27–28 baptismal theology is the starting point for a reconciling mission in the name of Christ, in whom we have all become one. *Practicing baptism* is therefore practicing reconciliation.

Re-imagining new ways of being church: There is potentially a strong missional move in baptismal theology.[85] At the same time the confessional identity, which arises from the baptismal community in post Christendom is increasingly something *liminal*, and the missional baptismal community becomes a *communitas*.[86] In such a context re-imagining new-old ways of being church is part of rediscovering the missional imperative in the concept of practicing baptism. This is a particular challenge in nation-state churches where the old parish structures do not necessarily allow for the potential missional flow in the concept. Ultimately, this must include opening up for a more pro-active mixed economy when it comes to ecclesial fellowships, where the church as a *communitas*—a fellowship even for the betwixt-and-between and for the temporary must be explored and given space.[87] Founded in the positive tension between the church as *communio sanctorum* and *congregatio sanctorum*—the church is freed to discover its missional baptismal impetus—its *vocatio sanctorum* for the life of the world.

Ora et labora: One possible example of the developing of such a missional identity may be how the practice of baptism opens the language of prayer. Baptism is the ultimate freedom to do nothing to deserve God's grace. Therefore faith becomes an active struggle—an *Anfechtung*—learning how to cling to the promise in the midst of suffering. According to the Large Catechism, using or practicing your baptism is not about turning theory into practice, or making potentiality into actuality (Aristotelian),

---

84. Van Gelder, *The Ministry of the Missional Church*, 28–29.
85. Schlink, *The Doctrine of Baptism*, 78, 81.
86. Cf. Kavanagh, *The Shape of Baptism*, 199–200.
87. Cf. for instance Archbishop's Council, *Mission-shaped Churches*.

but it is to return always to one's baptism, to the promise given in baptism. Returning to one's baptism has a strong performative aspect. Baptism itself is not prayer. Rather it is about performing the Word of baptism. Ultimately, prayer becomes a part of a missional baptismal vocation, where one is given to view life itself as a response to prayer.

Therefore developing and nurturing a missional baptismal vocation in ministry, re-imagining the church as a missional *vocatio sanctorum*, also has to take the *strangeness* of baptism as its point of departure; the fact that in baptism the triune God gets hold of the identity and destiny of the baptized. To live one's baptismal vocation is to expect that the triune God, in whose name baptism takes place, is at work in the baptized and in the world. It is about using the power of baptism against the powers of death, sin and evil. It is for the baptized always to be asking what God calls them to do. An ecumenical approach to this baptismal vocation is voiced in *The Nature and Purpose of the Church* (1998):

> All members of the Church, who on the basis of their common baptism, serve the world by proclaiming the Gospel, testifying to their faith through their way of life, and interceding for the salvation of the world. It is also part of their service to the world to feed the hungry, help the poor and marginalized, correct injustice, and care for the integrity of creation, together with all people of good will. In so doing, they are in harmony with the mission of the Church.[88]

NOT ABOUT PRACTICES AT ALL?

Why Christian Practices in an Emerging Post-Christendom Context?

Where the Christian practices paradigm and the Lutheran baptismal theology differ is in the *what* and *how* of baptism. What then does the *how* of baptism, using one's baptism, really look like? It is about the restoration and the amendment of life. I have argued that *practicing baptism* is about participating in what God does in his larger baptismal movement with the world. It is about being moved by God in baptismal ways.

Baptism and the Incarnation are events modeling Christian discipleship. Fundamentally, this implies at least two things. First of all,

---

88. WCC, *The Nature and Purpose of the Church*, 41.

missional Christian formation in a changing context should be rooted in the daily death-and-life community with the resurrected Christ that starts at baptism. Secondly, based on this, a renewed interpretation of Luther's distinction between the diffinitive and repletive presence of Christ may serve as a guiding principle for the life of the Christian—living as a beggar before God, both receiving and celebrating the salvific presence in the core church practices and honoring and stewarding the enhancement of the world in which Christ is continuously present.

One of the reasons why the Christian practices paradigm has taken on such momentum is because it reflects and resonates with the contemporary context on both sides of the Atlantic: In the churches of the Western world the last three to four decades have witnessed how new generations are not as literate and familiar with the Bible and Christian practices as previous generations. An important reason for this change in Europe is how Religious Education in schools has been altered. The engagement in Christian practices has therefore served as an attempt to recover and rediscover religious language in an emerging post-Christendom context. Another reason for the momentum in the engagement of Christian practices is that the focus on Christian practices has been an attempt to break out of the Kantian theory-practice split.

Comparing the current context in which the engagement in Christian practices is emerging with the context of the *Corpus Christianum* in which the Reformation took place, the contextual differences are noteworthy: Luther aimed to reform an old church complacent and loosing touch with its core identity. Christians in the Western world today are mostly faced with a defined a-religious state and a multi-religious society, in which re-creating communal and corporal Christian identity is *the* challenge. This calls for a more ambitious interest in the shape of Christian life, as the institutions which Luther trusted so deeply—in particular the family, but also schools—have been altered to an extent that in most cases have made them unable to offer faith formation.

Christian Practices Between Form and Freedom

One of the crucial questions related to the way of life-theology of the Christian practices paradigm is the question of form and freedom in the Christian life: Is the Christian life ultimate freedom or a set of spiritual disciplines? Or is this a false way to pose the question? The claim made in this study is that ultimate Christian freedom springs forth when we continually practice—receive—the gifts of God emanating from the center of congregational life—the church's core practices.

Compared with Dykstra's more Reformed scheme on practices, where the practices seem to serve to discipline the life of the Christian and his or her piety, and Dean's scheme where the practices serve as a tool to foster a passionate, cruciform and counter-cultural identity, in the Lutheran scheme there is always something secondary to the discipline that runs from a life formed by (Christian) practices. In the light of Lutheran theology, Christian freedom and faith comes first. This stems from the alien righteousness through the work of Christ, and which is imparted through the church's core practices, where the Holy Spirit is the true subject. The communitarian practices, which foster discipline, for instance in marriage, or in the church or in the realm of the state or public life are always something secondary. But first and foremost these practices, belonging to the second tablet, exist for the sake of the other, for the neighbor, and for the benefit and flourishing of God's will with creation.

In the light of Lutheran theology, a practice may not be particularly Christian but yet still be part of a Christian way of life. Reinhard Hütter emphasizes that the Christian life is life with the triune God, which is made possible by the life, death, and resurrection of Jesus Christ. This is a life of faith, hope, and charity, which is exercised in prayer, worship, and discipleship. Hütter also finds that there is ecumenical consensus to interpret the Christian life first and foremost from a pneumatological perspective.[89]

However, the question of form and freedom in the Christian life is a complex issue in the light of Lutheran theology. On the one hand, Luther admits that the Commandments are beyond human power to fulfill, but on the other hand he encourages Christians to "just concentrate upon them and test yourself thoroughly, do your very best, and you will surely find so much to do that you will neither seek nor pay attention to any other works or other kind of holiness."[90] Therefore Luther thinks, in line with the Jewish Shema- tradition, that we (the Christians) should keep the Commandments "incessantly before our eyes and constantly in our memory and to practice them in all our works and ways," and that "each of us is to make them a matter of daily practice in all circumstances, in all

---

89. Hütter, "The Christian Life," 285–86.

90. BC, 429.

activities and dealings, as if they were written everywhere we look, even wherever we go or wherever we stand."[91]

Ultimately therefore, one has to take "communtarian" or "pedagogical" considerations in balancing form and freedom in the Christian life. We see this clearly in how Luther deals with the observance of Sunday, Easter, Pentecost, and Christmas. Here Luther states that these days and festivals have been fixed in time in order for people to know when to come together and learn the Word of God. Luther underlines that it is not necessary even to keep these days or to regard it as sinful to do manual labor on them, but altogether it is well to keep them so that all people may know the time at which to assemble and to learn.[92]

The pursuit to re-discover the shape and theological bias for the Christian life as *practicing baptism* cannot rest assured with just referring to piety as a matter of freedom and spontaneity. At best this leaves the church with an individualistic, and even worse; elitist, approach to faith formation. Focusing the Christian life through the concept *practicing baptism* re-constitutes a communal way of church and faith as a way of life. The problem with the rather meta-idealistic attempt to frame Lutheran spirituality as mere spontaneity is that it fails to reckon with the concreteness of Luther's own approach to things—abundantly expressed in his Sermons and in the Catechisms. In the end this approach to Christian life may make the church sloppy when it comes to regaining the true freedom of a Christian. This is the radical freedom to love your neighbor based on the "happy exchange" where Christ becomes you and you become Christ—for nothing.

Developing Lutheran baptismal theology in the tension between the cyclic and the linear motif opens the way for a more narrative approach to the Christian life. In the light of such a baptismal theology the Christian life is an eschatological comedy, a story about hope, founded in the hope of baptism—the promise of the Christological movement from

---

91. BC, 431.

92. LW 40:304. Another example of this is how in the latter part of the *Visitation Articles* it is emphasized how daily worship in the churches should be conducted and how children should be divided in groups (divisions) as they learn the Christian faith. The most important element in this is that the teaching of Christian practices and Christian faith always takes into account maturity and experience, but it is interesting to note the role given to liberal arts, such as music, which children of all ages should practice. In teaching the central parts of the catechisms—saying the Lord's Prayer, learning the Ten Commandments and reading the Bible, learning the Creed—form the curriculum. Cf. LW 40:306–20.

death to the resurrection of life. In the light of such a narrative structure the Christian life is both tentative and formative. It is both a life with great freedom and spontaneity and a life shaped by distinct disciplines and practices, constituting and characterizing that freedom. It is both about a steadfast *cyclic* return to the promise of Christ's mercy in baptism, and a more *linear* and more peregrinational perspective on life, discovering the importance of these promises and the new life in Christ within the context of everyday life. In other words, the paradox of form and freedom in the Christian life needs to relate to the Christian life as a narrative, not as list of principles. This is particularly important in the context of ministry, where the developing of a narrative identity may be an important resource.

Growth and Christian Practices

The Christian practices paradigm offers an important challenge to a Lutheran understanding of the Christian life, particularly with regard to change, growth, transformation and conversion in the life of the Christian. One way to approach growth in the life of the Christian is to emphasize *practicing baptism* in narrative terms, the Christian life as an eschatological story. In this sense, the baptismal plot is about how the believer does not go on to anything after baptism, as baptism is the initiation into the community after which there is only the Kingdom. Therefore, the believer never advances beyond his or her baptism but instead falls behind it and must catch up with it.[93] Implicit in this cyclic scheme is also a linear scheme—the biographical narrative of the baptized. From this perspective returning to one's baptism is *always* the same, but for historical-biographical reasons it is *never* the same.

Practicing baptism may therefore, in the light of the linear perspective, be understood as the start of the journey home. Spinks concludes his two-volume history of baptismal rituals and theologies by underlining that baptism is the door into a new community, and that his community is on a journey to a promised land.[94]

Growth in the light of Lutheran baptismal theology has to do with keeping the indicative and the imperative in baptismal theology together.

---

93. Jenson, *Systematic Theology*, 2:297. Jenson here makes use of the new Finnish interpretation of Luther.

94. Spinks, *Reformation and Modern Rituals and Theologies of Baptism*, 211.

Biblical imperatives—like "do not quench the Spirit" (1 Thess 5:19) and "earnestly desire spiritual gifts" (1 Cor 14:1; cf. 12:31)—do not "annul the indicative which is valid because of Baptism, but they rather unfold it."[95] Therefore the logic of the Spirit also shapes the logic of baptism. Although the Spirit has been poured out through baptism, the life of the baptized is a life learning to depend on the constant receiving of the gifts of the Spirit:

> With the outpouring of the Holy Spirit the guarantee has been given for further gifts of the Spirit, gifts which the baptized is permitted to pray for and receive for his service in the church and to the world. It would be wrong to attempt to derive immediate possession of all gifts of the Spirit from the reception of Baptism, even though the baptized has been assigned to the sphere of the Spirit's influence.[96]

Ultimately, therefore, baptism is about being baptized into a whole life shaped by baptism. Quite simply, it is about *practicing baptism*. What may be problematic, however, is if the imperative with which God confronts the baptized is not drawn into the doctrine of baptism. This may lead to a magic understanding of the Spirit's activity and of baptism.[97] *Practicing baptism* is a paradoxical concept in the tension between freedom and obedience, as both Reinhard Hütter—and Edmund Schlink point out. Schlink emphasizes that the activity of the Spirit in baptism is not refuted by the disobedience of the baptized; rather the activity of the Spirit refutes disobedience.[98]

In the context of ministry, therefore, the Christian practices paradigm with its focus on a dynamic-holistic linear approach to the Christian life has important insights to offer in an emerging post-Christendom context. What are missing are clear criteria for distinguishing between

95. Schlink, *The Doctrine of Baptism*, 70.

96. Ibid., 63.

97. Ibid., 69.

98. Ibid., 70. It is from this perspective that Burgess's contribution falls short: Although offering an interesting and more balanced approach to (Christian) practices than many others, Burgess fails to take into account the full potential of baptismal theology. There is a tendency in Burgess's approach to underestimate the cyclic perspective and to interpret the maintaining and fostering of Christian identity only in a linear perspective. Burgess writes: "Baptism represents the beginning of our journey as those on whom God has bestowed an identity. The Lord's Supper represents God's sustenance along the way as well as the heavenly banquet that awaits us at the end" (Burgess, *After Baptism: Shaping the Christian Life*, 18).

the indicative and the imperative of baptism. Such criteria would avoid the unnecessary dissolution of baptismal theology in the claim that the waters of baptism may accomplish nothing. This theme should rather be discussed in the light of the tension between the indicative and the imperative of baptism and in relation to the tension between freedom and obedience that evolves from baptism. In the context of ministry, it is also important to keep in mind that growth and Christian practices have to be rooted in relations. More specifically, a practicing community is also an interpreting and mentoring community, taking into account how different life stories and different life stages influence the way different people approach Christian practices differently.

Too Much Practice?

This study has focused on discussing Christian practices theologically in relationship to ministry. But maybe a theology of ministry should not be about practices at all? Maybe the whole "practice talk" is a dead-end street? In an article in *Christian Century*, William H. Willimon—co-author with Stanley Hauerwas of *Resident Aliens* and *Where Resident Aliens Live*—criticizes the way he and others have focused on Christian practices. He appeals to what he calls a critical Kierkegaardian approach to practices. Willimon's worry is that by giving attention to practices our attention is deflected away from the living God. With this focus on practices Christianity morphs into a species of unbelief, where we take "revelation into our own hands."[99] Willimon's critique has launched a big debate in the blog sphere, which I will not include in the following discussion.

When the practices language is used in an attempt to recover religious language, the practices language may become hegemonic in the sense that it implicitly proposes that it is *only* through practices that we may encounter the present Christ. This is for sure one possible problem with the focus on Christian practices. But Willimon takes the critique too far. His critique of the potential damage of the practice-talk is as one-sided as he claims the same practice-talk to be: Focusing on practicing does not have to dissolve revelation, to put it mildly. In one sense though, it is important to underline that the Christian life is not (only) about (Christian) practices. Reinhard Hütter claims, probably including himself, that

---

99. Willimon, "Too Much Practice," 24.

> For theologians who are committed to substantive and normative notions of apostolicity, catholicity, and sacramentality, . . . the concept of practices always takes second place—albeit possibly an important second place—to the primacy of word, sacrament, apostolicity, and dogma on the one hand and the interiority of the Christian life constituted by the Holy Spirit's activity and shaped by the infused virtues of faith, hope, and love on the other.[100]

With my emphasis on the distinction between first- and second-tablet practices I largely agree with Hütter's point here. Willimon's critique, however, is less focused, and it does not really get to the core of this discussion.

Critically, one may also ask whether focusing on practices in the light of Lutheran baptismal theology is just a new way of *thinking* about practices, or if it also includes a reordering of the way ministry is done. But I will argue that by focusing on Christian practices in the light of a Lutheran theology of the presence of Christ and on baptism, both the theology of Christian practices and the way Christian practices are ordered and practiced in a context may change.

When we discuss the presence of Christ in Christian practices in the context of ministry, it is important to take notice of an alternative approach to interpreting the presence of Christ in ministry. This is found, for instance, in the works of Andrew Root. Root uses the Christology of Dietrich Bonhoeffer to rethink relational (youth) ministry. Root claims that Bonhoeffer's theology helped him discover that "Jesus Christ is concretely present to us in our relational lives, in our person-to-person encounters, in the *I* and *you*."[101] Root claims—quite daringly—that within the relational encounter Christ is concretely present: "Christ is not present as the other person, but because Jesus is the person *who* is incarnate, crucified and resurrected, he stands in between my person and the person I meet in the world." Root here makes use of Bonhoeffer's use of Luther's theology of the cross to advocate that Christ is "in between because he stands for and alongside the other, just as he stands for and alongside me (*pro me*)."[102] Therefore Root makes the claim that "relationships with

---

100. Hütter, "The Christian Life," 298.

101. A. Root, *Revisiting Relational Youth Ministry*, 15.

102. Ibid., 111. Root claims that Bonhoeffer "asserts that God in Christ is concretely present in the church and the world, where persons meet persons in being with and for each other in the construct of I and you." And "Jesus Christ is the *who*

others lead to our mutual transformation into the new humanity of Jesus Christ," and that "we partake in and taste the reality of Jesus Christ through person-to-person social relationships of place-sharing."[103]

For Root, ministry is therefore *not* "about "using" relationships to get individuals to accept a "third thing." Root argues that ministry is about connection, and about sharing in suffering and joy, about persons meeting persons with no secret motives. Therefore (youth) ministry is not about helping kids to be better Christians; it is about helping them become what God created them to be—human. Root claims that a youth ministry that understands relations as a means for influence represents the Christological heresy of docetism, "which believed that Jesus only *appeared to be* human in order to influence us."[104] Root proposes a ministry of place-sharing.[105] In the practice or ministry of place-sharing, Root underlines, "I take the self of the other into my own self," and he continues, stating that "place-sharing demands that I be completely *other* than the other (closed) while being completely for the other (open)."[106]

One possible critique of Root is that this may lead to a mere motif-centered Christian ethics. Here I will only point one crucial element, which is lacking in Root's elaborations—theological premises for speaking about the presence of Christ, and not just in the context of relationships. Root does not distinguish between different modes of presence. Root just continues to state that "for Bonhoeffer, Jesus Christ, and therefore God, is not locked in the past but is present among us now,"[107] and that "when we assert that God is present in Jesus Christ in relationship (not in where we take relationships), we are free, because God's presence is not dependent upon us—it's already a reality."[108] The question that remains unanswered is what kind of presence this relational Christological presence is. Therefore, Root's contribution, focusing on the relational presence of Christ, also needs to be complemented with a sacramental theology of the core church practices.

---

that encounters others through his own person, standing *pro me* for all humanity." Cf. ibid., 140, 170.

103. Ibid., 141, 171–72.
104. Ibid., 79.
105. "Place-sharing" is Root's creative translation of the German *Stellvertretung*.
106. Ibid., 127.
107. A. Root, *Relationships Unfiltered*, 113.
108. Ibid., 115.

However, Root's proposal may serve as a helpful point of departure for developing a theology of Christian practices in ministry: The "practice" of place-sharing is a practice which is not strictly sacramental, but which reflects the gifts of the sacramental community. It is a "practice" which celebrates the interconnectedness between the diffinitive and repletive presence of Christ, who gives himself for the life of the world in the sacraments, and who upholds the world through his constant presence. "Place-sharing" is a practice both celebrating baptism and the Incarnation as events modeling relationship.

In ministry, therefore, the "practice" of place-sharing is important, or focusing the engagement in Christian practices through relations, through mentoring and apprenticeship. But what is also important for a theology of Christian practices is to avoid making a dichotomy between opting either for a "God at the mall" or a "God in the Eucharist" theology. What should be developed is rather a mixed pattern of practices relating to the diffinitive presence and repletive presence of Christ—where the foundational perspective is the *Deus Semper Major*. In the light of this, revelation is not something we produce, rather revelation is like the church's core practices. It is something we suffer. It is a gift. "Suffering" here relates to what Luther calls the seventh mark of the church, the cross: In this world the presence of Christ and the practice of true "place-sharing" is revealed—and hidden—in suffering, in bearing the pain of the other.

Baptism Models Mission—some Concluding Remarks

The engagement of Christian practices in ministry and theological education from the late 1980s to the beginning of the twenty-first century is in many ways an ecclesiological insider critique within the traditional churches in the Western world. The paradigm has been developed as a response to a context where fewer and fewer people have knowledge of the Bible or Christianity as a practicing religion. In such a post-Christendom context it has been claimed that the church has to rethink its catechetical tactics. It has also been emphasized that the church can no longer lean on institutions like the family, or schools, to do catechesis, as many children and youth who come to catechesis in church have no or little knowledge of or experience with Christian faith.

The main advantage of the Christian practices paradigm in this context is its appeal to envision the Christian life as an embodied whole. A part of this holistic approach is also to picture the church fundamentally as a community of disciples. Shifts in time often bring about rethinking and reinventing of the practices and the structure of church. Cardinal Avery Dulles underscores this when he claims that the post-Christendom era re-evokes the pre-Constantine church model, which Dulles labels as a *community of disciples*.[109] According to Dulles, there is a strong "practice" element in this model: This discipleship model not only motivates the members of the church to imitate Jesus in their personal lives, but also it tries to make the member feel at home in a church that strives to find its way as a pilgrim church in a rapidly changing and fluid situation.[110]

Whereas the Christian practices paradigm understands baptism and Incarnation mainly as *models*, in the light of Lutheran theology, the Incarnation and baptism are events *modeling* the Christian life. This distinction is particularly important in the context of youth ministry, as it offers a criteriology and implies an ecclesiology, which draws the contours of a church with a clear center, but with purposely loose or open outer borders. As a result of this, structuring Christian communities socially through Christian practices is both an exercise in form (the first-tablet practices) and in great freedom (second-tablet practices).

The importance of the doctrine of sin in Lutheran theology, the *incurvatus se in se ipsum* of human beings, actually radicalizes the role of baptism and the role of distinctly Christian practices, as these practices liberate the baptized/the practitioner to a new life in Christ—freed to serve and love. Baptism is the source of Christian freedom. This freedom is soteriologically founded, and not a mere identity quest.

A benefit of the concept *practicing baptism* as a concept is how it tries to reformulate baptismal theology in an era of heightened personal autonomy. In the light of "the subjective turn in culture" authenticity is construed radically in an individualistic manner. This represents a particular challenge for a theology of baptism, particularly a Lutheran theology of baptism: The tension here is emphasizing the constituting part of baptism through the promise of Christ, or through the choice of the individual believer. The engagement in Christian practices has obviously served as an attempt to recover a religious language in a shifting context, where the church no longer holds the power of definition by the help of faith formation in schools and families. The fact that these institutions

---

109. Dulles, *Models of the Church*, 204–17.
110. Ibid., 214.

have been altered calls for a more ambitious interest in outlining the shape of the Christian life. In such a context, developing the concept *practicing baptism* has also been an attempt to rethink the importance of baptism and a life shaped by baptism.

My basic conclusion in this book is therefore that the concept *practicing baptism* envisions what it means to live a mature Christian life. *Practicing baptism* paves the way for a life where the triune God moves the baptized in baptismal ways, always dying and rising to a life shaped by giving and forgiving. There are several examples of how the concept *practicing baptism* envisions the shape of the Christian life in a more complex and comprehensive way than the concepts of *practicing passion* or *the life-giving way of life*. The concept *practicing baptism* is, as noted above, based on an engagement of Lutheran Incarnation theology, Lutheran baptismal theology, and partly also Lutheran creation theology. One of the chief findings here, by engaging the theory of different modes of presence and Luther's theory of *notae ecclesiae* in *On the Councils and the Church*, was how to distinguish between the diffinitive and the repletive mode of presence of Christ (in practices), and further between the first- and second-tablet practices.

This is important in a Western, post-Christendom context, as these distinctions allow for a more positive and constructive approach to contemporary culture than the Christian practices paradigm offers, as exercising the common order of Christian love through second-tablet practices is a very flexible exercise. At the same time this flexible approach happens without neglecting the importance of particular and distinct Christian practices.

Another important contribution from Lutheran baptismal theology to the engagement in Christian practices is that Christian practices do not bring Christ into the world, but through the church's core practices, the marks of the church, Christ acts on and in the practitioner. By distinguishing between the repletive and the diffintive presence of Christ, and by distinguishing between first-tablet and second-tablet practices, the distinction between practices on the economy of salvation and on the economy of creation is clarified. This also makes the distinction between human and divine agency in Christian practices clearer.

By making *practicing baptism* the guiding principle it is suggested that practices both of the first and the second tablet are Christian practices because they are a part of the triune God's baptismal movement with the world. Christian practices of the second tablet are not by necessity

Christian, but they may be(come) Christian practices when the triune God through these practices moves us in baptismal ways: Through death to restoration of life in Christ. On the other hand, the focus on an ecclesiological continuum, a holistic community, and not an episodic ecclesiolgy is the most important contribution from the paradigm to a Lutheran understanding of practices.

Engaging Christian practices in ministry has to be rooted in a missional view of what it means to be church. *Practicing baptism* is about being sent. It is about living by the grace of God for the life of the world. *Practicing baptism* is therefore a pneumatological missional concept, as the logic of the Spirit shapes the logic of baptism. Through baptism the Holy Spirit assigns the believer to Christ, and the same Spirit gives the believer a share in Christ's righteousness, holiness, life and glory. But since God's love in Christ through baptism has reached out to the world, no one should or has the right to keep the Spirit's gifts for himself.[111]

Finally, a missional baptismal theology unites the *womb*- and *tomb*-motif in baptismal theology. The potential dichotomy between the womb- and tomb-motif, including the anthropological implications of this dichotomy, is challenged. Therefore baptism and the Incarnation are the focal points of the *Missio Dei*. The Incarnation and baptism are both events that models and the models for what the triune God is doing in the world. The way the triune God continues to move his creatures in baptismal ways is a constant reminder that the gift of baptism is always both behind us (as a salvific promise) and before us (as an eschatological promise).

The pneumatological constitution of the Christian life arises from baptism. Ultimately therefore, baptism gives Christian life its indelible Christian character and is the source for ecumenical dialogue, as baptism is the initiation into the Christian life, and the sacramental seal of its eschatological character. This also implies that "every ecumenical step toward full agreement about the nature of baptism entails an increasing convergence on the nature of the Christian life."[112] The concept *practicing baptism* may therefore have a great ecumenical potential. Here even the radical openness of the outer borders of the community, which I have outlined previously, may serve as a help to start a dialogue on the different understandings of the nature and shape of the congregational center.

---

111. Schlink, *The Doctrine of Baptism*, 61–62.

112. Hütter, "The Christian Life," 300. Hütter here refers to Root and Saarinen, eds., *Baptism and the Unity of the Church*.

Concretely, this means that a common baptism should form the common ground for ecumenical interaction on Christian practices.

5

The Diaconal Telos of Christian Practices

SOMETHING IN THE WAY CHURCH MOVES

Where do We go from Here?

ONE OF THE MORE pressing questions in a religiously plural, post-Christendom context is the question "what do Christians do?" Fundamentally, the concept *practicing baptism* is an attempt to answer that question. With the concept *practicing baptism*, it is underlined that human beings are at the receiving end of practices, even when we look at the second-tablet practices: First of all, human beings' ability to practice in the first place is a gift. It comes as a result of the sustaining presence of the triune God, the giver of life. It is in this regard we speak of the presence of Christ according to his repletive presence. But secondly, human beings are at the receiving end of the second-tablet practices as their *telos* is diaconal. They are Christian, insofar as they serve the other.

The different circles of Christian practices therefore sketch out the social embodiment of the new self rising from baptism. The first circle of practices sketches out what this new self does by receiving (the first tablet practices). The second circle of practices sketches out what this new self may do (the second tablet practices). *Practicing baptism* is the movement of a life where the triune God moves the baptized in baptismal ways, always dying and rising to a life shaped by giving and forgiving. It is about living in Christ for the sake of the created world and the neighbor. Growing up as a Christian is growing up to be founded, over and again, in the promise of adoption to sonship (Rom 8:15). On the basis of this the baptized always returns to the gifts of God—gifts which by their nature and purpose opens the world and sends "the gifted" on a mission to face Christ in the neighbor, in suffering, and in all of creation.

This interpretation of the relationship between baptism and Christian practices and their interplay in constructing the (Christian) self also emphasizes a more ambitious missional impetus in engaging Christian practices in the context of practical ministry. It attempts to dissolve the dichotomy between church and contemporary culture, by insisting on the different modes of the presence of Christ, and how rooting the identity of the (baptized) self in the first tablet-Christian practices inevitably results in a missional sending to and for the world. This is particularly important in an emerging post-Christendom climate, where the particularity of the church has to avoid being captured in narrow sectarian terms.

In this final—and short—epilogue to the book I will sketch out the main implications of the argument that second tablet-Christian practices have a diaconal *telos*, that they are crucial to the church's service for the neighbor and the world, the larger, horizontal movement of the church and God's people in the world.

Practicing the Gift of Receiving

The whole Christian life is imbued with a gift character. This is basic to the concept *practicing baptism*. This implies that in relation to the triune God, both on the economy of creation and on the economy of salvation, human beings are *made receivers*. Therefore *practicing baptism* is about letting oneself be made a receiver, a beggar, over and over again. This opens up for a radically new approach to human freedom, which is a theme of great importance in the light of the subjective turn and heightened personal autonomy. In the light of the subjective turn of culture, freedom is defined in highly individualistic terms. *Practicing baptism* means exercising a narrative counter to the subjective turn. In baptism my ultimate freedom is a gift that I cannot produce, only receive, and through that act of freedom—salvation!—I am freed to a life where I am free to be bound and belong to my neighbor and the world. The Christian life is to *dramaturgically* practice your baptism as promise and gift—for freedom and for the benefit of the neigbor.

The concept *practicing baptism* offers a different narrative of freedom than that of the subjective turn. Rooted in the sacramental gift of baptism, that Christ becomes one with the sinner for nothing through the power of his death and resurrection, Christian freedom becomes the story about how to lose oneself. It is the story of the self, surrendered to Christ, the self that is freed through the process of becoming Christ-like (Rom 8:29). The big task in ministry, as in other contexts, is how to learn to exercise, or practice, this freedom in situations of ethical complexity, which is particularly important ministering to youth and young adults.

Ultimately, baptism restores life and liberates to a new life for the sake of the world. *Practicing baptism* continuously by celebrating the Lord's Supper also sets a new pattern or economy for consumption, replacing the usual consumer narrative.[1] This is not without relevance for an eco-sensitive young generation, but more importantly, crucial in sustaining creation in times of an ecological crisis. But this has nothing to do with becoming a better Christian. It is never about excelling in faith *coram Deo*. It is always about being a better human being: a better father, a better co-worker, a better neighbor, a better friend. Therefore *practicing baptism* is fundamentally related to *the gospel of renunciation*: It is by giving up something—greed for instance—that the triune God frees human beings to live. This it what it means practicing the gift of being a new self in Christ. This new self gives up the old self, and takes on Christ and the fruits of the Spirit.

Hence *practicing baptism* is the process of being brought into the presence of the kingdom of Christ again and again. This kingdom comes to human beings through the gifts of the triune God: In this kingdom the Holy Spirit calls and draws the baptized to Christ. When this happens, the lives of the baptized may be transformed—as they are gradually conformed to Christ, freed to practice the common order of Christian love, becoming Christ to the neighbor. *Practicing baptism* is therefore fundamentally a relational concept. Rooting the Christian life in this concept may be the starting point for the nurturing of a *mobile faith*—a faith crossing borders, shaped by the love of the triune God.

---

1. Cf. Cavanaugh, *Being Consumed*.

An Eschatological Community Practicing Missional Self-Giving Love

Implicit in the command to go and baptize in Matthew 28:18–20 is a sending. Looking at another post-resurrection narrative, John 20:19–23, the importance of Christian practices for this sending is highlighted, particularly the practice of forgiveness. *Practicing baptism* always means being sent. It (also) means preaching the gospel for baptism. Therefore *practicing baptism* has to be something other than a mere maintenance strategy. When the church practices baptism, the church is sent beyond its borders, as baptism shapes a community without borders, cf. Galatians 3:27–28.

Altogether, *practicing baptism* is about fostering missional self-giving love. It is about undying hope in the midst of despair. But missional self-giving love takes as its point of departure the abyss of sin and death in which this world is intertwined. It takes as its point of departure how the triune God in baptism makes human beings—used to entertaining themselves—radically dependent on the gifts of God. And then, when God is left to do "the god-job," human beings are freed to serve their neighbors and the world. This is eloquently elaborated in the document *The Nature and Purpose of the Church*:

> As persons are baptised, they "put on Christ" (Gal 3.27), they enter into *koinonia* of Christ's Body (1 Cor 12:13), receive that share of the Holy Spirit which is the privilege of God's adopted children (Rom (8:15f), and so enjoy in anticipation that participation in the divine life which God promises and purposes for humankind (2 Peter 1:4). In the present, the solidarity of Christians with joys and sorrows of their neighbours, their engagement in the struggle for the dignity of all who suffer, the excluded, the poor, belongs to their baptismal vocation. It is the way they are brought face to face with Christ in his identification with the victimized and outcast.[2]

Being baptized in the name of the triune God is the start of a sending to the world—a *missio*. It is to live one's baptismal vocation, expecting that the same triune God through Christ both calls the new self arising from baptism to always return to his or her baptism by practicing the first-tablet practices, and that the same self is freed to practice the common order of Christian love through the second-tablet practices. This is

2. *The Nature and Purpose of the Church*, 37.

the *vocatio sanctorum* of Christian practices. This is how the triune God moves the baptized in baptismal ways.

This also emphasizes the importance of relating to anthropological and ecclesiological complexity in ministry. This is crucial if the church as the public of the Holy Spirit wants to supersede being a public incurred in itself—and by doing so, ultimately refraining from being a public. Relating to these tensions in ministry, in combination with the radical openness of the outer borders of ministry, is of great importance particularly in youth ministry, particularly if ministry strives to build more than a ghetto. This implies that using Christian practices in the context of ministry means being radically open to all kinds of people. At times this may, however, also imply allowing for different kinds of community structures, ways, and places to engage people in Christian practices, serving the missional impetus of Christian practices.

The eschatological drive in the concept *practicing baptism* is therefore profoundly communal. As a communal concept *practicing baptism* has to do with practicing the foretaste of the kingdom to come, in which there will be no divisions, cf. Gal 3:27–28. Here also the communal-ethical aspect of the concept *practicing baptism* comes to the fore. As we are drawn to Christ through the Holy Spirit in the daily discipleship founded in the promises of baptism, we are also freed to be drawn to our neighbor. This communal-ethical aspect of the concept *practicing baptism* may be particularly important as it focuses on the fruits of the freedom in Christ as something which benefits the neighbor. It is an exercise in breaking divisions and making room for the kind of whole-making that Galatians 3:27–28 envisions.

Practicing Reconciliation

Fundamentally, baptism is a continuous call to reconciliation, as Christ in baptism has reconciled the baptized with God. One difficult but important part of this is the biblical call to love the enemy. Practicing forgiveness and reconciliation in the context of ministry also has to do with the practice of loving one's enemy. A crucial part in the Christian practice of forgiveness is to learn to love the enemy. There is not room to discuss this big theme in full length here, so I will only highlight a few important features of this practice. Loving the enemy needs to be defined broadly, not merely as those we may list as our enemies, but also those who count us as their enemies. There is a clear eschatological direction in this love of the enemy: The practice of forgiveness is preparing for the etiquette of the heavenly community, where all will dine with one another as forgiven forgivers.[3]

Therefore, practicing reconciliation in the light of baptismal theology has to do with fighting for the restoration of human dignity, the restored *imago Dei*. As *practicing baptism* proclaims the gospel of renunciation, it has to do with fighting for the just distribution of the gifts of the triune God, fighting for the poor and the marginalized. Similar to this, Luther seems to think that much more important than fasting is feeding the poor and the hungry.[4] *Practicing baptism* is hence not merely an individualistic concept, but both a personal and communal concept.

Discussing what it means to love one's enemy inevitably involves dealing with the powers of death, sin, and radical evil—both in you and around you.[5] But in which ways does the concept *practicing baptism* offer practices to face the powers of death, sin and radical evil?

Here it may be helpful to look at how US youth ministry theologian Russel Haitch elaborates on the potential connection and dis-connection between contemporary youth culture and baptism, underlining the potential of baptism and the Lord's Supper to become events and ways in which God destroys death and restores the material world, in order to make possible once and again an interesting communion with God.[6]

Forgiveness and reconciliation means putting into effect the *significatio* of baptism. For Luther the primary context for this was the humdrum duties of domestic life. In the midst of everyday life there is an arena for the dying, which is baptism, where this dying means serving the needs of your neighbor.[7] Practicing the ministry of forgiveness and reconciliation is therefore probably best learned through making forgiveness and reconciliation patterns in all aspects and situations in the context of everyday life and ministry. This is a crucial point, perhaps the most counter-cultural aspect in the whole *practicing baptism* concept:[8] In

3. Stortz, *A World According to God*, 107, 111.

4. LW 41:198–99.

5. For an excellent contemporary account of this, cf. Tutu, *No Future without Forgiveness*.

6. Haitch, "Bored to Death," 65.

7. Trigg, *Baptism in the Theology of Martin Luther*, 99.

8. For an insightful elaboration on forgiving as a counter-cultural practice, cf. Volf, *Free of Charge*.

the light of the two classic metaphors of baptism—baptism as *womb* and baptism as a *tomb, practicing baptism* by living *diakonia* may be a *womb* working for the enhancement of life. It may also be a *tomb*, addressing pain, brokenness and despair—the powers of death and sin—in the lives of ordinary people.

Practicing Baptism in Ministry: Confirmation

Post World War II youth ministry may be seen as a way for the church to make use of the evolving religious market in an emerging post-Christendom climate, where the subjective turn in culture and new claims on authenticity bring challenges to the church. The challenge for youth ministry in a market context is avoiding making young people into consumers, because this would ultimately jeopardize what being church is about. *Practicing baptism*—as a fundamental movement through death to life—naturally gives room for the practice of simplicity. When baptism becomes the focal point of ministry, the individual believer and the community is founded in their continuous dependency on the gifts of God. In the light of this, living simply becomes good news for young and old alike.

In the light of this, the developed concept *practicing baptism* may be a helpful resource in articulating what Christian Education with youth in a post-Christendom context is about in a more comprehensive and "sharper" way. Looking at confirmation in particular, this implies that rather than stressing that confirmation is *just* a rite of praying for and laying hands on the young confirmands, a theology on the rite of confirmation needs to rediscover confirmation as *confirmation*—a confirmation of baptism. From a certain perspective confirmation training brings us to the heart of what it means to be church: Confirmation training has to do with exercising the gifts of faith. This does not mean, however, that infant baptism needs to be confirmed by an act of personal choice or confession to be valid. Rather it means that being baptized, whether as an infant or as an adolescent, means leading a life where you constantly use or practice baptism. *Practicing baptism* means being *conformed to Christ* through the first-tablet Christian practices. Through that formative process the believer is freed to practice a wide range of practices in the common order of Christian love.

From this perspective, confirmation training—as all of the Christian life—is *confirmation in the passive form*. It is about letting the triune

God get to work. Dramaturgically, the rite of confirmation may then be interpreted as a climax in this particular process of *confirmation*. But confirmation training in this sense should not be restricted to the age of 14–15, rather the Christian life is a *continuous confirmation training*. But the benefit of making room for *months'* of confirmation training processes during particular stages in life is that it *helps to give birth to* a sense of vocation in a particular context: Confirmation training in the wide sense of the word means asking what Christ is doing in the life of the believer and asking what Christ is calling the believer to do in the name of the triune God. Narratively, one could even speak of the U-shape of confirmation, where the U-shape is typical of processes of change. Hence, confirmation becomes an exemplary process of change, formatting consecutive processes of change in the life of the Christian.

Practicing baptism as being conformed to Christ is always about being conformed to Christ in a particular context and in a particular lifestory. It has to do with how the gospel of baptism addresses the complex anthropology in a variety of settings. In this sense *practicing baptism* is about the continuous *embodiment* of baptism in the life of believer, on the dying to sin and the emerging of new life in Christ throughout new life stages and new contexts. From this perspective confirmation is also about *transformation*. By being conformed to Christ, the believer is transformed into a new Kingdom.

"Talk the Walk and Walk the Talk"—the Diaconal Telos of the Church

The engagement in Christian practices from the late 1980s to the beginning of the twenty-first century grew out of a self-critical evaluation of the situation within the traditional churches in the US: Not only numerical decline, but also a theological dissatisfaction with how the traditional churches approached an emerging individualistic approach to authenticity was an important impetus for the new Christian practices paradigm. In an analysis on how religious traditions in an era of heightened personal autonomy may still vitalize faith and practice in teenagers, so that they may choose church in later years, the findings showed that:

> Teens tend to choose faith when they live in families that "talk the walk" and "walk the talk." Moreover, church-related teens are most likely to "grow up into Christ" when they belong to

congregations that have learned to convey unchanging, eternal truths within a changing "culture of choice."[9]

The Christian practices paradigm may be interpreted as an attempt to "talk the walk and walk the talk," in the way that it seeks to both speak about Christianity as a way of life and to live that life in a consequential manner. But does this imply that the *telos* of Christian practices as *diakonia* is to offer a sort of strategic proclamation of the Christian faith as consequential? Do Christians do good deeds in order to convince others of a faith which "talk the walk" and "walk the talk"? This is problematic for several reasons. First of all, it implies an instrumental approach to *diakonia*. Secondly, it fails to make a faithful account of how the triune God moves the church.

There is something in the way church moves, or should be moving. But what is the primary move in the church? What is the *telos* of the church? What is the direction of the church? I have argued with Luther and Hütter that the church is constituted and characterized through first-tablet practices: the Word, baptism, the Lord's Supper, penance/forgiveness, service, prayer and worship, discipleship. These are practices, which are ordained by Christ through his promise of presence and through which human beings receive new life in Christ. Whenever these practices are practiced, church happens. This move to the Christological center of the church is the primary move of the church, or better, the first move of the church: We are called to *rest* in the presence of Christ's love and mercy.

But is this all there is to say? Is the church only called to rest in the core practices, or is there a horizontal U-move in the way the church moves - a move towards the world, towards the neighbor? In other words, what is the role of the second tablet Christian practices? Unlike those engaging Christian practices, I will argue that the primary *telos* of the second-tablet Christian practices, or practices on the economy of creation, is *not* meaning-making and identity construction. This is at best a secondary *telos*—practicing these practices may, at least at first, even challenge and confuse meaning-making and identity construction. However, the primary *telos* of such practices is the service of the neighbor and the world. The *telos* of these practices is *diaconal*.

In a sense therefore, *diakonia* is not a core church practice in the strict meaning of the word, but it is a practice, which pushes the limits and borders of how the church moves, by focusing on what the church

---

9. Lytch, *Choosing Church*, 202.

cannot *not* do: The church cannot *not* tell the truth, share goods, practice reconciliation and fight for human dignity etc. In this sense, *diakonia* is a creative, imaginative, and prophetic practice which is directed toward the other, as Christian existence is rooted in Christ but directed to the neighbor, cf. Luther's treatment of this in *The Freedom of a Christian* (1520).

Fundamentally, I argue that there are two Christian practices, which draw the contours of how the church moves, namely the practices of *rest* and *diakonia*. Both *rest* and *diakonia* are practices, which in a sense are negative definitions of church. They exist as two practices on each side of an ellipsis: where there is no *rest*, and where there is no *diakonia*, there is no church. They represent the two fundamental moves of being church, of a Christian existence rooted in baptism: Resting in Christ, serving the neighbor. The practice of rest focuses the fundamental *vita passiva* of the Christian life; that *coram Deo*, human beings are fundamentally receivers. Through the first tablet practices human beings suffers the work of the triune God. We become gifted. This starts in baptism, and continues, rooted in baptism throughout life. The Holy Spirit is *practicing baptism* with us. The practice of *diakonia* is the other move of Christian existence, the other move of the church. Radically, the new self emerging from baptism is not just obliged to help the neighbor, but this self exists in the other, for the other, called to practice *the common order of Christian love*.

Bibliography

Aagard, Anne Marie. *Identifikation af kirken*. Fredriksberg: Anis, 1991.
Antola, Markku. *The Experience of Christ's Real Presence in Faith: An Analysis of the Christ-Presence Motif in the Lutheran Charismatic Renewal*. Schriften der Luther-Agricola-Gesellschaft. Helsinki: Luther-Agricola-Society, 1998.
Asheim, Ivar. *Glaube und Erziehung bei Luther: Ein Beitrag zur Geschichte des Verhältnisses von Theologie und Pädagogik*. Pädagogische Forschungen 17. Heidelberg: Quelle und Meyer, 1961.
Asheim, Ivar. *Hva betyr holdninger? Studier i dydsetikk*. Oslo: Tano Aschehoug, 1997.
Austad, Torleiv. *Tolkning av kristen tro: Metodespørsmål i systematisk teologi*. Kristiansand: Høyskoleforlaget, 2008.
Bass, Diana Butler. *The Practicing Congregation: Imagining a New Old Church*. Herndon, VA: Alban Institute, 2004.
Bass, Dorothy C. *Practicing Our Faith: A Way of Life for A Searching People*. San Francisco: Jossey-Bass, 1997.
———. *Receiving the Day. Christian Practices for Opening the Gift of Time*. San Francisco: Jossey-Bass, 2000.
———. "Ways of Life Abundant." In *For Life Abundant: Practical Theology, Theological Education, and Christian Ministry*, ed. Dorothy C. Bass and Craig R. Dykstra, 21–40. Grand Rapids: Eerdmans, 2008.
Bass, Dorothy C., and Susan R. Briehl, eds. *On Our Way: Christian Practices for a Whole Life*. Nashville: UpperRoom, 2010.
Bayer, Oswald. *Living by Faith: Justification and Sanctification*. Trans. Geoffrey W. Bromiley. Lutheran Quarterly. Grand Rapids: Eerdmans, 2003.
———. *Theology the Lutheran Way*. Trans. Mark C. Mattes and Jeffrey G. Silcock. Lutheran Quarterly. Grand Rapids: Eerdmans, 2007.
Bonhoeffer, Dietrich. *The Cost of Discipleship*. Trans. R. H. Fuller. Rev. unabridged ed. London: SCM, 1959.
Boss, Marc. "What's Wrong with 'Communitarianism'? A Liberal Appraisal of Alasdair MacIntyre's *Ethics of Virtue*." *Svensk Teologisk Kvartalsskrift* 85, no. 3 (2009) 130–41.
Bourdieu, Pierre. *The Logic of Practice*. Trans. Richard Nice. Oxford: Polity Press, 1990.
———. *Outline of a Theory of Practice*. Trans. Richard Nice. Cambridge Studies in Social and Cultural Anthropology 16. Cambridge: Cambridge University Press, 1977.

Bibliography

Braw, Christian. *Mystikens arv hos Martin Luther*. Skellefteå: Artos Bokförlag, 1999.

Browning, Don S. *A Fundamental Practical Theology: Descriptive and Strategic Proposals*. Minneapolis: Fortress, 1991.

Braaten, Carl E., and Robert W. Jenson, eds. *Marks of the Body of Christ*. Grand Rapids: Eerdmans, 1999.

———. *Union with Christ: The New Finnish Interpretation of Luther*. Grand Rapids: Eerdmans, 1999.

Buckley, James Joseph, and David S. Yeago, eds.. *Knowing the Triune God: The Work of the Spirit in the Practices of the Church*. Grand Rapids: Eerdmans, 2001.

Burgess, John P. *After Baptism: Shaping the Christian Life*. Louisville: Westminster John Knox, 2005.

Cahalan, Kathleen A., and James R. Nieman. "Mapping the Field of Practical Theology." In *For Life Abundant: Practical Theology, Theological Education and Christian Ministry*, ed. Dorothy C. Bass and Craig R. Dykstra, 62–85. Grand Rapids: Eerdmans, 2008.

Carter, Craig A. *Rethinking Christ and Culture: A Post-Christendom Perspective*. Grand Rapids, Brazos, 2006.

Cary, Philip. "Why Luther is not quite Protestant: The Logic of Faith in a Sacramental Promise." *Pro Ecclesia* 14 (2005) 447–86.

Cavanaugh, William T. *Being Consumed: Economics and Christian Desire*. Grand Rapids: Eerdmans, 2008.

Certeau, Michel de. *The Practice of Everyday Life*. Trans. Stephen Rendall. Berkeley, CA: University of California Press, 1984.

Certeau, Michel de, et al. *The Practice of Everyday Life*. Vol. 2, *Living and Cooking*. Trans. Timothy J. Tomasik. Minneapolis: University of Minneapolis Press, 1998.

Clark, Chap. *Hurt: Inside the World of Today's Teenagers*. Youth, Family, and Culture. Grand Rapids: Baker Academic, 2004.

Coakley, Sarah. "Deepening Practices. Perspectives from Ascetical and Mystical Theology." In *Practicing Theology: Beliefs and Practices in Christian Life*, ed. Miroslav Volf and Dorothy C. Bass, 78–93. Grand Rapids, Eerdmans, 2002.

Cray, Graham, with Archbishop's Council. *Mission-Shaped Church: Church Planting and Fresh Expressions of Church in a Changing Context*. London: Church House, 2004.

Daniels, David D., III, and Ted A. Smith. "History, Practice and Theological Education." In *For Life Abundant: Practical Theology, Theological Education and Christian Ministry*, ed. Dorothy C. Bass and Craig R. Dykstra, 214–40. Grand Rapids: Eerdmans, 2008.

Dean, Kenda Creasy. *Almost Christian: What the Faith of Our Teenagers is Telling the American Church*. New York: Oxford University Press, 2010.

———. "The New Rhetoric of Youth Ministry." *Journal of Youth and Theology* 2, no.2 (2003) 8–19.

———. *Practicing Passion: Youth and the Quest for a Passionate Church*. Grand Rapids: Eerdmans, 2004.

Dean, Kenda Creasy, and Ron Foster. *The Godbearing Life: The Art of Soul Tending for Youth Ministry*. Nashville: UpperRoom, 1998.

Dean, Kenda Creasy, and Roland D. Martinson. *OMG: A Youth Ministry Handbook*. Youth and Theology. Nashville: Abingdon, 2010.

Die Bekenntnisschriften der evangelisch-lutherischen Kirche. [BELK]. 11th ed. Göttingen: Vandenhoeck & Ruprecht, 1992.
Dulles, Avery. *Models of the Church*. New York: Image, 2002.
Dykstra, Craig R. *Growing in the Life of Faith: Education and Christian Practices*. 2nd ed. Louisville: Westminster John Knox, 2005.
―――. "Pastoral and Ecclesial Imagination." In *For Life Abundant: Practical Theology, Theological Education, and Christian Ministry*, ed. Dorothy C. Bass and Craig R. Dykstra, 41–61. Grand Rapids, Eerdmans, 2008.
―――. "Reconceiving Practice." In *Shifting Boundaries: Contextual Approaches to the Structure of Theological Education*, ed. Barbara G. Wheeler and Edward Farley, 35–66. Louisville: Westminster John Knox, 1991.
Dykstra, Craig R., and Dorothy C. Bass. "A Theological Understanding of Christian Practices." In *Practicing Theology: Beliefs and Practices in Christian Life*, ed. Miroslav Volf and Dorothy C. Bass, 13–32. Grand Rapids: Eerdmans, 2002.
―――. "Times of Yearning, Practices of Faith." In *Practicing Our Faith: A Way of Life for a Searching People*, 1–12. San Francisco: Jossey-Bass, 1997.
Edie, Fred. P. *Book, Bath, Table, and Time: Christian Worship as Source and Resource for Youth Ministry*. Cleveland: Pilgrim, 2007.
Elert, Werner. *The Structure of Lutheranism*. Saint Louis: Concordia, 1962.
Ferel, Martin. *Gepredigte Taufe: Eine homiletische Untersuchung zur Taufpredigt bei Luther*. Hermeneutische Untersuchungen zur Theologie 10. Tübingen: Mohr, 1969.
Forde, Gerhard O. *A More Radical Gospel: Essays on Eschatology, Authority, Atonement, and Ecumenism*. Ed. Mark C. Mattes and Steven D. Paulson. Lutheran Quarterly. Grand Rapids: Eerdmans, 2004.
Frye, Northrop. *The Great Code: The Bible and Literature*. San Diego: Harcourt Brace Jovanovich, 1983.
Gadamer, Hans-Georg. *Wahrheit und Methode: Grundzüge einer philosophischen Hermeneutik*. Tübingen: Mohr, 1990.
Grane, Leif. *The Augsburg Confession: A Commentary*. Minneapolis: Augsburg, 1987.
Haga, Joar. *Was there a Lutheran Metaphysics? The Interpretation of communicatio idiomatum in Early Modern Lutheranism*. Göttingen: Vandenhoeck & Ruprecht, 2012.
Haitch, Russel. "Bored to Death: Entertainment, Violence and Sacramental Approach to Teaching Peace." *Journal of Youth and Theology* 4, no.1 (2005) 51–66.
Hamm, Richard L. *Recreating the Church: Leadership for a Postmodern Age*. Columbia Partnership Leadership. Saint Louis: Chalice, 2007.
Hammar, Anna Karin. *Skapelsens mysterium, Skapelsens sakrament: Dopteologi i mötet mellan tradition och situation*. PhD diss., Uppsala University, 2009.
Hauerwas, Stanley, and William H. Willimon. *Resident Aliens: Life in the Christian Colony*. Nashville: Abingdon, 1989.
―――. *Where Resident Aliens Live: Exercises for Christian Practice*. Nashville: Abingdon, 1996.
Healy, Nicholas M. "Misplaced Concreteness: Practices and the New Ecclesiology." *International Journal of Systematic Theology* 5, no. 3 (2003) 287–308.
Hegstad, Harald. *The Real Church. An Ecclesiology of the Visible*. Church of Sweden Research 7. Eugene, OR: Pickwick, 2013.

Heubach, Joachim, ed. *Luther und Theosis. Veröffentlichungen der Luther Akademie Ratzeburg.* Vol 16. Erlangen: Martin-Luther-Verlag, 1990.

Hoffman, Bengt Runo. *Theology of the Heart: The Role of Mysticism in the Theology of Martin Luther.* Trans. Pearl Willemssen Hoffman. Minneapolis: Kirk House, 2003.

Hütter, Reinhard. *Bound to be Free: Evangelical Catholic Engagements in Ecclesiology, Ethics, and Ecumenism.* Grand Rapids: Eerdmans, 2004.

———. "The Christian Life." In *The Oxford Handbook of Systematic Theology*, ed. John Webster, Kathryn Tanner, and Iain Torrance, 285–305. Oxford: Oxford University Press, 2007.

———. "The Church: The Knowledge of the Triune God. Practices, Doctrine, Theology." In *Knowing the Triune God: The Work of the Holy Spirit in the Practices of the Church*, ed. James J. Buckley and David S. Yeago, 23–47. Grand Rapids: Eerdmans, 2001.

———. "Hospitality and Truth: The Disclosure of Practices in Worship and Doctrine." In *Practicing Theology: Beliefs and Practices in Christian Life*, ed. Miroslav Volf and Dorothy C. Bass, 206–27. Grand Rapids: Eerdmans, 2002.

———. *Suffering Divine Things. Theology as Church Practice.* Grand Rapids: Eerdmans, 2000.

———. *Theologie als kirchliche Praktik: Zur Verhältnisbestimmung von Kirche, Lehre, und Theologie. Beiträge zur evangelischen Theologie.* Gütersloh: Kaiser, 1997.

———. "The Twofold Center of Lutheran Ethics: Christian Freedom and God's Commandments." In *The Promise of Lutheran Ethics*, 31–54. Minneapolis: Fortress, 1998.

Jenson, Robert W. *Systematic Theology.* Vol. 1, *The Triune God.* Oxford: Oxford University Press, 1997.

———. *Systematic Theology.* Vol. 2, *The Works of God.* Oxford: Oxford University Press, 1999.

Jetter, Werner. *Die Taufe beim jungen Luther: Eine Untersuchung über das Werden der reformatorischen Sakraments und Taufanschauung. Beiträge zur historischen Theologie.* Tübingen: Mohr, 1954.

Jones, Serene. "Graced Practices: Excellence and Freedom in the Christian Life." In *Practicing Theology: Beliefs and Practices in Christian Life*, ed. Miroslav Volf and Dorothy C. Bass, 51–77. Grand Rapids: Eerdmans, 2002.

Jones, Tony. *Postmodern Youth Ministry: Exploring Cultural Shift, Cultivating Authentic Community, Creating Holistic Connections.* Grand Rapids: Youth Specialties, 2001.

———. *Soul Shaper: Exploring Spirituality and Contemplative Practices in Youth Ministry.* El Cajon, CA: Youth Specialties, 2003.

Kalloch, Christina, Stephan Leimgruber, and Ulrich Schwab. *Lehrbuch der Religionsdidaktik: Für Studium und Praxis in ökumenischer Perspektive.* Freiburg: Herder, 2009.

Kavanagh, Aidan. *The Shape of Baptism: The Rite of Christian Initiation.* Studies in the Reformed Rites of the Catholic Church 1. New York, Pueblo, 1978.

Kelsey, David H. *To Understand God Truly: What's Theological about a Theological School.* Louisville: Westminster John Knox, 1992.

Kjølsvik, Idar. *Kreuz und Auferstehung als Geschichte—und Gegenwart? Die Bedeutung des Geschichtsverständnisses für die Lehre vom Christus Praesens in Jürgen Moltmanns Theologie.* Levanger: Kjølsvik, 2006.

Kolakowski, Leszek. *Religion, If There Is No God: On God, the Devil, and Other Worries of the so-called Philosophy of Religion.* New York: Oxford University Press, 1983.

Kolb, Robert. *Martin Luther: Confessor of the Faith. Christian Theology in Context.* Oxford: Oxford University Press, 2009.

Kolb, Robert, and Timothy J. Wengert, eds. *The Book of Concord: The Confessions of the Evangelical Lutheran Church.* Minneapolis: Fortress, 2000.

Kärkkäinen, Veli-Matti. *One with God. Salvation as Deification and Justification.* Unitas. Collegeville, MN: Liturgical, 2004.

Lathrop, Gordon. *Holy Things: A Liturgical Theology.* Minneapolis: Fortress, 1993.

Lathrop, Gordon, and Timothy J. Wengert. *Christian Assembly. Marks of the Church in a Pluralistic Age.* Minneapolis: Fortress, 2004.

Lexutt, Athina. "'. . . dass der böse Feind keine Macht an mir finde' Das Böse und seine Gestalten in Luthers Katechismen." In *Denkraum Katechismus: Festgabe für Oswald Bayer zum 70. Geburtstag,* 315–36. Tübingen: Mohr/Siebeck, 2009.

Lindbeck, George. *The Nature of Doctrine: Religion and Theology in a Postliberal Age.* Philadelphia: Westminster, 1984.

Lohse, Bernhard. *Martin Luther's Theology: Its Historical and Systematic Development.* Trans. Roy A. Harrisville. Edinburgh: T. & T. Clark, 1999.

Luther, Martin. *Luther Works.* Vol. 31, *Career of the Reformer I.* Ed. Helmut T. Lehmann. Philadelphia, Fortress, 1957.

———. *Luther Works.* Vol. 37, *Word and Sacrament III.* Ed. Robert H. Fischer and Helmut T. Lehmann. Philadelphia, Fortress, 1961.

———. *Luther Works.* Vol. 40, *Church and Ministry II.* Ed. Conrad Bergendoff and Helmut T. Lehmann. Philadelphia, Fortress, 1958.

———. *Luther Works.* Vol. 41, *Church and Ministry III.* Ed. Eric W. Gritsch and Helmut T. Lehmann. Philadelphia, Fortress, 1958.

———. *Studienausgabe.* Vol. 3. Ed. Hans-Ulrich Delius. Berlin: Evangelische, 1983.

———. *Studienausgabe.* Vol. 4. Ed. Hans-Ulrich Delius. Berlin: Evangelische, 1986.

———. *Studienausgabe.* Vol. 5. Ed. Hans-Ulrich Delius. Berlin: Evangelische, 1983.

Lytch, Carol E. *Choosing Church: What Makes A Difference for Teens.* Louisville: Westminster John Knox, 2004.

MacIntyre, Alasdair. *After Virtue: A Study in Moral Theory.* Notre Dame: University of Notre Dame Press, 1984.

Mannermaa, Tuomo. *Christ Present in Faith: Luther's View of Justification.* Trans. Kirsi Stjerna. Minneapolis: Fortress, 2005.

Martinson, Roland, Wes Black, and John Roberto. *The Spirit and Culture of Youth Ministry: Leading Congregations toward Exemplary Youth Ministry.* St. Paul, MN: EYM, 2010.

Mattes, Mark C. "The Thomistic Turn in Evangelical Catholic Ethics." *Lutheran Quarterly* 16 (2002) 65–100.

Mikkola, Teija, Kati Niemelä, and Juha Petterson. *The Questioning Mind: Faith and Values of the New Generation.* Tampere: Church Research Institute, 2007.

Muthiah, Robert. "Christian Practices, Congregational Leadership, and the Priesthood of All Believers." *Journal of Religious Leadership* 2 (2003) 167–203.

The Nature and Purpose of the Church: A Stage on the Way to a Common Statement. Faith and Order Paper No. 181. Geneva: World Council of Churches, 1998.

Norheim, Bård E. H. "From Ghetto to Communitas: Post-Soviet Youth Ministry and Leadership on a Pilgrimage to Emmaus." *Journal of Youth and Theology* 5, no.1 (2006) 67–84.

———. "The Global Youth Culture: Targeting and Involving Youth in Global Mission." In *The Church Going Glocal*, 168–75. Oxford: Regnum, 2011.

———. "'Have You Come Here to Play Jesus?' Å forkynna Jesus som førebilete." In *Grensesprengende: Forkynnelse for ungdom 15–18 år*, ed. Hans Austnaberg and Bård Mæland, 257–72. Trondheim: Tapir Akademisk, 2009.

———. *Kan tru praktiserast? Teologi for kristent ungdomsarbeid.* Trondheim: Tapir Akademisk Forlag, 2008.

———. "Practicing Baptism: The Church as Communio and Congregatio Sanctorum. Rethinking Ecclesiology in the Context of Nordic Youth Ministry." *Journal of Youth and Theology* 9, no. 1 (2010) 37–55.

Paul, Toomas. "Sanctorem Communionem." *Usuteaduslik Ajakiri* 48, no. 1 (2001) 38–59.

Pauw, Amy Plantinga. "Attending to the Gap between Beliefs and Practices." In *Practicing Theology: Beliefs and Practices in Christian Life*, ed. Miroslav Volf and Dorothy C. Bass, 33–48. Grand Rapids: Eerdmans, 2002.

Peters, Albrecht. "Busse—Beichte—Schuldvergebung in evangelischer Theologie und Praxis." *Kerygma und Dogma: Zeitschrift für Theologische Forschung und Kirchliche Lehre* 28, no. 1 (1982) 42–72.

———. *Kommentar zu Luthers Katechismen.* Vol. 1, *Die Zehn Gebote, Luthers Vorreden.* Göttingen: Vandenhoeck & Ruprecht, 1990.

———. *Kommentar zu Luthers Katechismen.* Vol. 2, *Der Glaube, Die Apostolikum.* Göttingen: Vandenhoeck & Ruprecht, 1991.

———. *Kommentar zu Luthers Katechismen.* Vol. 3, *Das Vaterunser.* Göttingen: Vandenhoeck & Ruprecht, 1992.

———. *Kommentar zu Luthers Katechismen.* Vol. 4, *Die Taufe, Das Abendmahl.* Göttingen: Vandenhoeck & Ruprecht, 1993.

———. *Kommentar zu Luthers Katechismen.* Vol. 5, *Beichte, Haustafel, Traubüchlein, Taufbüchlein.* Göttingen: Vandenhoeck & Ruprecht, 1995.

Peura, Simo. "Christ as Favor and Gift: The Challenge of Luther`s Understanding of Justification." In *Union with Christ: The New Finnish Interpretation of Luther*, ed. Carl E. Braaten and Robert W. Jenson, 42–69. Grand Rapids: Eerdmans, 1998.

———. "What God Gives Man Receives: Luther on Salvation." In *Union with Christ: The New Finnish Interpretation of Luther*, ed. Carl E. Braaten and Robert W. Jenson, 76–95. Grand Rapids: Eerdmans, 1998.

Rasmusson, Arne. *The Church as Polis: From Political Theology to Theological Politics as Exemplified by Jürgen Moltmann and Stanley Hauerwas.* Studia theologica Lundensia. Lund: Lund University Press, 1994.

Richter, Don, and Dorothy C. Bass, eds. *Way to Live: Christian Practices for Teens.* Nashville: UpperRoom, 2002.

Root, Andrew. *Relationships Unfiltered. Help for Youth Workers, Volunteers, and Parents on Creating Authentic Relationships.* Grand Rapids: Youth Specialities, 2009.

———. *Revisiting Relational Youth Ministry: From A Strategy of Influence to a Theology of Incarnation.* Downers Grove, IL: InterVarsity, 2007.

Root, Michael. "Continuing the Conversation: Deeper Agreement on Justification as Criterion and on the Christian as *simul iustus et peccator*." In *The Gospel of*

Justification in Christ: Where Does the Church Stand Today?, ed. Wayne C. Stumme, 42–61. Grand Rapids, Eerdmans, 2006.

Root, Michael, and Risto Saarinen, eds. *Baptism and the Unity of the Church.* Grand Rapids: Eerdmans, 1998.

Scharen, Christian. *Faith as a Way of Life: A Vision for Pastoral Leadership.* Grand Rapids, Eerdmans, 2008.

Schlink, Edmund. *The Doctrine of Baptism.* Trans. Herbert J. A. Bouman. St. Louis: Concordia, 1972.

———. *Theology of the Lutheran Confessions.* Philadelphia, Fortress, 1961.

Simpson, Gary. "Daunting Indeed! A Critical Conversation with the Promise of Lutheran Ethics." *World & World* 19, no. 2 (1999) 187–200.

Smith, Christian, with Melinda Lundquist Denton. *Soul Searching: The Religious and Spiritual Lives of American Teenagers.* New York: Oxford University Press, 2005.

Spinks, Bryan D. *Early and Medieval Rituals and Theologies of Baptism: From the New Testament to the Council of Trent.* Liturgy, Worship and Society. Aldershot, UK: Ashgate, 2006.

———. *Reformation and Modern Rituals and Theologies of Baptism: From Luther to Contemporary Practices.* Liturgy, Worship and Society. Aldershot, UK: Ashgate, 2006.

Stassen, Glen H., D. M. Yeager, and John Howard Yoder. *Authentic Transformation. A New Vision of Christ and Culture.* Nashville: Abingdon, 2006.

Steinmetz, David C. *Luther in Context.* Grand Rapids: Baker Academic, 2002.

Stolle, Volker. "Taufe und Busse." *Kerygma und Dogma: Zeitschrift für Theologische Forschung und Kirchliche Lehre* 53, no. 1, (2007) 2–34.

Stortz, Martha Ellen. "Practicing Christians: Prayer as Formation." In *The Promise of Lutheran Ethics*, ed. Karen L. Bloomquist and John R. Stumme, 55–73. Minneapolis: Fortress, 1998.

———. *Theology of the Lutheran Confessions.* Philadelphia, Fortress, 1961.

A World According to God: Practices for Putting Faith at the Center of Your Life. San Francisco: Jossey-Bass, 2004.

Stubbs, David L. "Practices, Core Practices, and the Work of the Holy Spirit." *Journal for Christian Theological Research* 9 (2004) 15–28.

Tanner, Kathryn. "Theological Reflection and Christian Practices." In *Practicing Theology: Beliefs and Practices in Christian Life*, ed. Miroslav Volf and Dorothy C. Bass, 228–42. Grand Rapids: Eerdmans, 2002.

Taylor, Charles. *The Ethics of Authenticity.* Cambridge, MA: Harvard University Press, 1992.

Trigg, Jonathan D. *Baptism in the Theology of Martin Luther.* Studies in the History of Christian Thought 56. Leiden: Brill, 1994.

Tutu, Desmond. *No Future without Forgiveness.* New York: Doubleday, 1999.

Van Gelder, Craig. *The Ministry of the Missional Church: A Community Led by the Spirit.* Grand Rapids, Baker, 2007.

Volf, Miroslav. *After Our Likeness: The Church as the Image of the Trinity.* Sacra Doctrina. Grand Rapids, Eerdmans, 1998.

———. "Community Formation as an Image of the Triune God: A Congregational Model of Church Order and Life." In *Community Formation in the Early Church and in the Church Today*, ed. Richard N. Longenecker, 213–37. Peabody, MA: Hendrickson, 2002.

———. *Free of Charge. Giving and Forgiving in a Culture Stripped of Grace*. The Archbishop's Official 2006 Lent Book. Grand Rapids: Zondervan, 2005.

———. "Theology for a Way of Life." In *Practicing Theology: Beliefs and Practices in Christian Life*, ed. Miroslav Volf and Dorothy C. Bass, 245–63. Grand Rapids: Eerdmans, 2002.

Volf, Miroslav, and Dorothy C. Bass, eds. *Practicing Theology: Beliefs and Practices in Christian Life*. Grand Rapids: Eerdmans, 2002.

Wannenwetsch, Bernd. "Lob der Äusserlichkeit. Evangelische *praxis pietatis* als gottesdienstliche Frömmigkeit." In *Denkraum Katechismus: Festgabe für Oswald Bayer zum 70. Geburtstag*, ed. Johannes von Lüpke and Edgar Thaidigsmann, 387–413. Tübingen: Mohr/Siebeck, 2009.

Wannenwetsch, Bernd. *Politcal Worship: Ethics for Christian Citizens*. Oxford Studies in Theological Ethics. Oxford: Oxford University Press, 2004.

Ward, Pete. *Liquid Church*. Carlisle, UK: Paternoster, 2002.

Ward, Pete, and Kenda Creasy Dean. "Practicing Passionate Theology! A conversational Review of Kenda Creasy Dean (2004) *Practicing Passion: Youth and the Quest for a Passionate Church*." *Journal of Youth and Theology* 4, no. 1 (2005) 95–111.

Webster, John. "Introduction: Systematic Theology." In *The Oxford Handbook of Systematic Theology*, ed. John Webster, Kathryn Tanner, and Iain Torrance. Oxford: Oxford University Press, 2007.

Webster, John, Kathryn Tanner, and Iain Torrance, eds. *The Oxford Handbook of Systematic Theology*. Oxford: Oxford University Press, 2007.

Wengert, Timothy J. *Martin Luther's Catechisms: Forming the Faith*. Minneapolis: Fortress, 2009.

White, David F. *Practicing Discernment with Youth: A Transformative Youth Ministry Approach*. Youth Ministry Alternatives. Cleveland: Pilgrim, 2005.

Willimon, William H. "Too Much Practice: Second Thoughts on a Theological Movement." *Christian Century*, March 9, 2010, 22–25.

Wingren, Gustaf. *Luther on Vocation*. Philadelphia: Muhlenberg, 1957.

Yaconelli, Mark. *Contemplative Youth Ministry: Practicing the Presence of Jesus with Young People*. London: SPCK, 2006.

———. *Growing Souls: Experiments in Contemplative Youth Ministry*. London: SPCK, 2007.

Yeago, David S. "The Bible." In *Knowing the Triune God: The Work of the Holy Spirit in the Practices of the Church*, ed. James J. Buckley and David S. Yeago, 49–93. Grand Rapids: Eerdmans, 2001.

———. "The Office of the Keys: On the Disappearance of Discipline in Protestant Modernity." In *Marks of the Body of Christ*, ed. Carl E. Braaten and Robert W. Jenson, 95–122. Grand Rapids: Eerdmans, 1999.

Yoder, John Howard. *Body Politics: Five Practices of the Christian Community before the Watching World*. Scottdale, PA: Herald, 1992.

Zizioulas, John D. *Being as Communion: Studies in the Personhood and the Church*. Crestwood, NY: St. Vladimir's Seminary Press, 1985.

Index

Aagard, Anne Marie, 82, 126–28, 136–37
agency, divine and human, 40–42, 50, 53, 56, 60, 94, 99–109, 113, 120, 140–44, 152, 160–62, 165, 171–74, 200
anthropology, 12–13, 35–38, 49–50, 96–100, 107, 116, 130–32, 156–57, 165–72, 178–80, 210
Asheim, Ivar, 97, 100, 103, 116, 121, 147, 151, 172–73
atonement, 49
authenticity, ix, 2, 174, 199
autonomy, ix, 1, 15, 199, 204, 210

baptism
  Corleone, 52, 167–68
  of Jesus, 117
  necessitas of. *See* why of baptism
  present tense of, 118, 134–36, 145, 150–51, 158–62, 174
  what of, 52, 156–57
  why of, 156–57
  as womb and tomb, 169–70, 201, 209
Bass, Diana Butler, 20, 43
Bass, Dorothy C., 2, 8–11, 17–23, 26–55, 67, 79, 82, 153–56, 160–67, 177, 179, 181
Bayer, Oswald, xi, 56–57, 76, 81–83, 109–13, 122–30, 147–48
Bonhoeffer, Dietrich, 44, 153, 157, 185, 196–97

Bourdieu, Pierre, 9–10, 17, 20–21, 31, 67
Browning, Don, 13–14
Burgess, John P., 157, 194

Cary, Philip, 59, 101
Certeau, Michel de, 9, 17, 20
Christendom. *See* post-Christendom
Christian love, *the common order of Christian love*, 90–94, 123, 133, 139, 145, 151–52, 161, 164, 176, 178, 200, 205, 209, 212
church. *See* ecclesiology
comedy, the Christian life as a, 149–51, 192
communicatio idiomatum, 80
communio sanctorum, 105, 117, 182–89
communitarian, vii, 2, 48, 173, 191
community, ix, xii, 3, 15, 17, 24–30, 33, 40–52, 61, 77, 79, 89, 108, 114–17, 120–29, 132, 144, 155–56, 167, 173, 179–80, 183–90, 193, 195 198–99, 201, 206–9
Confessio Augustana (CA), xiii, 3–4, 116–17, 156–57
Confirmation, ix, 209–10
conformitas Christi, 104–6, 151, 161, 175–78, 181
congregatio sanctorum, 115–17, 182–89
consumer society, 16, 46, 157, 165
conversion, 49, 110, 121, 174–76, 193

Corpus Christianum. See
  Post-Christendom
cosmology, 95, 99, 106, 128, 148, 169
cuius regio, eius religio, 115
cyclic, 58, 121, 130, 147–52, 192–94

Dean, Kenda Creasy, xi, 2–3, 8, 10–11, 17, 23–53, 55, 82, 154–68, 174–80, 186, 191
discipleship, 6, 15, 20, 24, 32, 45, 47, 51, 56, 90, 124, 153, 177, 187, 191, 199, 207, 211
diakonia, 125, 127, 152, 209, 211–12
Dulles, Avery, 187, 199
Dykstra, Craig R., 2, 7–11, 16–53, 55, 67, 79, 82, 154–67, 171, 177–80, 191

ecclesiology, 3–4, 12–13, 42–48, 49–50, 53, 57–60, 82, 108, 113–33, 151, 160, 162, 171, 178–89, 199
eschatology, 94, 109, 117, 122, 147, 150–51, 159, 167, 171–74, 178, 180, 184–85, 192–93, 201, 206–8
ethics, viii, ix, 8–10, 17, 55–58, 122–25, 129, 143–45, 172–73, 197
ex opere operato, 52, 156

fides, 81, 96, 136
fiducia, 96, 168
Finnish interpretation of Luther, 55, 59–60, 104–8, 193
Forde, Gerhard O., 57–58, 112–13, 143
forgiveness, viii, 2, 31, 62, 76–80, 89–94, 100, 115, 117, 121, 125, 131–33, 136, 143, 148, 153n1, 163, 178, 187, 206–8, 211
freedom, 12, 34–37, 55–58, 69, 74, 94–95, 100–101, 107, 112–13, 125, 132, 139, 143–46, 149, 161, 174–75, 178, 188–99, 204–7
Frye, Northrop, 150

Gadamer, Hans-Georg, 5–6
gift, practices as gift, 7n18, 41, 44, 71, 89, 92, 96–109, 125, 128, 130n267, 134, 138–39, 141, 150, 156. 161, 174–78, 181–83, 185, 191, 194, 198, 201–9
Grane, Leif, 115–17

hamartiology. *See* sin
Hammar, Anna Karin, 168–71, 187
Hauerwas, Stanley, 10, 17, 56, 174, 195
Hegstad, Harald, xi, 4, 118, 179
homo incurvatus se and *incurvatus se in se ipsum*, 98
Hütter, Reinhard, 6, 9–12, 55–60, 65–71, 75, 80, 82, 91–95, 101, 106–8, 114, 119n231, 123–36, 140–55, 160, 162, 171–73, 183n71, 191–96, 201n112, 211

identity, 2, 8, 24–25, 33, 38–40, 46, 49, 82, 95, 101, 108, 110, 113, 115, 126, 132, 157–78, 183–94, 199, 204, 211
  narrative, 5, 108, 185, 193, 204
imitatio Christi, 40, 79, 112, 122, 161, 166, 168, 175, 177–78, 180–81
inhabitatio Christi, 142

Jenson, Robert W., 5, 17, 48, 59, 83, 143, 175, 183, 193
justification, 4–5, 41, 55–60, 68, 82, 105–15, 119, 126, 130, 143–51, 173, 179

Kolakowski, Leszek, 166

Lahtrop, Gordon, 103n183, 119n229, 125n252, 155n2, 186n80
law,
  first use of, 170
  second use of, 68
  third use of, 57, 107, 143–47
lex orandi, lex credendi, 155
Lindbeck, George, 5, 17, 56
Linear, 44, 58, 117, 122, 147–52, 192–94
Lord's Supper, vii, 4–7, 56, 62–93, 102–9, 120, 123, 136, 147–48, 183, 194, 205, 208, 211

index 223

Luther, Martin, 4, 37, 45, 54–152, 54–152, 176, 208
   Confession Concerning Christ's Supper, 7, 65, 72, 86, 90, 103, 123, 131
   On the Councils and the Church, 6–7, 56–69, 79–92, 110, 120, 126–30, 136–40, 148, 200
   The Freedom of a Christian, 65, 68–69, 100, 144, 175n51, 212
   The Large Catechism, 4, 7, 63–78, 88–89, 102–10, 117, 120, 134–35, 140, 146, 188
   The Small Catechism, 4, 7, 62–77, 80, 97, 134–35, 157

Melanchthon, Philip, 4, 60, 110, 116, 154
Moltmann, Jürgen, 17, 39–40, 45, 159
MacIntyre, Alisdair, 6–10, 14, 17–20, 23, 27, 35, 42, 48, 55–56, 66–67, 116, 128, 152, 185
Mannermaa, Tuomo, 59, 104, 106
Mattes, Mark C., 57–58, 107, 129, 144
marks of the church. *See notae ecclesiae*
Methodist, viii, 26, 172
missional, 24, 45, 130–32, 186–90, 204–7
mobile faith, 114, 154, 205

Neo-Aristotelian, viii, 8–9, 14, 55–58
office of the keys. *See* penance
notae ecclesiae, 4, 6, 60–61, 82–83, 93, 103, 115–19, 122, 177, 200

passion, 2, 8, 23–25, 32–33, 38–52, 59, 69, 153–59, 162–68, 191, 200
passio, 67, 109, 150, 172
pathos. *See* passio
penance, 76, 119–27, 170, 211
peregrination, 58, 114, 193,
Peters, Albrecht, 62n18
Peura, Simo, 105
phronesis, 14n39
pneumatology, 56–57, 109, 191, 201
poiesis, 9, 12, 66

post-Christendom, v, 1–16, 47n153, 53–55, 113–15, 124–25, 129, 155, 164, 171, 178, 187–89, 194, 198–200, 204, 209
potentialis-actualis, 59, 150
practices
   church's core, 6, 12, 56, 60–71, 80–92, 107, 128–36, 140–43, 161–65, 171–73, 187–98, 200, 211
   first-tablet and second-tablet, 69, 82–94, 99–109, 131, 139, 142, 146–47, 151, 161, 164–65, 172, 199–200, 203–12
   social, 6–10, 19, 23, 31, 35, 44, 48, 55, 145–46
prayer, viii, 2, 4, 6, 28–32, 56, 62–63, 69–70, 77–81, 85, 87, 98, 124, 130n267, 137–42, 155, 188–92, 211
praxis, 9, 65–67, 110, 114, 130n268
Presbyterian, 25n40, 26n43, 49, 51, 157
presence, three modes of Christ's, 71–75
promissio, 76n70, 81
public (the church as the public of the Holy Spirit), 6, 119–20, 126–27, 133, 151, 207

radical evil, 53, 95, 99, 164–71, 177, 208
Radical Lutheranism, 57–58, 107–8, 112, 126–29, 143–47, 181
reconciliation, 170, 187–88, 207–8, 212
Reformed, 4n10, 41, 55, 64, 71, 157, 172, 179, 191
relational (youth) ministry, 185n78, 196–97, 205
rest, the practice of, 211–12
revelation, 92, 150, 195, 198
Root, Andrew, xi, 196

sanctification, 41, 82, 107–13, 120–28, 140, 145–48, 157, 168
secularization, viii, 1, 114, 133

Schlink, Edmund, 97n154, 128n261, 188n85, 194, 201n111
Simpson, Gary, 57
simul iustus et peccator, 99, 127, 149
sin, 2n6, 28, 34–38, 45, 49–50, 57, 62, 76–81, 89, 92–110, 113–20, 131–35, 139–51, 156–69, 172–73, 176, 180, 185, 189, 192, 199, 205–6, 208–10
soteriology, 4, 12, 34–42, 49–50, 53, 59, 67, 94–113, 119–21, 126–33, 156, 164–78, 180
Spinks, Bryan D. , 76n71, 95n143, 169–70, 193
spontaneity, 112–13, 132, 146, 149, 192–93
Steinmetz, David C., 63, 72–75, 96n149, 112–13, 120n233
Stortz, Martha Ellen, 55n1, 124–25, 160n17, 181, 208n3

Tanner, Kathryn, 10, 19–20, 142–43
Taylor, Charles, ixn2, 17n5, 185
telos, 6, 10, 17n5, 22, 36–37, 43n132, 50, 58, 67, 94, 128, 136, 147, 151, 203–12
theologia gloriae, 180
totus homo, 96
Trigg, Jonathan D., 74–76, 101n170, 118–21, 131n269, 134n278, 147, 208

U-shape, 148–51, 185
unio mystica, 176

verbum externum, 67, 111
vita passiva, 56, 65, 67, 71, 212
vocation(s), 28–29, 47, 83, 112, 122–25, 185, 188–89, 206–10
Volf, Miroslav, viii, 20–21, 31, 56, 100–101, 155, 182–84, 208n8

Wannenwetsch, Bernd, 125–30, 139
Webster, John, 13–14
Wengert, Timothy J., 4n8, 5, 60–63, 116–19, 129–30
Willimon, William H., 10, 17, 174, 195–96
Wingren, Gustaf, 83, 122–30
worship, ix, 28–29, 32, 34, 43, 84, 89, 96, 125–26, 139, 185, 191–92, 211

Yeago, David S., 55n1, 57, 67, 106–8, 120–21, 126, 143–47
youth ministry, vii, xii, 2, 7–8, 12, 23–26, 32, 39, 46, 49, 164, 167, 171, 174, 178, 182–86, 196–99, 205–9

Zizioulas, John D., 101, 183
Zwingli, 64, 71–72, 79

www.ingramcontent.com/pod-product-compliance
Lightning Source LLC
Chambersburg PA
CBHW062019220426
43662CB00010B/1397